Romanization in the Time of Augustus

ROMANIZATION IN THE TIME OF AUGUSTUS

RAMSAY MACMULLEN

Yale University Press/New Haven & London

Designed by Mary Valencia
Set in Quadraat by The Composing Room of Michigan, Inc.
Printed in the United States of America by Edwards Brothers, Ann Arbor, Michigan.

Library of Congress Cataloging-in-Publication Data

MacMullen, Ramsay, 1928–
    Romanization in the time of Augustus / Ramsay MacMullen.
        p.   cm.
    Includes bibliographical references and index.
    ISBN 0-300-08254-1 (alk. paper)
        1. Rome—Civilization.   2. Rome—History—Augustus, 30 B.C.–14 A.D.
    3. Rome—Provinces—Administration.   4. Acculturation—Rome.   I. Title.

DG 273 .M33   2000
937'.07—dc21   00-028108

A catalogue record for this book is available from the British Library.

The paper in this book meets the guidelines for permanence and durability of the Committee
on Production Guidelines for Book Longevity of the Council on Library Resources.

10 9 8 7 6 5 4 3 2 1

CONTENTS

Illustrations

PREFACE

My object is to point out and explain the appearance of a way of life in areas of the Roman empire outside of Italy just like that prevailing inside Italy. I focus on those decades in which Augustus was alive. My sketch should help to explain how Roman civilization eventually appeared everywhere, as one single thing, so far as it was ever achieved. The degree of achievement, however imperfect, remains a thing of wonder, familiar to everyone; but its processes have never been looked at in any comprehensive fashion.

A thing of wonder, indeed! It quite struck my imagination, many years ago, that I could pick up a book in Romanian and read it—"read" it, I admit, with some impudence and guesswork, drawing on what I knew of Latin, French, and Italian. The general subject of the book was already familiar to me, too. Had not Dr. Johnson once confessed of his student days, "I got the Latin from the sense, not the sense from the Latin?"

My experiment in so remote a tongue as Romanian thus succeeded, sort of, as with Portuguese later in the same manner and measure, approaching it through Spanish. Such was my personal encounter with the spread of Romance languages, from the Black Sea to the Atlantic—Rome's most enduring gift to the West.

Again, when I was last in Turkey, there was a market building, a *macellum*, still to be seen and in use as such, of a design imported from Italy of late Republican times (though with a minaret added!)—to be matched, among architectural reminders of the past, with many well-known bridges of characteristically Roman design still in use as such in western European countries.

It was striking to me also to learn that a fondness for wine had at a certain time spread from Rome's center westward to lands previously awash in beer, just as sweet water from the eastern inland replaces the salty Pacific in the Golfo Dulce as the daily tides recede.

And it was striking most recently in my reading to find the Romans' New

Year's festivities coming to prevail over all the western empire and much of the eastern too, there to prevail for centuries, along with the Romans' graveside festival, the Rosalia, still celebrated in certain festivals of eastern European lands.

To understand just how this all happened presented me with an inviting challenge. I addressed it even while inwardly acknowledging the likelihood that I might find little new to interest specialists. As I well knew, they had said it all already!—whether in works of smaller focus, describing the process in individual provinces, or more broadly, if tangentially, in the course of discussing Roman imperialism. How could I hope to gather and present so much that had been said in any readable fashion? Even if it could be somehow shaped into some huge lump, it would still be too little: meaning, that the evidence, so great a part of it being archeological, lacked a tongue. The living population behind it could be interrogated only indirectly as to the why of their behavior; and, beyond that principal obstacle to any real understanding, there were, there are, and will for ever be a thousand other gaps in our knowledge.

Really, I could see that I must narrow my curiosity to some more manageable scope, though without surrendering the broad interest of it. It was not, after all, the "huge lump" of largely archeological information that interested me for its own sake, so much as the processes that produced it. I needed therefore to deal only with such parts of it as would illuminate those processes; and they could be most conveniently found in the period of the later Roman Republic and early Principate. So there in that span of time I decided to fix my inquiry, calling it only for reason of brevity "Augustus' time" (Augustus, who started his life as Octavius in Cicero's consulship of 63 B.C. and died with his grand title in A.D. 14).

The story of those processes itself is one of many chapters. Let it begin at the beginning with the making of a core state, from Romulus' time forward; eventually, a confederation spreading over the Italian peninsula; next, conquest overseas; thereafter, the articulation of political and military control over subject lands; and, as an accompaniment expressed and reaffirmed at every moment, the Romans' sense of the need to master others: their drive for greaterness, maiestas. Never, however, was there greater progress made toward one single way of life, a thing to be fairly called "Roman civilization of the Empire," than in that lifetime of Augustus.

In parentheses I wonder if the word "progress" is the right one, or why, when biodiversity is so treasured, our logic is never brought to bear on the proliferation of our own species and its economic and cultural expression in "One World." Long live difference! say I. In any case, no end to all difference was achieved by the Romans, no single homogeneous "Roman civilization," partly because of the limits on their will and their administrative powers, partly because what they carried abroad in Augustus' day was a civilization already so full of differences, so broadly "Mediterranean" in a loose sense.

What precisely could "Roman" mean, then? Rather than struggle over terminology, let me simply lay out what evidence I can find of things newly appearing in the provinces, which are matched by their like, then or earlier, in Italy. "Roman" will thus be "Italian."

Most obviously and first, the new things to be described will be the emigrants from the peninsula themselves, bringing their material and intellectual culture with them; secondarily but of much more importance in the long run, new things, new thoughts, new patterns of behavior having their original in that Italian homeland but then naturalized among the provincial populations. I give attention to both of these phenomena, quite inseparable if only because of actual intermarriage; but I am most interested in the second. Readers may put any name they wish to the result—that replication of differing degrees of fidelity and completeness in different areas. Whatever it may be called, whatever its success, it represented a change in people's lives, and therefore, history, which is my object of study.

As to those lives that changed, they do not lie at the level of ordinary historical description. Their socioeconomic strata may be fairly, or very, respectable in their own provinces; but if one approaches Romanization from a stand in Rome, looking outward, of course they seem hardly worth notice. One can hardly avoid looking *down*. The stance seems common in discussions of the subject over recent decades, trying to determine the degree of conscious intent at the Roman top and center so as to explain cultural changes in the provinces. "Colonialism" and "ideology" are two terms that will suggest how a good deal of that discussion has been directed; and enlightenment has been sought among familiar texts, like Tacitus, and among familiar questions, especially regarding imperialism.

Entirely legitimate, such approaches, but they lose sight of the people themselves whose way of life embodied change. To a repair of this loss, the bulk of the evidence that tells us about Romanization points the way. It is not Rome-centered; it is not easily sought in literary texts; rather, it is archeological, and of the provinces. It has no heroes, no spokesmen, indeed no one to write so much as a word for us describing how and why Roman ways were adopted. Still, no one doubts that populations lying on the far side of stones, potsherds, and all the silent litter of the past have a story to tell.

I IN THE EAST

1. The immigrants settle in

Here in the east, as people saw their homeland pass into the Romans' power, they must have wondered just how life would change—now that the fighting was over and done with. There might or might not be new taxes to pay; and there would be loss of control over relations with other states. These consequences could be predicted from Rome's behavior in the past. But would there be much else?

Rome's leaders and spokesmen appeared to be civilized people, that is, like Greeks themselves. Surely, then, they brought with them no policy of cultural imperialism. Their personal servants were Greeks, that is, slaves. Besides masters and slaves in the conquering force there was of course the immense mass of soldiery, not to be counted on; but they might be capable of respecting what deserved their respect. Finally, on their heels or even in advance of them came civilians seeking profit. These moved or lodged where they pleased, while fitting in not too badly: and they too spoke Greek not only to do business but for the very good reason also that, as often as not, they too were Greeks in some sense—from southern Italy or Sicily, or freed slaves descended from once-Greek families.

You might almost suppose that Romans were only another folk among Alexander's boundless conquests, thoroughly digested into his legacy by the point in time with which the present study is concerned. For confirmation, a visit to their homeland in Italy and Sicily would have opened to view a degree of approximation between these, and the east, truly remarkable, in certain parts and strata. What had been for long called Greater Greece had received its settlers from Miletus and a dozen other cities centuries earlier; they had occupied the most promising southern coastal points from Syracuse and Palermo up to the Bay of Naples with a success that insulated them against much change, even after incorporation into the Roman state; while in that Roman state's very capital a majority of the population were of Greek descent, by the hundreds of thousands, through importation and manumission of enslaved captives.[1] Why fear the imposition of barbarism, then, when Aeneas' descendants began and steadily extended their subjugation of the Hellenistic world?

That unapologetic conqueror of Alexander's homeland, L. Aemilius Paullus, when he had a chance as governor later to share his own civilization with the population in Spain, chose instead to offer Greek gifts, works of statuary, out of a superabundance of prior pillage.[2] The date lay close to the mid-second century B.C., at a time when the Hellenizing of the Roman elite was still in its early phases. In the next century in what had been Gallic territory to the north, as the population of the Po valley was absorbed into the Roman state, some of the changes introduced into the way of life there can only be called Hellenistic. Items of fine pottery or sculpture manufactured there for export to regions further west might copy Hellenistic models.[3]

Roman admiration for such and similar models expressed itself through both import and imitation. By Augustus' day the resulting ascendance of the conquered Greeks over their conquerors in all but the public spheres of life was complete. Chefs, secretaries, interior decorators, physicians, were all from the east; likewise the most stylish of material comforts and artifacts. What leaders in taste and opinion were agreed on in calling civilization itself, humanitas, was to be sought among Greeks. "Even as we govern over that race of men in which civilization is to be found," Cicero remarked to his brother Quintus (in the days of Augustus' childhood, it so happened), "we should certainly offer to them what we have received from them . . . for we appear to owe them a special debt." He goes on to remind Quintus that he had been raised in that humanitas from his very childhood.[4]

In such a society with such an upbringing, it is no wonder that Augustus shared the consensus and eventually expressed it from his position of gigantic influence. He shared it in such little things as the quoting of Greek proverbs and literary tags, or in such big things as the celebration of a New Age in 17 B.C. by hymns in both languages.[5] That jewel of his reign, the Altar of Peace, was given a double staircase ascending it like the Twelve-Gods' altar in Athens; its reliefs were carved in the Athenian style; and the women of the imperial house therein portrayed had their hair done up in fashions most exquisitely derived from that of Hellenistic queens.[6]

To return, then, to my point of departure, asking what demeanor one might expect from Romans who appeared in one's streets in some eastern city: clearly no aggression should be looked for on the cultural level. The intruders would defer to local custom, they would be already converts to it, even if they were present, of course, principally as predators.

Their future intentions as well as the plain fact of their armed intrusions in the past must make their reception nevertheless somewhat chilly. For an advocate's reasons, Cicero might even claim that the average man in the agora (not of course the decent upperclass) "would freely seize the opportunity of inflicting some wound" on aliens among them "whose symbolic axes of authority are hated, whose name is bitter, and whose pasture-, land-, and import taxes are death."[7] Those western aliens are indeed found clustering, or it may better be thought of as huddling together, in neighborhoods and associations, whenever they were numerous enough to leave some mark on the historical record. The name they take in Greek is "The Local Roman Businessmen," sometimes merely "Resident Romans," the eastern equivalent of what in western provinces would be called *conventus* of Roman citizens. Mention of them begins in the early second century and runs down almost to the end of the period of interest to me, when "in the agora [of Gangra] the oath taken by the inhabitants of Paphlagonia and Roman businessmen" bound them publicly to the emperor and his descendants.[8] Scores of such associations are attested; they are spread over the Balkan peninsula, Aegean Islands, and Asia Minor, especially the coastal parts; even Syria, at Petra.[9] In Augustus' day they could be found in every city of any importance. No doubt the largest was Delos', terribly punished by Mithridates in 88, its survival barely detectible for a generation thereafter before its total disappearance. Another large one was in Pergamum. As the Augustan principate developed and Roman power advanced into Asia Minor, so too did the presence of immigrant citizens, to Phrygia or Caria.

To determine what influence these groups might exert if they chose, the more clearly to bring out how little was exerted in the service of cultural changes, perhaps the degree of their corporate organization should be considered first. At Delos in the second and earlier first century they formed several large associations of a sort quite common both in the east and Italy, defined by common occupation; these in turn elected presidents, *magistri*, and an agreed-on patron deity, Hermes=Mercury, Apollo, Poseidon. We may suppose they consisted of retailers, bankers, and shippers. Roman citizens in Narona in 48 B.C. elected their *magistri* and quaestors. With no sign of having formally titled leaders, associations here or anywhere raised money under duress, or did so freely as groups of good citizens for public projects; they expressed their thanks or offered their respects as groups to this or that political figure; were granted permission by Augustus to build a shrine to Roma and the deified Caesar; or they wangled corporate tax exemptions; from all of which, it seems fair to suppose that they could generally unite behind a common concern if they wanted to.[10]

In three small centers in Dalmatia in time of civil war the resident Romans appear to be in charge of the city itself. The exception tests the rule: they were influential not because of any constitutional position but because of the unusual circumstances, in which Roman citizens were expected to take an active part, to contribute, even to sign into the armies.[11] Their fellow residents without Italian connections looked to them to do the talking. Far more than by weight of numbers or formal organization, influence could always be brought to bear through personal ties to a governor, best, or to some past or present official or millionaire. Cicero is our witness to this in the 60s, 50s, and 40s B.C.[12]

The form of government prevailing in cities throughout the east remained very much as Roman conquest had found it, oligarchic. Roman senators controlling foreign affairs wanted to find their like in charge of the local scene, suitably conservative and deferential; but the natural drift of things even before conquest had long lain in that oligarchic direction anyway. A great conqueror like Pompey acting almost on a clean slate and as a good Roman in what had been Mithridates' kingdom, now to form the provinces of Pontus and Bithynia, organized the region along lines that looked pretty much like those to be found elsewhere in pre-Roman Anatolia. He raised several small rural centers to the official status of cities in the Hellenistic sense, which was also the Italian; and he invested these, and an additional handful of existing cities like Sinope, not only with authority over, but income deriving from, a farming territory around each. Like a Hellenistic monarch he renamed half of those he promoted after himself: Magnopolis and so forth; he created from nothing a Victory City, Nicopolis in Armenia.[13] Only the introduction of a censor to enroll the senators in these new centers, and life-membership for the chosen, had a Roman character.[14] In this region as in others needing no reorganization, thenceforward, there would be popular assemblies little listened to, and a council really in control, overseeing a small number of annual officials.

To these latter positions, even in cities where Roman associations were also active, inscriptions show a not inconsiderable number of Roman aspirants winning election. They are seen to act like the minority they were, accepting the majority structure of politics around them and seeking reward in ordinary terms: through public offices, priesthoods, pious acts to local deities, membership on civic boards, or the presidency of the gymnasium or festival games. They made big cash contributions to their communities.[15] The aqueduct-section across the

Marnas valley built for Ephesus in Augustus' reign by one P. Sextilius Pollio in his own name and that of his wife and children still stands today as a testimony to the civic ambitions of a family from Italy. They were 'playing the game,' one may say, by the local rules.

Further epigraphic evidence shows the children of such families beginning the ascent to office through participation in athletic competitions, in the age-old Hellenic tradition. They joined the upperclass Youth Associations and went on to further studies in Athens. A certain Mussius at Miletus is honored in a public decree for "his talent in rhetoric, poetry, and the arts generally," needless to say not Latin. And resident Romans married local women, they bought land and set up as farmers.[16] In sum, wherever they are found in the east, save in their own colonies, they seem determined to fit in, even to deny their ancestral culture if not the advantages of their Roman citizenship and connections.

It might be thought important to define more closely who "they" were: not all descendants of Aeneas, but many of them, as was indicated above, descendants rather of Greeks in the first place. The evidence on which to decide the proportions of the immigrant mix consists almost entirely of names in inscriptions. Here, distinguishing between a person of thoroughly Italian origin and Roman citizenship, and another whose own father or father's father had been born in Syria, reduced to servitude, and sent back east as agent for the interests of the family or of some tax-collecting company, may be impossible. Perhaps the latter, freedman category in "Roman" communities even made up the majority.[17] Add, the people of eastern origin who earned Roman citizenship and so took a Roman name—they too are indistinguishable. But what counts for my purpose is the fact that, regardless of their origin or civic status, the immigrants' behavior was the same. The superiority they asserted had nothing to do with the general style of life they found around them. That, they seem all to have accepted as the best imaginable. What they rather reserved to themselves was the pride of power, enjoyed either directly or indirectly.

For their part, Greeks seemed to invite more change than was attempted. Their readiness to fawn and flatter was often remarked on contemptuously by the rulers of the world. They liked to pass honorific decrees, a number of which Cicero mentions, while more still survive on stone; or they put up statues—of one of Antony's legates, most likely when he was a governor in the early thirties, or of Agrippa in Sparta, commissioned by a civic leader.[18] They organized festival games in compliment to a proconsul, renamed a voting unit of the citizen population after some great man, instituted a cult group—all this before and during Augustus' lifetime and ultimately centering on him.[19] Latin names thus appeared increasingly in the public record and might be called a form of Romanization; yet the customs, social or political, which accounted for their appearance were entirely Hellenistic.

Certain little habits died hard. In Delos the Italian originals imported quantities of wine from Apulia and pottery from Etruria and Campania; in another generation or two the residents of Corinth, mostly Roman colonists, imported Italian lamps for their parties, along with the drinking vessels named for their north Italian manufacturer, "ACO" cups, and elegant relief-decorated ceramic ware from Arretium, some by that late-Augustan potter with a splendid name, Publius Cornelius. In Pergamum there was even some local imitation of Italian ceramics, presumably for the resident Italian or Roman population.[20]

Naturally, too, when civil war commanders in the east needed cash to pay their troops, their troops insisted on something with a familiar look; so mint-men at campaign headquarters, wherever that might be, issued Roman silver pennies, *denarii*, even in the midst of a sea of eastern city- and royal issues. The experiments were at first only that. They helped to familiarize eastern markets with Roman units of reckoning in silver, and encouraged cities to respond with their own experiments in equivalences. It is natural to suppose that, as money was raised for war or as taxes, it should be payable in Roman terms, for example, in Illyria in the 30s or in Galatia in the 20s. An inscription of 27 B.C. indeed records Augustus' mandating of *denarii* as the unit of payment in Thessaly. How widely he meant to be heard is not known, but the measure left no sign in any other context. Well into his reign Augustus himself still put out large numbers of the traditional eastern *cistophori*. Bronze coinage continued to be minted by a hundred local mints, for centuries, without any imperial interference, side by side with Roman bronze.[21] Indeed, the fact that at the end of Augustus' reign the whole region had come under a single precious-metal currency system with only compatible local issues in non-conforming local bronze—this great fact arose out of no central pressure or policy at all. It was a result rather of unhurried market behavior and the realities of power expressed in numberless situations ad hoc, showing once again a surprising degree of acceptance of the Greeks on their own terms, applied in the realm of money as elsewhere.

The fact is surprising only to a modern mind. True, Romans as private individuals in the east were overwhelmingly active in business, not torpid rentiers, and many were connected with tax companies that handled huge sums, having therefore liquid capital to invest as, in effect, bankers. But it is not easy to see anything in their situation that would have suggested the desirability of displacing local currencies. Payment of armies was another matter; and it was for these, ultimately, that requisitions and taxes alike were demanded. For change toward a unitary system, then, the most likely engine was administrative convenience, but only slowly acknowledged by local mints. They first modified their issues to be compatible with the Roman and then, at least in silver, ceased activity for good, one by one.

2. Effects on public institutions

The civil wars just invoked as the setting for currency innovation did most horribly embroil the east. Extraordinary efforts were made by all participants to increase the size of their forces. After what appeared to be decisive victories, in fact only in preparation for more fighting, the winners had repeatedly to pay off their men in cash or land or both. That story has been often told. Its outline will have to be recalled again so far as it concerns the west; but in the east, its effects can be seen especially after Philippi in 42 and after Actium in 31. Even before Philippi, before his death, Caesar had soldiers in relatively manageable numbers to find a home for, as he did at Sinope and elsewhere. Afterwards, the scale of demand sharply increased. It could be easily predicted that the sudden planting of Roman veterans in clusters of a culturally viable mass would have some effect on the accommodation so far described.

On the map, forty-odd locations can be identified to which Caesar gave a Roman form, like Sinope or Antony did, later, or Augustus at that same time post-Philippi or in the early twenties B.C.[22] Some settings were little comparable, for example, Beirut compared to Arba in Dalmatia; yet no doubt the group of seventeen to which Arba belonged on the Balkan coast from Nicopolis northward did rather closely resemble each other; likewise a second group of eight in what is now south-central Turkey: Antioch-in-Pisidia and its neighbors. A few foundations represented the amalgamating of two or more small populations, in the old tradition of synoikismos (Patras or Augustus' own Victory City, like Pompey's); others were previously existing centers to which some small number of settlers was added, along with a charter as a *municipium*. Municipal status insured Roman citizenship to the families and persons of elected officials. At some sites, a second infusion of settlers might be added to a first, as at Buthrotum, where the displaced inhabitants in revolt drove out the colonists for a time, or at Dyme, where Augustus added his own men on top of Caesar's, with some re-surveying involved; elsewhere we hear of small infusions of men to towns in no other way reconstituted (Attaleia and others).

Most *coloniae*, numbering at least a score, were Augustus'; perhaps a further

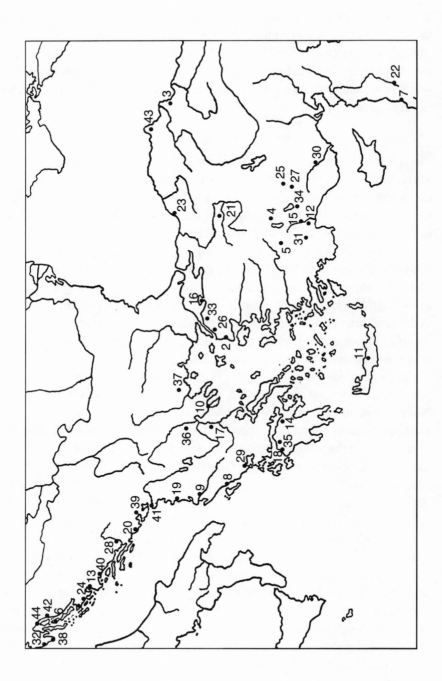

half-dozen, too, unless they were Caesarian or triumviral. To the citizens of a small number was granted the tax status of an Italian town, that is, immunity from direct taxes though not from import duties.[23] It is possible to identify the particular legions from which Augustus drew the settlers for some of his eastern colonies, and at Antioch-in-Pisidia, to see where he got the land for them: by confiscating temple estates.[24]

The demographic and institutional impact of all this activity, involving forty to sixty thousand veterans within some twenty years, was predictably serious. It

FIGURE I. The colonizing effort in the East in Augustus' time

IN THE EAST:

C = Caesar-founded;   c = colony;
A = Augustus-founded;   m = municipium

1	Aenona *Am*	23	Heraclea Pontica *Cc*
2	Alexandria Troas *Ac*	24	Iader = Zara *Ac*
3	Amisus *Cc*	25	Iconium *Ac*
4	Antioch-in-Pisidia *Ac*	26	Lampsacus *Cc*
5	Apamea Myrleia *Cc*	27	Lystra *Ac*
6	Arba *Am*	28	Narona *Cc* or *Ac*
7	Beirut *Ac*	29	Nicopolis free city, synoecized
8	Buthrotum *Cc* / *Ac*	30	Ninica *Ac*
9	Byllis *Cc* / *Ac*	31	Olbasa *Ac*
10	Cassandreia, triumviral then *Ac*	32	Parentium *Ac*
11	Cnossus *Cc* or col. triumviral	33	Parium *Cc*
12	Comama *Ac*	34	Parlais *Ac*
13	Corinium *Am*	35	Patras, synoecized *Ac*
14	Corinth *Cc*	36	Pella, *Cc* or *Ac* or triumviral
15	Cremna *Ac*	37	Philippi triumviral then *Ac*
16	Cyzicus *Cc*	38	Pola *Ac*
17	Dium *Ac* or triumviral	39	Risinium *Am*
18	Dyme = Iulia Dumaeorum *Cc* or triumviral	40	Salonae (Martia Iulia S.) *Cc* / *Ac*
19	Dyrrhachium *Cc* or *Ac* or triumviral	41	Scodra *Ac*
20	Epidaurum *Cc*	42	Senia *Ac*
21	Germe *Ac*	43	Sinope (Felix Iulia S.) *Cc*
22	Heliopolis *Ac*	44	Tarsatica *Am*

should not be exaggerated. Around it was, after all, an East of five hundred cities or more, with their own ways deeply embedded in the past. Yet it introduced a good number of non-commissioned officers who counted as middle class, a certain mass of purchasing power, ties to Italy and higher personages, and patterns for self-government which replicated the Italian, more or less.

The colonies' population would be divided into voting units and a minimum age set for eligibility to office. There would be a standard Italian pair of *duumviri* assisted by aediles, the four together sometimes called *quattuorviri*.[25] With these changes in place, added to Pompey's foundations in Pontus and Bithynia, Roman rule may thus be said to have brought a significant minority of the population under its own forms of urban government.

But notice how little different from Hellenistic patterns the realities of power remained, oligarchic and close to plutocratic; also, that voting units were nothing new in a Greek city, and in at least one of Augustus' colonies they are even called *phylai*. By Pompey's arrangements in Pontus and Bithynia, later replicated in several Galatian cities, the college of officials might vary from three to five, with one member among them preeminent, a president; and other quite non-Italian anomalies can be occasionally glimpsed in other areas. Following the usual practice, to leave as much in place as could be accommodated within the central purposes of rule, but to be as flexible as possible, the Roman founders of cities not only satisfied the new settlers but the prior residents, too. The latter were, after all, numerous, and now citizens, too, and in many instances a majority.[26] They could not too arbitrarily be subjected to new forms and governmental practices; nor were they, after all, mere barbarians.

The territories over which pre-conquest cities ruled might vary enormously in size. No comparison with these is very helpful, in understanding the new settlement patterns. The extent of the colony Antioch-in-Pisidia has been reckoned at about 540 square miles; of Philippi, at about 730. For administrative purposes newly settled cities, like the old, recognized and dealt with the surrounding villages. Some enclosed formerly independent little towns. Land declared vacant became public and could be bought by individual citizens.[27] Over new and old alike presided governors, for whose convenience certain cities were named as centers of juridical areas.[28]

The logical consequence, that conquest led on to the imposition of Roman law, did not follow, because in Augustus' day there were so many exceptions negotiated by treaty at the time of individual cities' surrender to the conqueror, and such a very great latitude of action enjoyed by governors. These officers in effect *were* law and could impose or more often permit whatever they chose. The result is in fact a confusion made worse by the lack of adequate evidence; and most of the little that survives dates to post-Augustan periods. For my purposes, what counts is how much alien legal practice was introduced into people's lives, and so became a part of their thoughts; but my question, even a little limited in this fashion, cannot be very well answered. Even the best scholarly survey of what is known or knowable makes that clear.[29]

To begin with, Roman law recognized the individual's right to be judged according to his civic status, which might depend on treaty-arrangements in turn governing the status of his place of residence. Resident Romans, however, may be seen waiving the rights they were entitled to, preferring Greek law; and the high jurists in the empire's very capital considered and accepted degrees of *mos regionis* so far at least as private law was concerned. Augustus' edict of which a translation was found inscribed in Palestine gives us an illustration: the crime of breaking into someone else's tomb is forbidden partly in Roman, partly Hellenistic, terms. There were distinctions in treatment usual between criminal and civil cases; also levels of gravity of offense, the lesser falling under local authorities, the more serious even in a Roman colony having to await a hearing by the governor; and it was his choice whether or not to follow or allow local customs. Local authorities would tend to apply their own, of course, which would be traditional Greek law; and if they spoke for a "free city," at least over non-Romans their jurisdiction might rise to quite severe penalties.

No one disputed the Romans' right to command, and under the Principate of course that principal *imperium*, held by the emperor, might be exerted ad lib. Examples are well known: the Cyrene Edicts, and so forth.[30] What does not emerge from even these, however, and still less from all the exceptions, reservations, and complications just reviewed, is a Roman will to unify all subjects under a single set of regulations. The fact will recur in a later chapter. For the eastern provincial population, plainly, it sufficed that things were made easy and familiar for the people that counted, beginning with the supreme authority on the spot: a representative of the state embodying the right to rule, *imperium*, or the delegates of such a person: under the Principate, proconsuls, or propraetors. Next beneath such officials lay the upper ranks of Roman citizens; then, non-citizens.

The introduction of an alien legal system began with administrative law, settling the affairs of communities, not of individuals. The shaping of city government, settling of boundary disputes, taxation—these and the like followed on conquest almost as a part of the act itself. All could be handled exactly as the Roman authorities liked. When we look rather at people's relations with each other, however, the effect of conquest is not easily demonstrated. The rights of a tenant against her landlord, of a father over his deceased daughter's dowry, or of one farmer against another who struck him in a quarrel regarding the goats of the one and the fields of the other, seem to have been determined in the traditional ways, undisturbed by imported novelties, unless it were a Roman who sued. In that latter case, of course litigation might carry the dispute to a praetor in the imperial capital, even to the emperor himself, at every step obedient to Roman procedures.

Access to Roman law was the privilege of Roman citizenship, as every reader of St. Paul's life well knows. It had been for centuries within the gift of the highest officials. As reward or incentive in the period of the civil wars it had been given out to individual local leaders like Eurycles, mentioned above, or P. Caninius Agrippa—despite his name, a son of some certain Alexiades. War not manumission no doubt explains some fair proportion of the endless Romans named Iulii in the eastern provinces, and Antonii, too, and Vipsanii and Barbatii and so forth.[31] Perhaps these newly enrolled, added to prior immigrant totals, approached one per cent of the population (excluding Egypt) at the time Augustus appeared on the scene, and his program of colonizing thereafter doubled that total.[32]

Granted, such immigrants and Greeks raised into the ranks of citizens would set an example, exert influence, advertise Rome—yes, but not to the same effect as veterans. Beyond their numbers, these latter constituted quite a novel element through their cohesion and distinctness from the context around them: they are often seen joining or initiating some particularly Rome-loyal motion. In particular, they brought a knowledge of their institutions which a naturalized citizen would lack; they could not fail by their presence and disproportionate power to raise the general knowledge and consciousness of their law, whether or not it was much sought out or applied among non-Romans.

Methodical efforts to make it known appear in our principal sources themselves, which are on stone or bronze, and survive not only because of the pains taken to inscribe them on durable materials but to make copies of them as well, and to order their distribution and display. But the effectiveness of these routines in Romanizing, that is, in making non-Romans act and think in some awareness of Roman law, depended on reading the document put up on walls and bulletin boards. In short, it depended on knowing Latin. In the long term, descendants of Italian immigrants to the east lost their Latin (suggesting an eventual fate for Roman law); and in the short term, we have the anecdote of the Greek judge, therefore a prominent and educated person, yet ignorant of

Latin—this, a generation after Augustus. He was evicted from his judicial panel by an indignant Claudius. In a like case, an envoy from Lycia was stripped of his Roman citizenship for being unable to address the Roman senate in its own language.[33] The two men together serve as reminders of a Greek reality, which could get along very well in the old ways.

With the exception of a narrow zone along the Via Egnatia in southern Macedonia, and Beirut, rightly called "an island of Romanism" by reason of its determined loyalty to the ruling tongue, Latin did not take root for ordinary communication. It generally vanished within a generation or two in immigrant families. In the long run, not even veteran colonies in the east succeeded in establishing it in their own streets, to say nothing of the surrounding region.[34] That is, imperial officialdom spoke as always in Latin; technical terms generally dealing with public life and administration made their way steadily into Greek; translators and interpreters of Roman law begin to be heard of in the east, nomikoi; and the emperor's loyal army veterans in the conduct of their colonies' official affairs, including their coinage, used Latin. Yet on the other hand both emperor and veterans alike made concessions in the form of translation. Bilingual inscriptions are not uncommon especially in Roman colonies. Augustus' official autobiography offers the most famous instance, while an Italian family immigrating to Philadelphia during his reign, to be sure of their being understood, recalled the founding members on their tomb in Latin at the top, but Greek beneath.[35]

In Augustan Latin epitaphs of Antioch-in-Pisidia, the names of women are generally absent. The fact is best explained by assuming they were Greeks of the area, and were as such not fully integrated into the veteran community. "Do we not have, here, one of the reasons for the rather rapid disuse of Latin?"[36]

Yet across the eastern provinces, Latin loan words did enter Greek. The fact was just mentioned, along with the limitations on it. People had to get used to calling themselves collectively by Roman names, because they were now enrolled as Roman citizens in a Roman voting tribe, or as residents of a Roman colony, in city voting units. At Corinth, there were ten or more such: called Atia (for Augustus' mother), Agrippia (for his son-in-law), Calpurnia (for his adoptive mother, Caesar's wife), and so forth; and the parts of the city might be called after those of Rome itself: in Antioch-in-Pisidia, precincts like Velabrus, Tuscus, Cermalus.[37] The whole city itself might be renamed in honor of some Roman lord: not Soloi, home of malapropisms, but now Pompeiopolis; not Anthedon but Agrippias, not Karana but Sebastopolis, not Anazarba or Mazaca or Antioch-in-Pisidia but Caesarea. There were a very great many Caesareas, a great many Augustus = (Greek) Sebaste-towns scattered around the eastern provinces and minor kingdoms.[38] Pola became Iulia Pietas. As flattery, they all struck familiar, by now rather reedy notes, in echo of all those places earlier recognizing Hellenistic rulers: Antiocheia, Seleukeia, and so forth. They represented the Hellenizing of Roman conquest quite as much as any Romanizing of Greek geography.

Flattery infected not only place but time itself: time was declared by popular vote in many cities to have begun only with the benign appearance of, let us say, Pompey; so the coinage of this or that city proclaimed a new era's commencement in 66, 65, or 64 B.C. by which civic business was to be dated (so, for example, in his six Pontic foundations).[39] The good news would be printed on the local coins. Months too might be renamed, as we all know: Sextilis made August, another instance of Rome's own Hellenization. Augustus' father had been recognized similarly: Quintilius made July. To the son, because of his endless reign and his unique celebrity, a great deal more was eventually due, and duly offered: the commencement of local eras at Amisus, Anazarba, or Ancyra, to go no further than the letter A; the renaming of all twelve months in Cyprus after the ruler and his family, running on to his tribunician power (the month Demarchexousios), Aeneas, Anchises, and the Capitolium![40] Though he asserted no accession day, his birthday on September 23rd was celebrated everywhere, and in Egypt, the 23rd of every month whatsoever. Actium and other high moments of his ascension and reign were widely remembered for thanksgiving.[41] In particular, in 9 B.C., the governor of the province Asia made the irresistible suggestion that all the cities there should commence their year from September 23rd, and they were so delighted with the idea, they voted him a gold crown.[42]

The novelties thus introduced within a relatively short period appear to have affected most urban centers by the latter days of the reign, and would have to be noted by anyone who dealt with public documents. Otherwise, who cared? Observances might, however, take a more visible form: of hymns sung in a prominent point of assembly at Pergamum on September 23rd, or festivals on Samos on the date of Augustus' accepting the consulship after a lapse of many years. In the new province of Paphlagonia in 3 B.C. the entire population swore to a long declaration of loyalty.[43] There were festivals with games established in many cities to take official notice of this or that day honoring the reign. Games honoring great benefactors, sometimes kings, occasionally Roman commanders, had long been at home in eastern cities.[44]

The offering of cult to Caesar, Augustus, and the abstraction Roma has been made the object of special studies which there is no need to repeat or even to summarize. The attendant rituals and beliefs developed along traditional lines. If there was any public introduction of Roman civilization, it cannot have amounted to much more than the acquainting of the audience with the physical appearance of the imperial family, occasionally in characteristic moments, e.g. at worship.[45] Everything else was purely Hellenistic. To express gratitude in proportion to both gifts and givers, to please the powerful and so to incline them to favor, to acknowledge their more than human greatness, had long been the custom of the Greek-speaking world, giving rise to a rich language of symbolic gestures: thanks, praise, speeches, song, communal activities, monuments, and worship in seamless series. All in good time had been offered to the Romans, the most emphatic and precious ones being, in the end, no less than the due of Augustus.

Hence, notably, the request in 29 B.C. from the Asian cities that they be permitted to establish his cult. His permission was qualified: the object should be Roma and himself, conjointly—perhaps in line with the veneration recently established in Mytilene, of Roma and Caesar; but only the latter cult was declared proper for Roman citizens.[46] Two years later, Mytilene followed up with a decree establishing its own version of emperor worship; and copies of what was voted were sent round to several other eastern cities, to the emperor in Rome, and to several western cities.[47]

By the introduction of imperial cult nothing alien to the east need have been added. In fact little was; but that little, displays some curious features that deserve mention. Chronologically first: around 190 B.C. a prominent Chian citizen commissioned a relief in marble showing the "genesis" of Romulus and Remus (so, perhaps being suckled by the wolf?). It was to be a compliment, a very expensive compliment as he made plain, to the resident Romans and an offering to the goddess Roma, whose cult had recently been established there.[48] He had recently returned from an embassy to Rome, had there perhaps seen the wolf-statue on the Capitolium or noticed the wolf and twins on Roman coins. He had learnt something about his hosts, so knew how most appropriately to honor the divine essence of the state. His gesture saluted its history very much as the coins of Apamea had done, showing the wolf and twins, in the triumviral period. Similarly, the honor paid to Aeneas and Anchises: those names were attached to months in a fashion mentioned above; depiction of them appeared on coins of their home, Ilium.[49] And it was a historical event very dear to Augustus, the capture of Alexandria on the 1st of August, that was signalized by a day set apart in Egypt (his victory at Actium, he had honored according to his own dictates).[50] Regarding all these honorific gestures, however, the point needs to be made again: though they were given a distinctly Roman character by Rome's Greek subjects, showing how features of Roman history had become public knowledge, they were nevertheless a distinctly Greek gift. And when we see Greeks on other occasions advising the cities of Italy on how best to shape similar compliments, we are reminded of the currents of influence flowing in both directions across the ancient world.[51]

3. Roman structures for Roman novelties

A once-notorious case of compliment carried to excess may be found in the reign of Antiochus IV of Syria. He had taken the title "God Manifest," Epiphanes, but was nicknamed "Epimanes," "Maniac." His mind awhirl with images of the conquering civilization picked up during a long sojourn as a hostage in Rome, he returned to his own capital determined to show his subjects the world of the future. Indeed he succeeded, but ahead of his times. It was in the 170s B.C.: "he put on a gladiatorial exhibition in the Roman manner at first for an audience unused to such a show, so responding with more horror than pleasure," Livy reports; but as they grew used to it, they liked it. Volunteers came forward to perform, where at first the performers had to be imported at great expense from Rome.[52] Whether or not, thereafter, an occasional Romanophile in some other city than Antioch-on-the-Orontes followed his example, or Roman generals before Lucullus indulged their national passion, we cannot say; but Lucullus at least did exhibit gladiators in the major cities of the province Asia, a century after Antiochus; and with an increase in both the Roman presence and our sources we hear rather casually of gladiatorial exhibitions in a scattering of Greek cities over the course of the next generation.

Now, as Vitruvius says, the rectangular Roman style of forum and the spacing of its columns could serve for such shows, but not the Greek; and if there were to be anything done in style, it must be in proper accommodations. Oval race-tracks would do, not very well, perhaps: they could be found at Tiberias or other cities. Most likely it was something of this sort that Herod built in Caesarea "Maritima" toward the middle of Augustus' reign, as he had earlier, in 28 B.C., built a suitable facility in Jerusalem and probably in Samaria, too.[53] The Caesarean structure survives in part and allows a correct interpretation. It is only by chance that we have this to explain our texts, or know of an amphitheater built in Antioch-on-the-Orontes by Caesar and one in Alexandria under Augustus.[54]

So the evidence adds up: Romans in particularly Roman and triumphant mood liked this bloody sport, along with wild beast hunts; it would find its most

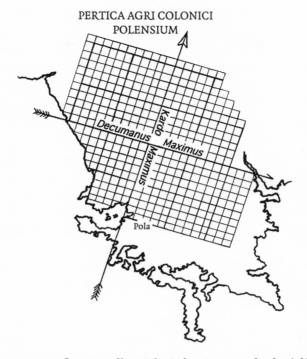

FIGURE 2. A page from Kandler: "The Polans' surveyed colonial land."

natural patrons in great generals, its most natural audience in colonies like Beirut, its frequent occasion on imperial cult days; and it caught on. Antiochus' enthusiasm received a sort of delayed vindication in the increasing audiences of the east. Corinthian potters found some general market in such eastern cities for depictions of its scenes.[55]

The indications provided by the Caesarean ruins is a reminder of the obvious: physical structures once had people in or on them doing things characteristic to the setting. Archeology and philology, stone and text, go naturally together in a description of the changes wrought by Rome.

Beyond gladiatorial combat, there is a second illustration in land surveying. A farming people, the Romans of course developed their own system of measurement. It began with the length of furrow an ox could comfortably plow (an *actus* of 120 feet), which, doubled, made a ploughing or *iugerum* 120 by 240 feet; that, doubled, made a family plot of land (a *heredium*, 240 feet on a side); and a hundred *heredia* made a *centuria* of 2,400 feet on a side, or about 710 meters. Division of large expanses was *centuriatio*. It has been called "the sign and symbol

of the effects of conquest on preexisting rural structures,"[56] producing still-de-
tectible marks from the clearing of fields and the accumulation of stone-dumps
in lines along the edge; sometimes in weaker growth of crops over the obliter-
ated remains of such lines, showing up as a weaker color; or the stronger color
of stronger growth in lines left by ditches, filled up over the course of time by
blown soil; or by surviving stretches of roads, especially crossing at right an-
gles; and other hints too many to mention, recognizable from air-photos since
the second World War.

But before that, to recognize the patterns, it took the knowledge of someone
trained in the old way, able to read Roman training manuals in their very difficult Latin, and the eye of a sailor, used to reading the surface of broad planes.
Such were Christian Falbe, Denmark's consul-general in Tunis, publishing in
1833 on centuriation around Carthage, and Pietro Kandler of Istria, fifteen years
later detecting tell-tale squares in the countryside around Pola.[57] These con-
formed to the most usual dimensions such as Kandler found also around Padua,
where he lived for a time; and they had the same orientation. In Italy centuriation went back at least to the fourth century B.C., detectible at Tarracina, with
many other areas receiving a similar imprint for ease of distribution after Roman conquest in the third and second centuries, though with particular clarity
in the Po valley around new urban centers like Padua and Ariminum, Mutina and
Parma.[58] The checkerboard of air-photos visible there is spectacular.

For this most ancient and quite un-Hellenized practice of Italy there was little occasion in the course of the Romans' empire-building in the east. Here, inventory had long been made before them, the population was settled into its
own divisions and title to land. Yet at Corinth in perhaps 44 B.C., at Patras somewhat later, the survey signs can be read.[59] Then in the north and west, apart
from the whole of the new province of Pannonia in A.D. 10, we have that string
or cluster of colonies including Dyme in 44 B.C., Pola, Salona in 39/33, Iader in
35/33, Cassandreia, and Nicopolis after Actium, all parcelled into squares of
ordinarily a hundred heredia.[60] If other information and probabilities were lack-
ing for their dates, there survives at least at one of them the honorific title accorded to Augustus, "father of the colony." And surely traces of Augustan centuriation, or Caesarian or triumviral, will eventually be found also at settlements
in Asia Minor like Sinope.

Surveying in the Roman manner introduced new units of measurement.
They were only words, one may object, with effects on nothing but speech. Yet
they determined just how land transfers were handled in Roman law courts,
which were not only set over colonists but available to non-citizens, too, and

sometimes required of these latter. Furthermore, surveying in traditional fashion distinguished between several types of land, for farming or wood-lots or grazing or common use, with consequences, when the job was done, for the farming practices of the area's population; and room was reserved on extra-wide bordering paths for heavy wagons, or for irrigation ditches.[61] From such provisions, improvements in agriculture would follow.

At Pola as at Nicopolis, the identity of the colony's network of main streets and the line defining the network of plots in its territory indicates how centuriation sometimes proceeded along a line of travel that ran straight through a new settlement and into its fields beyond. At Corinth excavation indicates even the survey center, the point fixed by the surveyor and his *groma*, which determined the city grid; Parentium and Iader were gridded, too, the latter with a Roman forum in the middle.[62]

A familiar feature of Roman occupation was of course good road-building, such as could be seen in the 70s in southern Anatolia and under Augustus among his Galatian colonies, to join them together.[63] The network received his name. Another Roman touch was city-wall construction such as Augustus undertook for colonies in Italy, certainly not for military use but more as a declaration of full urban character and status. Examples of such that he received credit for building can be seen at the colonies of Antioch-in-Pisidia, Tergeste, and Iader.[64] Aqueducts, too: built for Antioch-on-the-Orontes by Caesar, by Augustus for Ephesus with contributions from a local citizen.[65] And a principal reason for aqueducts was of course baths—not that such public facilities were new to the east, but that their arrangement, size, place in the day, and disengagement from strictly upper-class gymnasia were to be all new and typically Italian. A baths-building was paid for by Caesar in Antioch; two more by Agrippa; and, to a city of Cappadocia, another was presented by Augustus in honor of its faithful ruler.[66]

The intimate connection between warfare and so much of Roman construction or amplification of cities in the east introduces the army engineer. Caesar, Antony, Octavian-who-became-Augustus on campaign or in its intervals would all have had their Commanders of Engineers at hand for the works just reviewed: roads, bridges, centuriation, laying out of streets, walls, towers, aqueducts, and the drains and so forth in baths—quite evidently, not only because no alternative to these figures readily suggests itself but because, even under Augustus, instances begin to appear among inscriptions. C. Fabricius Tuscus was in charge of "building operations in the colony [of Alexandria Troas, no. 2 in Fig. 1] by order of Augustus" in 4 B.C., a prefect at the time, then a military tribune; and another Augustan military tribune, M. Cassius, turns up as *architectus* after his demobilization.[67] Anyone who has read Caesar's *Commentaries* well knows what inventive and sometimes very difficult tasks were required of army experts, over the river Kwai or the like, and there is even good second century B.C. archeological evidence of military skills in stone construction, in Spain, or anywhere else one cares to look, under the Empire.

Review of the evidence must take into account not only characteristically Roman capacities but preferences in design as well. Those that governed baths have been mentioned; add, Caesar's, which governed the basilicas he put up in Antioch-on-the-Orontes and Alexandria—they were not Hellenistic in plan— and an occasional temple on its high Italian platform, like the Capitolium at Iader built by the Appuleii, Herod's Jupiter temple in Heliopolis (no. 22 in Fig. 1) or a smaller building in Ephesus of perhaps the 20s B.C.[68] Corinth was equipped with a speaker's platform, a marble *rostra*, like that on the Roman forum.[69] Triumphal arches were an alien novelty, of the type put up by the family of the Sergii at Pola, with Victories in the reliefs and dedicatory inscriptions in the attic. One of them gives us the name of L. Sergius Lepidus, military tribune, who fought on the winning side at Actium. Michelangelo and Piranesi depicted the edifice in a less damaged form, and so we know it the better. It still stands today.[70]

Municipal senate chambers in the east from the mid-first century sometimes took advantage of Roman or Italian features in their seating arrangements; the results fitted better and more flexibly into a close urban site;[71] and the Roman style of theater-cavea with a 180-degree curve and other characteristic features was introduced, first by Caesar or Augustus at Antioch-in-Pisidia; likewise of an early date at Sparta by Augustus' loyal friend and supporter at Actium, Eurycles. The emperor richly rewarded him, and in the 20s B.C. he spent some of his wealth on gifts to cities: on baths at Corinth, and so forth. At Sparta, one of the indications of date for the theater is a pair of statues found in it, their bases inscribed with the names of the two imperial princes, Gaius and Lucius. One of these, Augustus for a time intended to appoint a successor; but both predeceased him.[72] In Syria there are no Hellenistic temples at all; the building does not exist until the area comes under Roman influence; and its presence as well as its form may be fairly called an import.[73]

A particularly striking illustration of a good Roman design exported is the food-market building, the *macellum*, realizing the Roman liking for the orderly concentration of activities in structures meant for them only. The imperial capital with its many specialized commercial forums, not to mention other types of utilitarian edifice, demonstrated this impulse in a very striking manner. The tradition of it reached back to the third century, finding imitation in dozens of Italian cities. Pompeii's is only the most famous—there, the early structure went up in the second century, only to come down in the much later, post-Augustan earthquake.[74] *Macella* were closed rectangles made up of porticoes along all four sides in which vendors could rent the stalls; and there might be a stone stall or two in the center, and water laid on for the cooling of perishables. There is a Caesarian example, if rightly identified, in Athens, to which Augustus later made contributions.[75] Of Augustan date, other examples can be seen in Corinth with grand proportions (175′ by 140′), put up principally as a fish market by a Roman family, the Cornelii, and on the city square of Mantinea some miles away, where, again, construction costs were covered by the city and "the Roman Businessmen."[76]

At the level only of architectural detail lie drains and sewers, paving of streets and squares, or a fondness for marble which can be seen here and there in the period and area.[77] Roman materials and techniques were introduced bit by bit over the last half of the first century, including the use of brick and cement, the latter serving as fill and strength behind a facing of small stones ("petit appareil," as archeologists generally call it) with the stones at the surface of the concrete sometimes arranged in a net pattern (*opus reticulatum*).[78] The evidence comes from Miletus, Pergamum, Ephesus, Sparta, Corinth. . . .

For my purposes what is most interesting is not the presence of these construction-practices as dating indicators but as indicators of how Roman techniques were diffused; for the evidence generally turns up in structures with some identifiable Roman connection: dedicated to a Roman end, perhaps cult, or paid for by a Roman, or occurring in a project of a more or less Roman plan. What is implied is both the impulse in the commission to replicate what had been seen or reported in some Italian city, most likely Rome, but also the presence of the workmen to do the job. They would have to take on others who were local and trained in local habits. Much of the use of stone, brick, and concrete in eastern projects is not very good, not very convincing; and the lack of the proper ingredients for the cement may be to blame; but then, the laying of stone cannot have been always or entirely by an Italian hand; so it is likely that the imported ideas were being realized by artisans used to their own ways, learning the new. They would represent Romanization exactly as I mean the word.

Why a person with money to spend might commission something of Italian plan, let us say a *macellum*, is one thing; choice of technique, another thing entirely. This latter would lie with the architect, who in turn hired the labor—at

which point, quite different considerations arose. Some plans could not be realized without terracing to level the surface, the lower parts supported on vaulting. Roman builders were at home with this, and examples in the Augustan east
are clear if not numerous. Or again: a plan like Agrippa's Odeion in Athens involved an enormous span, unparalleled in Greek architectural history but well
within the powers of Roman technicians.[79] Or yet again: Herod's needs for a
grand big harbor on the coast of Palestine at what had been the tiny port of Stra-
tonis Turris, now Caesarea, could only be filled by cement that hardened under
water. That required something unheard of outside of Italy: *pozzolana*, cement
made of vulcanic sand. Gigantic quantities of the material were shipped over
from the Bay of Naples, gigantic quantities shaped into blocks 45′ × 25′ × 13′
put down in layers as breakwaters into the sea to form one of the most capa-
cious harbors of the ancient Mediterranean.[80] The whole was a monument to a
superior alien technology.

A review of Herod's activities as a builder, drawing both on Josephus and ex-
tant remains, may serve as a summary of all that has been said so far on the city-
building and architectural aspects of Romanization in the east. Since the general scope of his program has been most thoroughly reviewed recently, there is
the less reason for detail here; but a catalogue drawing out the imported features alone might logically begin with his founding or renaming of a dozen
cities and more, as Caesarea, Iulias, Sebaste=Augusta, or Agrippias, walled like
Caesarea merely for show, equipped like Caesarea with sewers and aqueducts
carried on arches, an amphitheater that was mentioned earlier, a theater of Roman style, a great pedimented temple, abundant use or imitation of marble
throughout, use of reticulate walls and vaulting to form foundations and concrete for the theater.[81] Virtually all of these features can be found in his kingdom
elsewhere; and elsewhere he paid for paving of public areas, too, and built baths
of a Roman type. In the theater he put on Greek musical and athletic competitions and horse-races; also gladiators and wild beasts in Roman fashion—
everything that one might see in the most costly style in Rome itself and with
every sort of equipment supplied to him from imperial resources by Augustus
and Julia.[82] In the baths, of course people bathed in a Roman manner; in his
amphitheaters at Caesarea and Jerusalem and other cities, they watched entertainment of a Roman sort: gladiatorial combats and fights with wild beasts.[83]

4. Behavior

Herod was a great builder of gymnasia in the cities he founded or favored. In
gymnasia lay the essence of the Greek way of life. Similarly, in honoring his

great Roman friends with statues, he chose for imitation the famous Zeus of Olympia and Hera in Argos.[84] Comparing his Greek enthusiasms with his Roman, the question naturally arises, just what were his loyalties or intentions?

We can get no closer to Herod's thoughts than Josephus will allow, who, however, does offer a clear reading of the king's nature: "he imitated everything, though ever so costly or magnificent, in other nations, out of an ambition that he might give most public demonstrations of his grandeur."[85] Herod's governing aims, his towering aspirations, expressed themselves in proportionately grand acts calculated to bring him fame. The corresponding terms used in description are familiar in decrees of thanks and praise: philotimia and megalopsychia. In confirmation of Josephus, an extraordinary list of royal acts of generosity can be compiled out of his narrative, many of them visible in their remains today.

But it is no less Greek and understandable that, as his biographer adds, Herod wished to win the favor of those above him, his Roman friends, as much as the favor of those whom he benefitted. So he advertised the titles and triumphs of Augustus, for example, on the walls of the theater he built in Jersualem (AJ 15.8.1 [279]). There was flattery explicit; but he saw it as equally flattering, equally sure of a good reception, that gestures of expenditure should be on things appropriate to the recipient, that is, in some way Roman. The same calculation underlay a Greek citizen's commissioning of a relief of the Capitoline wolf for the local community of Roman Businessmen (above, at n. 49)—no considerations of cultural loyalty in the man of Chios, neither in the king at Jerusalem.

Rather, the source of energy accounting for Herod's actions was one and the same, that radically Greek philotimia. It inspired all public benefactors in their defining activity, "euergetism" (a neologism so important in describing how the Greco-Roman world worked that it may by now be used almost without apology). Romans in their eastern sojourns had seen ambition for honor and magnificent public giving on display everywhere; they had picked it up from their noble eastern friends; and some of them had acknowledged the two together in their own conduct in Greek lands, so early as the second century and more lavishly in the first: Lucullus, Pompey, Aulus Gabinius in the 50s, Caesar, Antony, and inevitably Augustus; witness for example his paying for the pefection of the propylon in Athens, to which Caesar had earlier contributed. The coadjutors of these great figures, men like Agrippa, or their very freedmen (men like C. Iulius Heliodorus), came forward as benefactors, εὐεργέται, of favored eastern cities.[86] Of at least Caesar's and Augustus' gifts, a good number have been recalled earlier; likewise, of local citizens like Eurycles, the Appuleius or Sergius family, or P. Sextilius Pollio, above.

Augustus was understood by Herod personally to favor *philotimia* and its expression in the conduct of his friends. Certainly his friends closer to home understood, and richly endowed Augustan Italy. An instance is L. Cornelius Balbus, constructing a theater in Rome in which to greet the emperor on his return from abroad. It was recalled by Suetonius long afterwards as an example of how Augustus "urged everyone according to his resources to adorn the city with new or renovated buildings."[87] Such projects and grand donors demonstrate the continued operation of Hellenistic influences upon non-Greeks, such as are of course evident also in the reign of Herod.

The currents of influence, however, flowed in both directions, east and west. The fact was pointed out earlier and needs to be recalled here, too, in the context of prevailing values. Of those that particularly characterized Roman civilization, three stand out: those attaching to superiority, to favors, and to triumphal display. They are all three somewhat mis-labelled here. We lack the words the Romans might have used (*maiestas*, "greatness"; *fides* with an assemblage of related terms like *gratia, amicitia, clientela, patronus*, or *patrocinium*; and *philotimia*, gaining historic force only under the teaching of the Hellenistic world and of Augustus' example). Of these three, what signs can be read in the east in the period of this study? Was the east in these terms "Romanized"?

For my purposes, perhaps enough has been said about the last, *philotimia*. As to the first, *maiestas*, it need not occupy me at all; for how could it have any place among a conquered population? They had acknowledged their inferiority, at least in arms; their position was the result and reward of the Romans' drive to be acknowledged masters; and when at last the hunger for "greatness" had been appeased, when everybody had been overcome and the Temple of Janus closed by Augustus in token of a universal *pax Romana*, the historical role of that impulse was played out.

The second characteristically Roman value, however, attaching to *fides*, was on display from the first moment of the east's encounter with its conquerors. It had to be understood. It engaged the latter themselves in a network of mutual obligations; if *pax* were ever to prove tolerable for the conquered, they too must find some place within that network. Its influence on the operations of law and government have been touched on, above.

The logic underlying it all was not hard to understand, in those days, nor even among ourselves; for when a politician or anyone at all today, in some moment of personal need, says he "has to call in all his chits," meaning, to remind anyone who owes him a favor to be ready with its repayment, we sense in outline what *fides* was all about. The Roman phenomenon may be called only a particular form of something common to a hundred societies (as *noblesse oblige*, likewise, which was at the moment of its introduction into English nevertheless seen to be in some way or degree different from anything at home among Anglophones). What made an economy of favors so peculiar to Augustus' world was the importance placed on it, its centrality in power relationships, and its consequent articulation in its own vocabulary. Passages in an early Latin writer like Cato, many in Cicero, many in post-Augustan moral philosophers like Seneca, openly explain what right conduct was and so enable us to grasp how society could function as it did.

It is important to get clear what the terms of description mean. Much scholarly effort has been given to that end, with or without some trimmings of social-scientific method; but what begins in dictionaries needs to get beyond lexicography to real life, especially life as it was lived by people who needed to know how to behave in a Roman way, but spoke no Latin!—or spoke it as a second language.[88]

To illustrate the Roman introduction of the Greek world to the Roman way of acting we have in particular the letters of Cicero down to the mid-40s, referred to above (at n. 12). Let one further text suffice.[89] It is a copy of a letter from Augustus written at some point in the later 30s B.C. to the city of Rhossos, a little north of Antioch-on-the-Orontes. The letter attaches another of a few years earlier to a citizen of Rhossos, one Seleukos. He had served in Augustus' fleet (Octavian's, to be precise about his name) perhaps in 36 B.C., as Eurykles did later, and was rewarded accordingly with Roman citizenship. The letter defines what it means, and informs Rhossos of the reason for the gift: "for such men increase my zealous good will toward their native cities. Be assured that I shall do more gladly everything possible for you, because of Seleukos, and send to me confidently for whatever you wish." Notice, in addition to the importance of the *beneficium* bestowed on him—that is, citizenship itself with all its tax advantages and security of special treatment—he is declared to be the future key to further *beneficia* for his city or anyone else in it; and this is obviously an enormous boost up in the world for this brave and useful man.

Though Roman ideas often looked like a more strictly spelt-out form of moral behavior in traditional Greek terms, and though they are correspondingly hard to identify in their eastern contexts, their penetration into interpersonal relations cannot be doubted. One clear proof is the adoption into Greek of at least a part of the Roman terminology, in the form of the word "patron," *patronus*, πάτρων. It appears in votes of honor and thanks to a governor or any other mighty person: to a son of Eurycles, for example.[90] An even better indication of the spread of Roman ideas is the success of eastern clients in dealing with the mighty of the Roman world.

A favored path upward into the ranks of the influential lay through the imperial cult. To be a priest declared a devotion beyond the mere acceptance of the conquerors. There is no indication that the rites were anything but traditionally Greek, though on Delos the Roman or Italian residents paid homage to Roma with some admixture of their own imported ways.[91] Perhaps as much was true of whatever forms of worship were usual in Roman-style temples. Those known have been mentioned; and there are temples more or less surely to be called Capitolia.[92] It is probable that no-longer-extant Capitolia or close equivalents with Roman rituals could be found in veteran colonies like Antioch-in-Pisidia or Beirut, where in due course room was found for a variety of deities like Mater Matuta, Liber Pater, Mars. . . . [93] But the most striking devotion to their ancestral gods appears among the Delian Romans, in practices attested over a period too early for this study, but carrying down to the very edge of the 60s.[94] They can be read in mural paintings, down to the details of ritual gesture and dress in accord with what can be seen in Pompeii; but here too there is some identifiable admixture of Hellenistic practice. I suppose we would find pretty much the same little domestic altars and shrines and frescoes and contexts of living piety in Antioch, again, if we could visit such sites across the gulfs of time. In these ways and sites, religion was imported to the east—not very much.

One striking little exception is the Roman recollection of the year's beginning, on January first, by the choristers of Pergamum mentioned above, the hymnodes who chanted the praises of Augustus on his birthday. Its rites at home in Italy involved thanks-offerings but no one deity in particular. Family and neighborhood celebrations were the larger part of it; and there is no indication of the prevalence of these in the east.[95]

Much better attested is the Rosalia on a day in May, when families brought roses to the graves of their dead and sat down together over grave-side banquets. We know of these because they were important enough to Italian feelings to require careful provision: a sum of money bequeathed for any expenses involved, or a small vineyard bought to yield the wine each year. Details are spelt out in inscriptions from around Philippi in the first century (by chance, none clearly Augustan); again, across the straits into Asia at Thyatira (a day's ride from Pergamum, where the hymnodes also celebrated the Day of Roses) in the late first century B.C. or first half of the first century A.D.; and thereafter in various other Bithynian and Phrygian towns of the second century and so into Christian communities and centuries, to the present day. In Bithynia even the native villagers picked up the celebration; in Asia, celebrants are as likely to have clearly Greek names as Roman.[96] The Rosalia serve as a reminder that the evidence for the ancient way of life is capriciously presented to us by Time, and what relates to the private sphere is most likely to be largely or entirely withheld. There is a general warning here, of course.

Tangible memorials for the dead, since they were designed to endure, do sometimes succeed in their purpose sufficiently to show us Roman practices preserved in Greek lands. At Antioch-in-Pisidia and the less urbanized areas of Anatolia, gravestones have reliefs on them showing a doorway with the epitaph inscribed to one side, in a fashion brought from northern or central Italy in late Republican times.[97] An Antiochene funerary inscription put up by a freedman advertises the contribution he made to his former master's interment, in a manner and form of declaration normal in Italy.[98] The deceased had been one of the original veteran settlers. So private pieties preserved the past.

5. On balance

Looking back, now, on all the miscellany of graves and grids, pottery and pozzolana, surveyed in the preceding pages, the impact of one civilization on another can certainly be discerned. In succeeding centuries its effects would become more marked, and another survey might then note the greater use of *terra sigillata*, the alterations in theaters to accommodate gladiatorial combats, and so forth. On balance, however, in Augustus' time the historical significance of what I have presented seems still quite minor.

True, many people from Italy visited or settled in the east. At the moment of their largest living total, they certainly exceeded a hundred thousand, if veterans of the civil wars are added to those civilians who had emigrated or were sent out from Italy on business. Regarded as so many little packages of their own culture scattered about, no doubt one could say they constituted in their own persons some degree of Romanization. But they died. At that point, without their somehow having inculcated their ideas into their neighbors, their effect was at an end. It was as if they had never lived. An approach to acculturation through prosopography thus yields nothing but names upon names.

Some indicate something more than immigration. There are the hybrids: "Gaius Iulius Pericles" (to invent one), showing how someone given citizenship by the emperor or by his adoptive father took the donor's praenomen and nomen. Such a man was Romanized at least in terms of law. His *tria nomina* went with his registration in a Roman tribe, unavoidably. Registration in turn meant liability to taxes. The spectre of imperialistic compulsion rises over the scene, to make everyone and everything Roman.

Was it more than a spectre? Taxes would be levied in a form the Romans chose; but they imposed no uniformity in that; and, if their exactions had been much lighter or heavier than in the past, we would expect some indication in the sources; but none appears. There cannot, then, have been much change. Antecedent inventory of real property might be in Roman form, here and there, to be seen in centuriation—but only around a handful of reconstituted cities. And certain taxes were payable in coins compatible with the Roman; so Greek issues modified their weights. There is no sign they were compelled to. Enforcement would have to lie through governors, assize districts, and law. As to the weight of that, however, the quite limited realities were explored, above. In sum, the effects on the population's way of life resulting from Roman exploitation and administration seem to have been quite limited.

Most areas of life lay beyond the reach or the conquerors' intent of compulsion; and here, some acculturation undoubtedly took place. Our invented Gaius Iulius Pericles might present his city with a structure which was in some important way Roman. Instances have been given at Ephesus and elsewhere. They show a natural advance from legal status to a wider cultural loyalty—an advance so natural, one would expect to see it more often. But, where differences between Roman and Greek ways could be perceived, what was needed to make converts was something more than a natural fit. What was needed was some manifest benefit. For example: to watch men duel with real weapons afforded tremendous excitement, pleasurable to many in the audience; or again, the genuine best Italian table-ware afforded more pleasure to the eye than local products; and Roman concrete in its several forms and uses did the job better than traditionally eastern cut-stone construction. Delivery of water into drains and sewers and, better yet, into great big swanky baths-buildings constituted a distinct improvement of life. These and a few other points of difference drew converts to the Roman way without the least compulsion. The points were few, however. That is what most needs emphasis.

The explanation of course lies in the fact that the east was, in Romans' own terms, civilized. Solutions to ordinary problems had long been worked out more or less satisfactorily. Proof of this perception lies in those impressively many colonies, most of them founded for veterans (some with an admixture of the poor from Rome; most or all with incorporation of natives of at least the richer sort). Here from the start Italian towns were to be replicated: in ritual of foundation, form of government, layout of streets, circuit of walls, division of lands around them into *centuriae*, and law and language. So it would appear. But it was not really so. From the start, there was bilingualism and intermarriage; little Hellenistic touches show up in every sort of institution or artifact; the immigrants forget their own names, or accept Hellenizing distortions, even give their own children Greek or Greek-sounding names.[99] Gradually the east transforms these colonies. It makes them and their manners and customs a part of itself; it digests them.

The process is in part attributable to mass, or the lack of it. In the long run that mass even in Roman colonies proved to be not viable. More of the explanation may have lain rather in the perception of difference by Romans who were in positions of power and could have asserted it through example, command, or expenditure; but in eastern city settings, they did not do so. They did not see civilization in the abstract as much different from what they found already in place in the east, themselves having been long accustomed in their own homeland to value Hellenistic ways as the best, the most to be admired. That point was made at the head of the chapter.

The two civilizations being thus pressed against each other through the course of conquest show rather nicely what certain points stuck out and wouldn't fit. They allow a competing pair of profiles to be drawn. The Romans, to no one's surprise, won out where arms, administration, and practical technology were in question. As to the rest, in familiar words, captive Greece took Rome captive.

II AFRICA

1. The occupation of the land

Along the coast of North Africa in Augustus' time from Leptis as far as Tingis, the urban centers had all been absorbed into the empire. They appeared to be almost all that was worth absorbing, excepting only the hinterland of Carthage; and that, too, was taken over. Each port of course had some farming territory around it, and might seem to invite occupation on that account; certainly Carthaginian lands were very inviting, and steps had been taken to open them up to Roman settlers in the second century; but the decisive advance was made only by Caesar, with his veteran colonies.

"Old" Africa had been no more than that Carthaginian territory. At Thapsus, however, in 46 B.C. Caesar emerged as victor over his enemies, both Romans and their African allies; and in so doing he gained control over the allies' domains of gigantic size lying behind the coastal parts. A "New" Africa was formed out of the eastern part; most of the western was given in reward to a supporter, and by 25 B.C. had passed into the hands of Augustus' favored Juba II.

A small slice of territory between the two parts was awarded to P. Sittius after Thapsus for his assistance to Caesar. It received a special constitution and bore the title, the "Four Cirta Colonies." They were the colony of Cirta and three smaller places. Their defining names, "Sarnia" added to the proper local name of the site of Milev, and so forth, were all drawn from the region of Italy that Sittius and his followers came from. He and his men were among the first from Italy to take up their lives in Africa at any distance from the coast. A large colony was established in Carthage in 44 B.C., made up mostly of civilians from the poor of the imperial capital. Other colonies established by the dictator's provision for his veterans included Thapsus itself and at least eight more, all on the coast or close inland; and many veterans were settled in little walled villages, *castella*, no less than eighty-three of these scattered around the territory lying just west of Carthage.[1]

Two thousand has been proposed as a representative figure for the core group of a veteran-colony. That would mean some twenty-five thousand soldiers turned into farmers on seized land, now Roman state land, through Caesar's provision, enjoying citizenship in the urban center to which they were assigned; and there they (or certainly ex-officers among them) could count on being an instant elite; for officers got extra-large plots of land.[2] Some settlers had families to swell their presence. Throughout the territory round about them, upon their arrival, new boundaries must be drawn, incumbents evicted, and all this in the space of a year or two. The pattern can be seen on the map (Fig. 3).

Augustus in his turn in the 30s and 20s B.C. faced the dictator's problem of indebtedness to troops, but on a larger scale and in more than one post-war predicament; so his responses were on a larger scale and more urgent. What was left of his Twelfth Legion went to Thuburbo Minus or Maius; of his Thirteenth, to Uthina, of his Eighth, to Thuburbo Minus, of the Fifth, to Thuburnica;[3] veterans of other units went to one of several other places, while a further three or four colonies received a second settlement on top of Caesar's (Carthage, Cirta . . .). Sometimes it was a pre-existing town that had to make room for the immigrants, for example, at Thuburbo Maius; elsewhere, a colony might come to life *ab ovo*: Thuburbo Minus for one. The Augustan total in "Old" and "New" African colonies came to a dozen or more. And there were veterans not assigned to any colony who were given a share in land around native centers in a village of their own or in one pre-existing: at Suturnica for one, a couple of days' ride southwest of Carthage. There, an inscription records "the veterans of the village Fortunalis whose ancestors received Suturnican land by Augustus' act of grace," his *beneficium*.[4]

He appears to have avoided the demotion of towns within the old limits of Carthaginian territory—avoided also, to the extent possible, the confiscation of their lands. Added to Caesar's, however, the new settlers of Augustus' act brought the total above fifty thousand. Disruption in rural ownership must have been considerable—and yet, in an over-all population approaching four millions.[5] They were all nailed down in a census taken by agents drawn from the army. One military tribune of the Third Legion won praise for overseeing the process among no less than forty-four cities, and honestly![6]

Augustus' times saw a number of cities walled and others connected with good highways. Of this latter work, much was done by the Third Legion. It was Vergil who foresaw how Aeneas would provide cities with walls; and Roman military engineers and often military labor had long been engaged in road-building.[7]

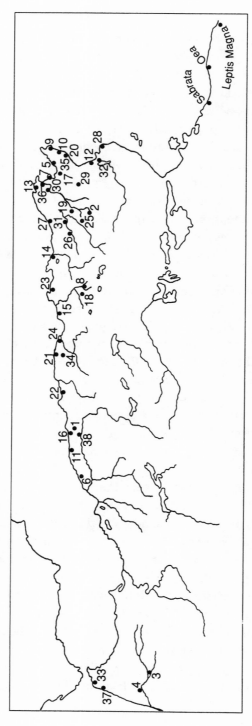

A final task of the army was surveying. The instrument used was a sort of staff, the *groma*, first planted at some convenient point of commencement chosen for its relation to a highway or a city center, or both if they were aligned. The process, first noticed in remains visible around Carthage in 1833, was described in the preceding chapter; and the original publication has since been supplemented on an enormous scale through air-photography especially in Tunisia inland from the southeastern coast. The purpose served by "gromatics" was administrative: both of land distribution and taxation.

Effects on the landscape are at many points easily read even in detail. At Thysdrus, not only can the units of a hundred *heredia* be identified through existing

---

FIGURE 3. The colonial effort in Africa

AFRICA:

C= Caesar-founded;   c=colony;
A=Augustus-founded;   m=municipium

 1 Aquae Calidae Ac   21 Rusazus Ac
 2 Iulia Assuras Ac   22 Rusguniae Ac
 3 Babba Ac   23 Rusicade Ac
 4 Iulia Valentia Banasa Ac   24 Iulia Augusta Saldae Ac
 5 Carpis Cc   25 Iulia Sicca Veneria Ac
 6 Cartennae Ac   26 Iulia Augusta Numidica
 7 Concordia Iulia Carthago Cc   Simitthus Ac
 8 Iulia Iuvenalis Honoris et Pietatis   27 Victrix Pia Iulia Thabraca Ac
    Cirta Ac   28 Thapsus Cc
 9 Iulia Clupea Cc   29 Thuburbo Maius Ac | Am
10 Iulia Curubis Cc   30 Thuburbo Minus Octavanorum Ac
11 Gunugu Ac   31 Augusta Thuburnica Ac
12 Hadrumetum Cc   32 Thysdrus Cc
13 Hippo Diarrhytus Cc | Ac   33 Tingis Am | Ac
14 Hippo Regius Am   34 Iulia Augusta Tubusuctu Ac
15 Igilgili Ac   35 Iulia Tertiadecimanorum Uthina
16 Iol Caesarea, Ac   Ac | Am
17 Maxula, Ac   36 Utica Cc | Ac
18 Mileu=Mila Ac   37 Iulia Constantia Zilis=Zulil Ac
19 Musti Cm   38 Zucchabar Ac
20 Neapolis Cc | Ac

walls and so forth, and the tell-tale measurement of 20 × 20 *actus* = 2400 feet
(ca. 710m), but sub-units of *bina iugera* (ca. 2ha) or even sub-sub-units of a single *iugerum*, with every possible combination of numbers of *iugera* to make up
different sizes of farm. The very olive trees obeyed. They were planted four per
square *actus*.[8] Elsewhere it is possible to estimate the size of an entire colony's
territory: one, for example, of 80 centuries, rather on the small side.[9] The orientation of the grid varies from one broad region to another according to when
the land was parcelled out, whether in the later second century or in the 40s or
under Augustus. A striking case of difference can be seen at Carthage where the
groma was fixed atop the city's acropolis for the laying down of division marks
across the land in one direction, and for the lines of streets within the city in another, the two dates being respectively in the 120s and 40s B.C.[10] For my purposes, chronological uncertainties matter little; rather, it is the fact of a strict or-
dering of thousands of square miles according to the most characteristic of
Roman acts of conquest, inventory. Definition of boundaries on some sort of
grid there had been, here and there, before the Romans came;[11] but what they
introduced gave a uniformity to measurement. It declared even to a peasant
population that they had new masters; for centuriation was extended well beyond colonies, wherever Rome claimed an area as state land. As a later chapter
will show, the results were plain not only through boundary-stones and eventually through ditches and so forth along the edge of properties, as they were
marked out and became established, but also in public maps ready to be consulted. From these, civil officials would make colonial assignments and non-
colonial as well, at times of sale and re-sale.

Ownership of African lands by Romans can be traced back well prior to the
age of major colonization: even to the earliest years of Augustus' time. In "Old"
Africa a friend of Cicero's had certain large investments. Freedmen representing his interests and bearing his name, Caelii, turn up especially around Hadrumetum and a few other towns, just as Rabirii in great numbers turn up in another region, suggesting investment by Cicero's client C. Rabirius Postumus;
and there were quite huge estates formed in the period of my study by those six
unnamed persons whose descendants Nero later stripped bare. Also, perhaps,
by Agrippa.[12] Inevitably, a hero of Actium is a candidate for reward carved out of
state land: M. Lurius Varus, commander on the left flank, to be detected behind
the estate name, Villa Magna Variana; and there would have been a profiteer of
the civil wars to give his name to the "Domitian Estate," *saltus*, and some other
(the emperor Tiberius' father?) to own the Neronian, and the Lamian.[13] The
very name *villa* is of course a Latin one, indicating the unit of agricultural ex-

ploitation most characteristic of the Roman well-to-do, and of a characteristic plan at its center, a characteristic organization of labor and farming techniques. Of all these there is no proof so early, only reasonable presumption;[14] but reasonable presumption may go further, with some little evidence, to imagine the selection of only the very best soil raising the best crops for the "best people," as first Caesar and then his heir adjudged them in the time of victory. They are to be added, though as absentees, to the immigrants who we know were settled in colonies or villages. The latter got their nine or ten acres each, not, of course, nine or ten square miles, and perhaps not the best, either.[15]

Highly praised though Carthaginian agriculturalists had once been in the past, the conquerors are not likely to have given up their own methods in deference to local custom. The main business of Africa, farming, was thus no doubt Romanized wherever Roman citizens owned the fields and farmed them personally or through their slave or freedmen managers. The total area subject to change in "Old" Africa must have been huge, perhaps approaching a quarter by the end of Augustus' principate. To judge from the century following, the principal effect here would have been the introduction of olive culture and some admixture of slave-labor.

2. Leptis Magna

The far larger area of "New" Africa was for a time little affected by conquest, yet that little, in a significant direction: toward sedentarization. The signs are best and earliest read in the hinterlands of Tripolitania, especially south of Leptis Magna. There, by the mid-first century A.D., the early phase of a great rise in prosperity is evident, derived from the extension of acres under olive-orchards; and its beginnings can be traced to the latter years of Augustus' principate. To some extent, an estimate of the change depends on the estimate of pre-Roman nomadism, which appears to have been misread and exaggerated in the past: oleiculture in the backlands, not grazing, may predate the Roman era.[16]

Regarding urban Romanization, too, there are difficult questions to consider. An increase in "Old" and "New" African settlements calling themselves cities, and doing so in Latin, civitates, is obvious. In any language, such centers can perhaps be counted to a hundred in Caesar's day, but to five times that number in Augustine's, due to entitlement of what had once been villages. The progress and chronology of the increase remain largely hidden. Processes leading to it were evidently set in motion in the period of my study, but just how strongly, touching what number of potential "cities"?

The surviving record will of course not show changes in size of urban populations, only changes in form of government. Augustus initiated a policy in "Old" Africa of granting autonomy to villages, thus preparing them for eventual recognition as cities.[17] Caesarian colonies naturally had normal colonial government, meaning *duumviri* at the head of a college of four magistrates, as at Curubis or in the smaller three of the "Four Cirta Colonies." These, Augustus later raised to full colonial status.[18] He and Caesar before him conferred the status of *municipium* on several centers, for example, Utica. In Utica, as at a small number of coastal sites, Roman businessmen and traders had long resided. An early name in Leptis shows up through Cicero's mention. They formed associations with which Caesar and his enemies dealt, for support. Collectively they are called, as elsewhere, *conventus*, and prepared their towns for promotion in form and title.[19] Some population centers, upon settlement of veterans, remained double: a native town side by side with a chartered Roman one at Thuburbo Maius, Carthage, and elsewhere.[20] All of these various forms of organization and compromise are little reported. Taken together, however, they explain the far better known processes of the first and especially the second century A.D., leading to that total of five hundred cities in Augustine's day.

Steps taken toward Roman city form were on occasion incomplete. Under Punic influence the more conspicuous sites had all had Punic governments, and, by Augustus, were left (most of them) free to run themselves; so they retained the officials and procedures they were used to. Citizen associations called *curiae*, serving what civic purpose is not clear, can be found in scores of places of Punic heritage; and Curubis was not alone in retaining its old Punic assembly, senate, and *sufetes*.[21] Tripolitania was clearly conservative in these respects. Oea and Sabratha and its chief city, Leptis, were administered by *sufetes*; they were apparently retained at Leptis long after the city won *municipium*-status; and its citizens continued to convene in a Punic style of assembly.[22] The differences from Roman forms may have appeared not much more than nominal to Roman governors, seeing before them an annually elected college of magistrates, a senate, and an assembly pretty nearly on the model of the Italian towns with which they were familiar. In any case, they didn't press for change.

Among the *sufetes* of Leptis under Augustus was a certain Annobal Tapapius Rufus, son of Himilco. He held other municipal offices as well. It was he that paid for a *macellum*, as he made known in a Punic inscription on its walls and a Latin translation of that text. The specially Roman significance of the building-form was indicated in the previous chapter, and its Italian derivation is clear in a comparison with Pompeii's (Fig. 4).

Tapapius' gift was made in 8 B.C., followed up on two occasions a little later

LEPCIS MAGNA

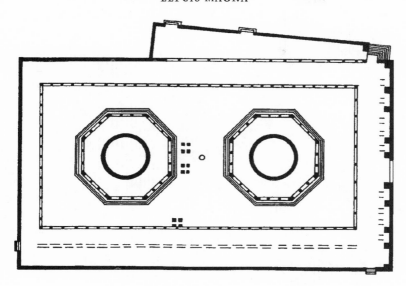

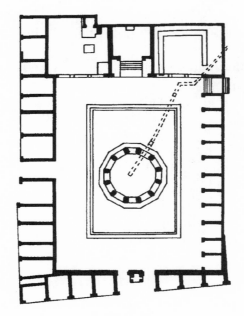

POMPEI 2

FIGURE 4. *Macella* of Leptis and Pompeii.

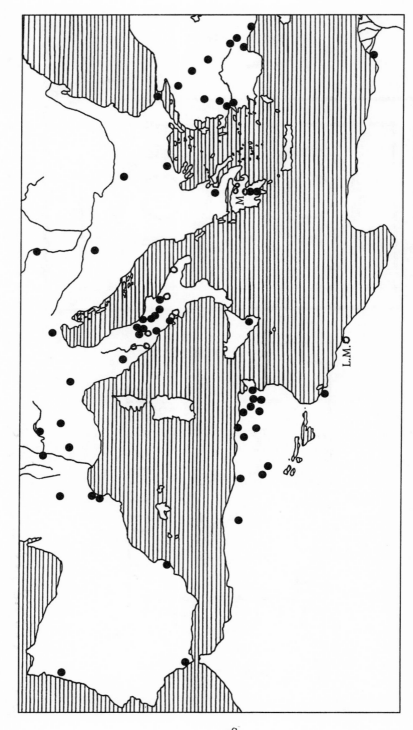

FIGURE 5. Distribution of *macella*, Augustan and later ○ Augustan *macellum* ● Post-Augustan.

with contributions to theater construction. His theater followed the plan that Romans favored and had a Roman touch along the uppermost rim: a portico in which were displayed the emperor's name and titles; and it was perhaps Livia who was also honored there, in the shrine to Ceres Augusta. Aligned with it to the rear of the stage-building was a small temple, no doubt for the imperial cult, enclosed in a three-sided portico. This too—this close union of facilities for entertainment and worship, especially of the imperial house—was very much of the times.[23]

Iddibal Caphada Aemilius, son of Himilis, was another great donor at Annobal's side, putting his name on the chalcidicum next the theater and on a portico, gate, and main avenue of the city in A.D. 11–12. Throughout these projects there is abundant use of local marble in emulation of Augustus' boast that he had found the imperial capital itself mere brick, and left it clothed in the more precious stone.[24]

It is striking to see the mixture in these building-activities of two civilizations, the Punic and the Roman, reflected in the rolling names of the donors. It characterizes the building types themselves: to begin with, the macellum, the ubiquity of which was noted in an eastern context, and of which Africa was to provide the most examples outside of Italy. Leptis, however, had a pair of Augustan temples on high platforms of an Italian type. One of them was dedicated to Liber Pater, whose image dominates in the municipal coinage of the time. The other might be expected to be a capitolium, such as rose in Sabratha or Carthage at the time; and so it was first termed by the excavators; but in fact it originally served a native deity before it was remodelled to serve Roma and Augustus. It had a pair of staircases at each side of the podium in imitation of the Temple of the Deified Caesar on the Roman forum, and marble ships'-beaks on it, too, to make a rostra for Lepcitanian speakers (in neo-Punic or perhaps Greek?) just like the rostra in the Roman forum.[25] A municipal senate hall was also remodelled to an Italian form.[26] Column capitals incorporated in the great projects of the time follow the pattern to be found in Italy.[27]

It is uncertain when the "Old" Forum took on its marked regularity: well before Augustus, probably. It was too nearly square for Vitruvian rules, with three temples, not one, facing a basilica, and with porticoes along the basilica's front and the other two sides. The orthogonal layout of Leptis' more central streets is more Hippodamean than Roman.[28] Still, it was a new idea to displace so much ordinary urban activity from the city center into a separate macellum for retail trade and a chalcidicum, a spacious columned barn of a building, perhaps serving shipping and wholesale trade. As to the forum, now, it was reserved for politics, with administration accommodated in the basilica. All very tidy, very new and Roman. The governor added the finishing touch. He provided paving of big triangular limestone slabs across its whole expanse, for which he took credit in a bronze-lettered inscription.[29]

On a plan of any Roman city and here on the plan of Leptis Magna, one notable characteristic strikes the eye: the proportion of space given to public buildings. The *macellum* and *chalcidicum* alone bulked larger than the whole of the "Old" forum; so did the theater and the temple-plus-portico to its rear.[30] Even without an amphitheater such as Carthage boasted, or public baths, the area occupied by such handsome construction accessible to every citizen far exceeded what we in modern cities are used to. An important consequence followed: the effectiveness of the city as a draw, as a display-window advertising novelties, was dramatically enhanced; and the novelties were of Roman inspiration, including the urge to build, itself. At another site transformed by the Augustan age, a colony of Caesar's planning, Curubis, the *duumvir* L. Pomponius Malcio "saw to the building of the whole city wall in cut stone." *Pax*, prosperity, and *philotimia* combined in such transformations.

From about 10 B.C. forward, Leptis issued its own currency. It chose to do so, as did Oea and Sabratha and a number of other cities in "Old" Africa, beginning around the time of Actium, all on the Roman standard. That had become generally familiar through the coining and paying-out of *denarii* by commanders in the time of the civil wars, in Africa as in the east. Some issues celebrated Caesar as triumphator; others chose to imitate bronze issues from Rome in exact detail, legend-form included; but there were also a number of touches that declared purely local loyalties.[31] Hadrumetum's coins showed its favorite Ba'al Hammon; also, Livia bearing the insignia of the local goddess Tanit. The same insignia honor the empress in Utica, Carthage, and Thapsus, all, loyal colonies but also far longer Punic. Liber Pater appears on Sabratha's coins, but beneath his venerable name no doubt most citizens saw and thought of the older Shadrapa.[32]

The term the Romans themselves later used for such an assimilative vision of Shadrapa, *interpretatio Romana*, introduces a large subject—large in its reality, affecting the lives and thoughts of many people, and almost as large in the modern discussions it has given rise to. When an image or ritual or site of cult of some older deity is given the name of another more recent, or at least more recently imported, what image occupied the worshipper's mind? Was he thinking of the old god or the new? Was he thinking *like a Roman*?[33] Though ancient polytheism was not seriously troubled by this question, modern monotheistical ap-

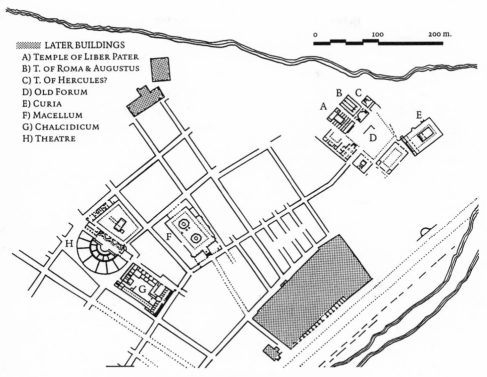

FIGURE 6. Augustan elements of Leptis Magna.

proaches want an answer. In the nature of the evidence any answer to it in individual instances can be little more than speculation. On the other hand, there is no denying real conceptual change when it is reflected in the general prevailing of Roman forms over against pre-Roman; and this may certainly be seen in the centuries post-Augustus; so the early stages of such prevalence, even if they appear only in isolated indications, do have historical significance.

The opening up of African contexts to Roman religion can be seen at Leptis in the position of honor accorded to the temple of Roma and Augustus on the "Old" forum. Before it was rededicated under Augustus, the building had been the home of Shadrapa and Milk'ashtart. The two had long been the special protectors of the city, its "ancestral gods." Now they were displaced—and diminished. For, adjoining their home, now lost to them, was only a smaller temple dedicated to Milk'ashtart alone.[34] The governor who paved the forum before them also set up a dedication to Mars Augustus in a prominent position; and Leptis was the first city of its status, a *civitas libera*, to institute the cult of the emperor's *numen*.[35] Its public accommodation to foreign worships was thus much more than punctilious.

Another deity of greater fame in Punic settings was Ba'al Hammon, named in Latin Saturn. Infant-sacrifice to this god began to give way in Augustus' time to symbolic equivalents, at Sousse, and, under Augustus' successor if not much earlier, at Carthage.[36] In the same period, Saturn's cult began to be enclosed in a built home, a temple, though traditionally it had taken place in open-air settings.[37] The evidence invites the interpretation that the influence of Roman ideas was felt by the city's leadership. Carthage would have contained a share of Roman citizens of wealth, therefore of some weight. One such we find erecting a Tellus-temple in 40 B.C.[38]

3. Juba's kingdom

As the eastern parts of Roman Africa were anchored in Leptis and Tripolitania, so were the western in Iol Caesarea and Mauretania. The latter province, seven hundred miles across as the crow flies from near Igilgili to a little beyond Tingis, was formed in 33 B.C. by Augustus and eight years later entrusted to the young C. Iulius Juba II, who reigned forever (25 B.C.–A.D. 23). Juba was descended from the line of native rulers; but having been taken to Rome as a captive when he was a little boy and there raised to manhood in the setting of the imperial court, indeed in its inner circles—having fought at Actium and owing his return home and the obedience of his kingdom all to Augustus—he must have seemed as unnatural an import to his subjects as Antiochus Epiphanes to his in Syria, many generations earlier.[39]

In the kingdom given him, what counted were no doubt principally its coastal cities. In a number of these Augustus settled colonies of legionary veterans: of the Seventh at Saldae, Tubusuctu, and Rusazus; the Ninth in Rusguniae, the Thirteenth at Uthina; praetorian cohort-members in Gunugu, and so forth; and Uthina and Tingis were given municipal status, too. That was in 38 B.C. The totals per site were probably modest: in the hundreds, not thousands.[40] Various dates have been proposed for the founding of the settlements other than Tingis, falling between 33 and 25 B.C., perhaps even a year or so later. The sharpest need would have been felt immediately after Actium in 27, before Juba had taken over; and only three of the colonies are given the title "Iulia," from which it is argued that they come before the majority that are titled "Iulia Augusta" ("Augustus" of course being the title born by the emperor only from 27 B.C. on). Counting Tingis, a total of a dozen seems sure; another four, probable. The king on his arrival would have seemed reassuringly Latinate to these Roman settlers, whose interests he would specially consider. They came to prevail in due course—to make their towns recognizably Roman—though in most locations the earliest effects of Augustus' colonizing have left little trace.

Juba was a good deal more than Latinate. He was after all brought up in an aristocratic Roman manner, therefore bilingual. He liked his studies and excelled in them, and when he had the leisure, seated on his Mauretanian throne, most improbably he dictated books in Greek with titles like "Roman History," "Congruences" (between the Greeks and the Romans), and "History of the Theater," from which surviving quotations show a special interest in music. His works suggest a large royal library. They prepare us also for the presence of a mima, a female recitalist, and a dresser among the palace slaves, and a certain famous tragic actor, Leontius of Argos, hired for a visit.[41] Juba was given by Augustus in 20 B.C. a good Greek wife with that rather common Macedonian name, Cleopatra—daughter, however, of the very uncommon Cleopatra of Egypt. She may have had something to do with the temple to Isis erected in the capital. Their son was named Ptolemy. All in all, a good Roman court, which is to say, once again, much Hellenized.

Juba's capital city was bound to have a theater on the Roman model. So did Lixus, far to the west, and no doubt other or all chief cities of his kingdom. Caesarea's, however, was one of the earliest in Africa and the finest: its orientation strictly on Vitruvian principles, its stage-works sheathed in Carrara marble, its marble Corinthian columns supporting rich entablatures imitative of the temple to Mars Ultor in Rome. Somewhere in the structure, place was found for a colossal statue of the emperor; and high in the seating area was a small chapel, such as could also be seen in Rusicade, later—and earlier, in Rome: the famous theater built by Pompey there providing the model for such a linking of theatral and cult spaces at scores of sites in the empire. Among Caesarea's ruins are unfinished stones including column parts, some signed by the mason, P. Antius Amphio. . . . Importation of Italian experts explains the level and style of much of Juba's building campaign; also, clearly, support from the emperor. Augustus had recently opened up the Carrara quarries at Luni to a new level of exploitation, and it was from there that Juba drew, with additions of local stone, for not only his theater but his palace, too. In Carrara marble, lying about Caesarea, there survive scattered architectural elements such as cornices, soffits, and pilasters imitating a range of recently constructed buildings like the temple of Divus Caesar in the imperial capital or elsewhere in Italy.[42]

Caesarea was a fully equipped Roman city. It had an amphitheater bigger than Rome's, uniquely elongate, almost a race-track. It has been suggested that here wild beast fights were staged, while gladiatorial combats went on in the forum, in the old Roman manner.[43] Juba gave the city water, too, by an aqueduct, and baths-buildings fed by it and probably all three of them of an early date, since they conform to the grid of the streets. Gridding was not a uniquely Roman feature of urban planning, but it was a normal one, to be seen elsewhere in Roman colonies.[44] He supplied a new circuit of city walls on a gigantically ambitious scale, enclosing no less than 370ha. In Africa, urban areas seldom exceeded 30 or 40.[45] Walls, as can be seen in the east as well, were declarations not of readiness for war but of completeness of urban status.

At Sala, on the very western edge of Juba's kingdom, the forum had a range of half a dozen chambers on one of the shorter sides reminiscent of the layout of a legionary camp center. Construction of this has been assigned a date under Juba (with the same feature in other forums of the kingdom in post-Augustan times). The hand of military surveyors may be seen here; but Sala's forum is more likely of the same later date as the other instances, drawing my account into a period better attested in Africa, when indeed the army did do a great deal of city-building.[46] Timgad constitutes the classic example.

Some more or less direct imperial assistance in Mauretanian construction is certain. It has been shown already in Juba's access to the resources of Luni which had come under Augustus' control; and if not demonstrable, at least it is probable in the derivation from Rome of building plans and the architects to explain them. Assistance can be glimpsed also in the personnel of the palace. Epitaphs of the servants there show how they were sold or lent or somehow made available to Juba from the imperial palace staff; the court physician was brother to the emperor's own. Juba had a bodyguard modelled on the emperor's, and even an urban cohort.[47]

Even before his appearance on the scene, his predecessors on their native thrones minted their silver on the Roman standard. His own issues of course followed that example.[48] He chose to honor his queen on both sides of coins with full regal symbolism, and indicated his debt to Augustus by depicting the Capricorn of the emperor's birthdate on coins; also, depicting a temple dedicated to the emperor's cult and an altar in a sacred grove near the capital.[49] Other cities besides Caesarea in his reign built temples to Roman deities.[50]

Between these grand public gestures in stone and precious metal, and the smaller signs—let me instance the circle and its nine holes inscribed on a paving slab of Leptis' "Old" forum, on which the loungers of the day played some game—there is an enormous gap.[51] The play-board is undated, most likely Augustan. It is in the nature of evidence about the mass of any civilization, or about its masses, to be less well or less often recorded; to be ambiguous, without context. It invites comparison with all the foregoing record of this chapter, describing the actions, or the effect of actions, of local authorities, Big People. Only these are able to build temples, mint coins, erect statues, stage theatrical performances or ritual parades in honor of the emperor.

In all their actions, because they were in the public eye and had much to lose from any clumsiness, a sort of artificiality may be suspected. Big People do not willingly reveal the ordinary little people who are within them. The modern observer thus finds two obstacles to understanding the empire's way of life: so much below the top is hidden by accident, and even at the top, so much is hidden on purpose.

For illustration, take the donor of Leptis' *chalcidicum*, Iddibal Caphada Aemilius, son of Himilis. His gift was noted, above. Naturally, the eye lingers on that "Caphada *Aemilius*." The man or his father who named him wanted a Roman touch to raise him in the general estimation, though he was not a Roman citizen. At Leptis to call one's self after some prominent, popular figure unconnected with any gift of citizenship was especially common. Clumsinesses resulted of a ridiculous sort: the mis-placing of what the Romans would have called the *nomen*—enough, certainly, to make a real Roman like Cn. Papirius Carbo smile.[52] He will be recalled as the governor, Aemilius' contemporary. In the second century A.D. a visitor in the next-door town of Oea found another person with a Latin name, Pudens, who nevertheless spoke nothing but neo-Punic, to that snobbish visitor's disgust; still later, Septimius Severus, Latin-speaking son of Leptis but with a Punic accent. It was remarked on by Romans of Rome.[53] Leptis' cemeteries from Augustus' time forward for long preserve the confusion of families that gave the commemorative formulae in neo-Punic but added "*vixit annos*" in imported fashion; similarly, the Roman legal term appearing in a bilingual inscription, "adopted by will," indicates a posthumous adoption in a family of Punic name that in fact did not follow Roman legal usage. Obviously there was an important sector of the population that was not really at home in Roman ways, though in the surviving evidence as a whole the imperfectness of its acculturation is covered up. It continued prominent if not dominant; for neo-Punic texts appear in Tripolitanian municipal decrees and notices and on coins into Tiberius' reign (as also in "Old" Africa).[54]

Notice, "into Tiberius' reign"—indicating that in time they disappeared. So did other non-Roman customs. Clumsinesses in the process only represented steps along the way. In the east, by contrast, it was the Roman intruder's ways that were eventually forced off the stage; yet the percentage of sons of Italy and their descendants in Caesarea-in-Pisidia within the total urban population was no less than that of the Romans of Leptis whose ways prevailed. The same proportions no doubt obtained in Augustus' colonies to the west, such as Simitthus: compared with Caesarea-in-Pisidia, there would be no greater number of natives admitted to citizenship among the new settlers, yet the new settlers imposed their own ways, sooner or later.[55] The civic leaders in fact led the way to surrender.

What can be read in the scanty record of Tripolitania is revealed also in "Old" Africa. Names and language on inscriptions provide the proof. Like the clumsy texts of Leptis, one from a small town near Thuburbo Maius is filled with bad Latin, apparently through translation from the Punic of the people listed in it.[56] It may be Augustan. Still, it cannot be dated more closely than to the first century. The subject of language as an indicator of cultural change slips away into later times, too late to illuminate my chosen period of study.[57] All that can be said, in the most general terms, is that beneath a growing depth and circulation of Latin (and of Roman nomenclature, whatever that indicates more broadly), there was a stratum of neo-Punic both spoken and written; and beneath that in turn, but by Augustus' time to be found only in rural, southern areas, was a native tongue also spoken and written, but so little recorded that its importance is hard to estimate. Its surviving inscriptions number under a hundred, compared to over 30,000 in Latin. What alone is certain about it, paradoxically, is its survival to the present day where Punic and Latin have left no trace. The cultural "middle" which is so important to understand, lying between the urban leadership and the idle poor playing checkers on the public squares, thus reveals itself only in the most puzzling and imperfect glimpses.

4. Acculturation through the plastic arts

One exception is suggestive, though it too offers only a glimpse: in a number of sites in Mauretania, from the start of the first century B.C., potters can be detected at work whose language is Latin. They can only be Italian immigrants to Sala, Banasa, and so forth, whose numbers multiplied under Juba. The vessels they make are used, and stamped in Latin, for oil, wine, and the usual flavoring sauce (*garum*); and they make not only containers but fine dishes and cups for the luxury trade, inscribed with their names. This local production could not satisfy demand. To Caesarea itself and to the east, in "Old" Africa, importation from Italy of its most famous fine ware, *terra sigillata*, began toward the middle of Augustus' reign and picked up rapidly from that point on.[58] As in the east, it gained a share of the market through its intrinsic qualities of pleasing luster, finish, shape, and decoration. Also price: techniques of mass production perfected in Italy kept that low.

The African market not only for vessels but ceramic lamps as well also brought in Italian manufactures, including a model that had in molded relief the golden Shield for Manly Honor (not a good translation of *clipeus virtutis*) awarded to Augustus by the senate in 27 B.C.[59] One such lamp was found at Carthage. In Carthage, too, a relief in stone showed up, with the Roman Earth Goddess, Tellus, seated in just the usual posture but more particularly in the fashion of the relief on Augustus' Altar of Peace; only, her various symbolic accompaniments have been simplified and Africanized.[60] The question suggests itself, comparing the ceramic with the stone relief, to what extent did the article and its market demonstrate intrinsic superiority, as opposed to political correctness? The same question is suggested by the relief of Romulus and Remus mentioned in the first chapter, above. An answer would help to explain motivation underlying cultural change.

It is plain, at least, that the Tellus figure and the twins were commissioned by persons prominent and seeking to be more so; therefore, sensitive to the climate of power around them. Since people of this sort could command art that lasted, art that was large and durable and beautiful, it must dominate, indeed almost seem in itself to characterize, the whole body of surviving evidence; hence a natural inference, that what art conveyed to the audience of the time was principally a political message, calculated to induce the powerful to like and favor you, and to make persons around you think you resembled the powerful and were really one of them.

To draw illustrations from the three African cities which have been the special object of my focus: on a public building of Carthage a relief represented the deified Caesar with Mars and Venus, recalling the cult statues seen in the temple of Mars Ultor in Rome.[61] It is obviously a public—a political—piece of art. From Augustus' time there is little else touched by Roman inspiration that might demonstrate change in the material culture of the host city. In Leptis, shortly after Augustus' death, a collection of marble statues of the emperor and his family was set up in the porch of the temple of Roma and Augustus on the forum. Of other statuary there is hardly a trace. The emperor himself was shown in larger-than-life size, the style properly Roman of Rome.[62] And at Caesarea in Mauretania, a colossal cuirassed statue of Augustus was found near the theater. It recalls the Prima Porta masterpiece. There was apparently a shrine there for the imperial cult, since a statue of another member of the imperial family adjoined it; and other statues of the emperor and his wife have turned up elsewhere in the city.[63]

The emperor is portrayed as he would wish, of course, in Roman style. We have portraits of Juba, too; and differences marking them off from those of the previous native dynasty have been pointed out. The earlier portraits had favored Hellenistic styles and symbolism: a fillet around the head in Alexander fashion, and so on. Juba now follows Rome; more, his official portraits replicate that much-noticed detail in Augustus' usual image: the divided locks of hair over the forehead near the center. Juba's son the crown prince imitates the hair-style of Augustus' heir apparent.[64] Loyalty in Caesarea thus extended beyond the exhibiting of the imperial family and its head; it extended to style as well.

The king's palace has yielded a considerable quantity of art, more than any other site in Africa except Leptis alone. It mirrors in mosaics and statuary the cultural ambition of some grand senator in his villa—of Cicero, let us say, more gourmand than gourmet, snapping up all the antiques he could afford for his "Tusculanum." Juba's collection included antiques as well, or rather, good copies; Egyptian works also to represent Cleopatra's heritage.[65] The drowned cargo of a ship off the African coast, carrying bronzes, furniture, marble statues and statuettes, architectural fragments and inscribed plaques, doubtless all from Athens, helps us to picture just how king and courtiers of Caesarea got what they needed to decorate their homes.[66]

The king's tastes and example were more or less imitated by the rich of his capital, so far as they could afford it. They too had imperial portraits in their houses. In the stelai they erected in suburban cemeteries, carving of purely native tradition is the exception, not the rule.[67] But Caesarea in Augustus' time was itself exceptional. Around Carthage, burial monuments generally maintain their Punic quality; likewise in Tripolitania.[68]

A page or two earlier, a question was raised regarding the intrinsic superiority of imported art, as opposed to its political correctness. It cannot have been the latter quality that accounted for the sale of lamps showing the emperor's *clipeus virtutis*. The buyers, not necessarily of any high class at all, without consideration of their loyalties, simply liked what they saw. A second question then follows: whether the preferences on display in grand monuments communicated purely political messages, or whether they may not also have taught taste, quite apart from any political message. They could not fail to teach *something*, because of the position they were accorded in public. The answer must follow the logic of cultural transfer on other planes: in technology, mores, military arts . . . What was seen as better in terms of its own area of function, without regard to any other implications, would find a market.

III Spain

1. Transformation of the land

In the Iberian peninsula ("Spain," as I will use that term), the Romans' way of life beyond mere warfare had become familiar in at least some areas by the mid-second century B.C., or no doubt earlier in the form of an occasional merchant. Immigration in really significant numbers did not have to wait, as it did in Africa and the east, for the civil wars. The trickle of merchants increased; remnants of Roman armies received their discharge locally, at Graccuris, Carteia, Corduba, Valentia, Italica, Pompaelo. Particularly mining in the south attracted immigrants, who turned to the slave markets for their labor force.[1] The Baetis=Guadalquivir valley was rich not only in metals, but agriculturally, and its coast had ancient cities worthy of the name, notably Gades=Cadiz. The Carthaginians had brought their commercial and administrative skill with them, so that the Romans could claim to occupy but not to raise in civilization this whole quite densely urbanized region. In the larger port sites on the east coast, too, the same was true: a high level of civilization whether thanks to early Carthaginians or Greeks. In the Ebro valley, cutting up northwest toward the mountains, clusters of Celtiberian dwellings often deserved the name of towns through their service as points of exchange, tax-collecting, minting, and jurisdiction. Yet the unsettled conditions around them are sometimes suggested, too, by their elevated sites and the defenses around them.

Further north and west the conquerors could fairly call the country backward or "barbaric." The native inhabitants huddled on hilltops behind their earthworks or walls; they referred to their home by a word eventually rendered in Latin as *castellum*, and had to be driven down into the plains before they could be effectively controlled. What the Romans wanted in the end is shown in the proliferation of little places raised half-way toward city-status and useful for administrative purposes: *vici*. But only three new proper cities in this vast region were founded by Augustus: Lucus Augusti, Asturica, Bracaraugusta. Almost meaningless in their number, they call attention to a fact obvious on the map: acculturating activity in the period of this study touched only a small portion of all Spain, as likewise in Africa and Gaul; but indeed across all of the Roman centuries to come, areas beyond the reach of water-transport and most particularly areas of mountain remained little susceptible to the necessary impulses of imitation.[2]

In the more habitable parts of Spain in Augustus' time the flow of immigrants from Italy was sharply increased by the predictable after-effects of civil strife: groups of discharged soldiers and their families were given land to live on in the territories of already established towns; and some of the latter were rewarded for the part they had borne in wartime by being issued charters to reshape their government on an Italian model and to bestow citizenship on all or at least the upper classes of their populations. The process went forward over the course of no more than a generation but over a considerable area. Beyond the three colonies in the northwest, it involved some seventy identifiable sites. Little urbanization entirely de novo was attempted (as exceptions, Valentia, and a few other towns developing out of or adjoining Roman legionary camps).[3] Most of the effort was concentrated in Baetica (at thirty-odd sites); the rest, with rare exceptions, lay on the east coast (twelve) and in the Ebro valley (ten). Their pattern emerges clearly on the map (Fig. 7).[4]

At somewhat more than half these sites, Caesar was the agent of change. The total of his colonists has been set at about 80,000, added to some 30,000 Roman civilian immigrants already resident. Augustus' veterans amounted to less. They included remnants of his Fifth Alaudae, Fourth Macedonian, Sixth Victrix, and Tenth Gemina legions, after the Cantabrian wars.[5] The total would come to 150–175,000 Romans within a peninsular population of 3,500,000. Such are the best estimates. But even the best, like Easter Island gods, may inspire awe short of conviction.

Change at any rate was on a very significant scale. It should not be thought of as wholly benign, of course; even after slaughter and enslavement ceased, people were driven off their land to make room for in-settlers, to what extent, we cannot say.[6] But the locus chosen for colonization was generally where the Roman face had long been familiar, thereby in fact preparing the way for more welcome contacts. Early *conventus* of Roman citizens turn up from time to time in the historical narrative, prominent and prosperous in native cities from which Pompey or Caesar or others could raise troops. Gades had an astonishing number of Romans of equestrian rank, among whom L. Cornelius Balbus, chosen suffect consul in 40 B.C., was only the most spectacular success.[7]

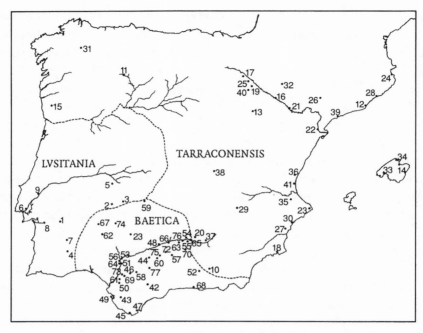

FIGURE 7. Urbanization in Spain

A= founded/chartered by Augustus   m= municipium
C= founded or chartered by Caesar   c= colonia
R= founded or chartered in Republic   con.= conventus-center
?= form of charter uncertain

Lusitania

  1 Ebora *Cm*
  2 Emerita *Ac*
  3 Metellinum *R? Cc*
  4 Myrtilis *Cm*
  5 Norba Caesariana *Cc*
  6 Olisipo *Cm*
  7 Pax Iulia *Cc*
  8 Salacia *Cm*
  9 Praesidium Iulium Scallabis *Cc*
 10 Iulia Gemina Acci *Ac*
 11 Asturica *Aco*
 12 Favent IulAugPiaPaterna Barcino
     Ac 55 Isturgi *Cm*

 13 Bilbilis *Am*
 14 Bocchorus *A?*
 15 Bracara *Acon*
 16 Caesaraugusta *Ac*
 17 Calagurris *Am*
 18 Iulia Victrix Carthago Nova *Cm/Cc*
 19 Cascantum *Am*
 20 Castulo *Cm*
 21 Victrix Iulia Lepida Celsa *Ac*
 22 Dertosa *Am*
 23 Dianium *Am*
 24 Emporiae *Am*
 25 Gracchuris *Am*

An accurate inventory of conquered territory according to the conquerors' usual routine began really not before the time of Augustus. It was he that more carefully divided Spain into three provinces and assigned to each a capital: Tarraco, for one, titled *Iulia urbs triumphalis* in keeping with its dignity. Also he divided the provinces into *conventus*, giving the term a second meaning, as assize centers for juridical purposes: Pax Iulia serving Pacensis, Lucus Augusti serving Lucensis, and so forth. The territory around cities which they were in charge of,

26 Ilerda Rc/Am
27 Ilici (Elche) Ac
28 Iluro Am
29 Libisosa Ac
30 Lucentum Am
31 Lucus Acon
32 Osca Am
33 Palma Rc | Am

34 Pollentia Rc | Am
35 Saetabis Am
36 Saguntum Cm? Am?
37 Salaria Ac
38 Segobriga Am
39 Iulia Victrix Triumphalis Tarraco Cc
40 Turiaso Am
41 Valentia Rc

Baetica

42 Acinipo A?
43 Caesarina Asido Am | c
44 Augusta Firma Astigi Ac
45 Baelo A?
46 Callet C?
47 Carteia Rc
48 Corduba Rc | Cc?: | Ac?
49 Gades Cm? | Am?
50 Hasta Cc
51 Iulia Romula Hispalis Cc
   Tarraconensis
52 Iliberri Am
53 Ilipa C?
54 Illiturgi Cm
55 Isturgi Cm
56 Italica Cm
57 Virtus Iulia Itucci Cc
58 Lacimurga C?
59 Lucurgentum C?

60 Munda Cc
61 Nabrissa C?
62 Nertobriga Cm
63 Obulco Cm
64 Osset Cm
65 Ossigi Cm
66 Sacili Cm
67 Seria C?
68 Sexi C?
69 Siarum Cm
70 Aug Gemella Tucci Ac
71 Iulium U . . . C?
72 ClaritasIulia Ucubi Cc
73 Ugia Cm
74 Ugultunia C?
75 Ulia Am
76 Urgao Alba Am
77 Genetiva Iulia Urban. Urso Ac

on the model of those in Italy (and, long before Italy, as in Greek lands), was me-
thodically parcelled out. In Lusitania it was left largely to villages (Strabo
3.2.15); similarly in the northwest (3.3.5); but around colonies and especially in
Baetica, rural areas were marked off into *pagi* that helped in administration,
usually reflecting their Roman origin in their Latin names: "Augustus" or "Sub-
urbanus."[8]

Organization of responsibility under cities was no new thing in Spain; its
common presence in the Ebro valley was mentioned, above; but it was new in
the recently conquered parts, west and northwest. In spite of it, people for
decades continued there to regard themselves just as they had always done, as
members of a tribal group, a *gentilitas*. They would declare, We are the family of
such-and-such a name within such-and-such a *conventus* and such-and-such a
civitas within it, in the town or village or strong-place called so-and-so, of the
such-and-such clan. Old tribal boundaries were acknowledged by the new government, in the form of stone markers; but the new membership patterns had
to be learned because they determined whom one dealt with in land-registra-
tion, law suits, or tax-paying. Inscriptions show that in fact they soon became
familiar, without suppressing the memory of older patterns.[9]

A further common Roman process, that which assigned plots of land within
centuriae, has been described in other settings. For reasons having much to do
with irregularity of terrain, fewer signs of centuriation can be read in Spain than
in Tunisia or the Po valley. Still, much is detectible: surviving ditches along the
edge of the main lines of demarcation, *kardo* and *decumanus*, indicating quite
minute sub-divisions, near Emporiae=Ampurias, or the area taken in around
Corduba, 120km across to the northwest, 65 to the south. Augustus was himself
the driving force behind much of the program of inventory in Spain, intent on
taxation. Where there had been recent military activity there were Commanders
of Engineers available for the work. Surveying naturally characterized the territories of colonies but spread to native cities as administrative purposes might
suggest, and without respect for city boundaries. In colonies, Roman citizens
occupied much of the farming acreage and, according to their own law, any sale
or inheritance required location on a centuriated plan. Of such a thing, a little
bronze fragment has turned up near Hispalis=Seville.[10] In addition, they occupied the local magistracies, and so made decisions about the administration of
the city's territory; and they had army engineers among them, handy to do the
surveying. That said, it is striking that, for the familiar Italian units of measurement (the *actus* of 120 feet and the *iugerum*), the Baetican population sometimes

substituted their own term, and a unit of measurement, too, that was all their own.[11] No doubt some of them remained loyal to their traditional agricultural practices, too. Nevertheless, Roman colonists both on their own farms and by the force of their example, disciplined as it was and well thought-out, certainly introduced changes to the rural scene.

Just what the Roman presence meant can be learned from the bits and pieces of the archeological evidence. To begin with, landowners in some parts took up oleiculture and viticulture in response to the draw of the market in Italy as early as the second century B.C. There was money to be made there. First to respond, and with wine not oil, was the coastal area in the extreme northeast, behind Barcino, Emporiae, and Baetulo=Badalona. Where there had been importation, the tide of trade shifted to export by the first century. Large farmhouses of the Italian *villa* type appear by the mid-first century and begin to crowd out some of the smaller Iberian farms. Here and there, even a village fades away. *Villa*-owners could see the value in difficult but rich lands requiring a more disciplined labor force, and their methods imply agriculture on Italian lines. Kilns of the area in the same period begin the production of large containers needed for shipment. All these indications of change grow more numerous and obvious from the beginning of the Augustan period. Cn. Cornelius Lentulus' name shows up on amphorae found at Emporiae, in southwest and southeast Gaul, and in Italy including Pompeii. They were manufactured on his great estates in what is now Catalonia—Lentulus, consul in 14 B.C., known from Tacitus as hugely rich, an intimate of Augustus, an Arval Brother.[12] We may suppose him typical of the commercial energies on display in this region and up the Ebro valley—brought in by Italians, not locally generated; for in those agricultural sites of most evident wealth the preferred pottery is of the sort Italians would want, Campanian, and in shapes that suggest Italian food and drink on the table.[13]

With a little delay, the same story unfolds in the Baetis valley and behind the southern coasts of Baetica, most spectacularly behind Gades: that is, subsistence and cereal farming are outstripped by olive-culture for export in the hands mostly of immigrants, to judge from the rural residences they built and decorated; but among them the elite of the native population could find their fortune, too.[14] Strabo (3.2.6) signalizes the production of oil there. The transformation of the rural scene was extremely rapid, most notably so from mid-point in Augustus' reign.

"The latter years of Augustus' reign marked in Spain the grand period of villa development" in Baetica, for example, around Hispalis. A few names of individ-

ual owners may be found in the record, destined to establish the family fortunes: Sextus Pomponius in Pliny's *Natural History*, or the uncle of Columella.[15]
Around Emerita the colonists were especially favored by a territory of more than
2,000 square kilometers and, within it, double-sized *centuriae* (100+ha) implying generous allotments.[16] From here south to Gades and Baelo, the economy
was evidently improved by a new landed aristocracy, farming in their own ways
on their own scale and generating and enjoying a new level of wealth. A late Augustan rural residence near Carthago Nova=Cartagena provides an illustration
of how the owners lived, not exactly on a Vitruvian, Italian model but very comfortably and well suited to the climate: in cool, closed-in rooms protected to the
north and south by galleries.[17] This general plan became the rule for later times.

An overwhelmingly large percentage of the Spanish economy, even in a
province famous for its mines, rested on agriculture. This latter grew more productive in Augustus' times, not in a way that can be quantified but as can be inferred with certainty from a thousand signs of prosperity both on the land and
in the cities. An end to the waste of war must constitute one large part of the explanation; as a second, improvements in the road system which opened up
wider markets. Then, too, conquest and occupation brought taxes, and taxes,
ultimate benefit. The idea that taxation may be good for you is, to say the least,
counter-intuitive; but, once proposed, it survives discussion. It assumes a con-
structive response by subsistence farmers: therefore, occupation of empty areas
such as certainly existed in the south-central parts of Spain; clearing of under-
utilized land; application of techniques for the exploitation of swampy tracts
seen (above) in the northeast.[18]

All this was in some degree tax-driven. But our uncertainty, how much of
taxes was collected in cash, how much in kind, makes interpretation difficult. If
in kind, then the stimulus of taxation played directly on agriculture, and farmers raised more than before so as to hand over a part of their crops to the collec-
tor; whereupon, it left the country. Its value was lost to the local economy. Alternatively, if taxes were payable in cash, the cash had to be earned by selling part of
the crop. That would make people reach out for sales beyond the local markets,
especially to Rome and Italy. Coinage in circulation was perfectly adequate for
the latter purpose, meaning, tariffed in Roman units: if of silver, then largely
consisting of imperial issues by Augustus' time, while small change in bronze
continued to issue from a great number of city mints. They were left free to respond to local needs.[19] Given the lack of evidence, however, which might tell us
how the economy worked, all that can be safely concluded is that the methodical
raising of tribute worked in the same direction as the other two factors just

mentioned, the *pax Romana* and improved communications. To what extent taxes affected the circulation of money must remain unclear.

As to communications, road-building in Spain of course long antedated Augustus' time. The earliest sign of Rome's presence in the Ebro valley are in fact milestones of about 114 B.C. on the road connected to the even older coastal Via Herculea, renamed Via Augusta. Rebuilt beginning in 8/7 B.C., this principal artery ran from the edge of Gaul to Emporiae, on to Tarraco, and so to Saguntum and Carthago Nova.[20] By the same name it then bent west, to enter the head of the Baetis valley at Castulo and follow the left bank of the river to Gades. Augustan construction of this southern section dates from the years around 2 B.C. Passage across provincial boundaries was marked by grand arches, the southern one called, inevitably, "The Augustan Janus." It stood at one of two crossings of the Baetis, on the detour that tied in Castulo.[21]

In the same reign, road-building went forward in the northwest to connect the three new cities there and two other little towns, one of them a Caesarian municipality: Iria and Salacia.[22] Work on the northeastern network involved the Fourth and Sixth Legions, and it is safe to assume both military engineering and labor for the system in every region.[23]

The two bridges over the upper Baetis were not the only ones built under Augustus. Not many miles west of Barcino there was another, still in use today; a good number elsewhere in Spain; and a famous one at Emerita which the traveller sees from afar, directly in his sights as he approaches that handsome city on the north bank of the Anas. The highway, in a straight line of a thousand meters, steps across two streams and an intervening islet, passes over the Anas, and becomes Emerita's main avenue, its *kardo maximus* cutting through town. Similarly, the Via Augusta leading to the Augustan colony of Ilici, up the coast from Carthago Nova, and earlier at the port-settlement of Gades: highway and urban *kardo* flow into each other in a line. At Caesaraugusta, the streets are laid out in blocks oriented on the same lines as the farm plots in the surrounding territory. Explanation for such identity lies in the practice observable elsewhere also, of planting colonies on main lines of communication, where a foundation *de novo* was intended, and of extending the logic of cadastration onto the network of city-blocks.[24]

Before conquest, Spain did not entirely lack anything the Romans brought with them. At least here and there, its fields had marked boundaries; it had roads and bridges, old-established urban centers, centralized markets, silver and bronze coinage adequate for commercial purposes; a rural population served thereby; crops of every variety, oil and wine included. But nothing in the list diminishes the importance of the changes wrought in Augustus' time. Being concentrated in regions of dense habitation, they promptly reached the very great majority of the population; even in the most backward corners of the northwest as well, they were detectible. They put on display the particularly Roman way of doing things, bigger and better. They advertised, taught, and so affected daily routines. Without any human presence to observe, one could have told from the tangible signs alone that the land had been made Roman.

Since no written story survives, however, to tell us about that human presence, there is no saying to what extent the Romans brought with them from Italy the use of slave labor in agriculture, nor the interplanting of cereals, vines, and olive trees in a single field such as is recommended in their farming books. The shifting balance of small as against large farms, successfully traced by archeologists across southern Latium, for example, has not been traced in the same detail in Spain. Names and fortunes of the major landowners are not so well known as in Augustan Italy. Despite an extraordinary increase in the vitality of archeological discovery from the 1970s and a corresponding increase in what is known, the rural scene in the great river valleys, in the Meseta, everywhere, thus remains very much more obscure than the urban, even though it held eighty or ninety per cent of the population.

2. Urban structures

The familiar ancient and medieval icon of a city as a ring of walls brings the Spanish picture into focus: a pre-Roman land some parts of which lacked even the word for peace (Basque) and had to borrow *pax*. Our earliest accounts show the native centers armed with some sort of fortified circuit, and archeology confirms that general fact, providing details about technique: of earth-works, mudbrick, stone without mortar, sometimes squared stone, taking advantage of natural features.[25] At first the Romans didn't like such provisions for war, destroyed them in the course of conquest, and generally forbade them to be built, as Appian happens to specify in his account (*Bell. Hisp.* 6.99).

When the conquerors, on the other hand, built their own towns in Spain, they gave them the same sort of massive walls that were to be found at home in the third or second century, sometimes importing Italian masons, and masterfully oblivious of terrain. Carteia's walls went up at the time of its first settlement, in the third century; Tarraco's, a little after the turn of the second century; fifty years later, those of Valentia, or of the site called La Caridad; later in the century, Baetulo, Emporiae; and so on to Augustus' time with Segobriga, Corduba, Barcino. . . . The walls of Emerita are depicted on its coins and dedicatory relief sculptures. But at these latter sites the fortifications were lighter and more for show, or even entirely dispensed with; and the magistrates of a native town near Corduba might offer it a fortified gate in 49 B.C., unopposed by higher authority. Surely Italian practices provided a model or a validation; for in the last generation of the Republic a great number of Italian cities, often thanks to some particular native son, received their stone circuit not so much for defense as for definition and pride of urban status.[26] At Corduba the rich donors were Binsnes son of Vercellionis and M. Coranus Alpis son of Acrinus, serving respectively on the Board of Ten, and as aedile, both of them inspired by patriotism and *philotimia*. A number of instances appear through inscriptions of Augustus' time to show the connection between a gift to one's city, and election to one of its offices.[27] The phenomenon was to have a long and effective life everywhere in the empire.

Since suburban housing is not often investigated and, besides, was likely to be made of poor perishable materials, estimates of a city's size must generally work with the durable defenses around it; whereupon, a few of the colonies win the prize: the immense Clunia (130ha) or, not so strikingly, Emerita. Over-ambitious circuits might remain empty for a generation or two, or more.[28] In general, however, the planners stayed within the limits familiar to them in Italy.

Within the circuit, wherever city-building started from scratch, it was possible to impose a system of orthogonal streets of the sort prevalent in Italy from the third century on; and Augustan planners favored this and made it the mark of a Roman foundation.[29] In the grid of streets a set of four blocks might be reserved for the forum, each block measuring one by two *actus* of the standard dimension, 120' × 240'.[30] Occasionally the decision was made to attach a new settler population to an old, perhaps even separately walled off, allowing the old to stand but the new to be laid out in the Roman way: pre-Augustan examples are less rare than the Augustan.[31] For the most part, however, the Romans chose established centers for colonizing or other imperial favors, where restructuring on such a fundamental level was out of the question; so it would be the very center and not much more that underwent significant modification.

Caesar (BC 2.20) mentions that at a point in the early 40s B.C. two legions, one of them made up of local levies, "camped in the forum and its porticoes." This was at Hispalis, reminder of the Italian style of enclosed space that might be expected at the center of a town owing its birth to the Romans. Most Spanish fora that are known in some completeness date, however, not to Hispalis' time but to Augustus'; and by then the model was thoroughly familiar. Vitruvius (5.1.2) recommended a rectangle with sides in the ratio of 3:2 such as is generally realized, for example at Conimbriga. At this site, however, a basilica lies along one long side, as in some Italian towns, though the normal practice would place it at the end. More characteristic is the ambition shown in extending the plane of the forum on a cryptoportico, over lower ground. Such terraces supported on vaulting were a common expedient of Roman engineers in Spanish town centers—once again, with familiar illustrations in Italy (at Palestrina, for one) but beyond the capacities of pre-Roman science. Centered on Conimbriga's cryptoportico is a temple for the imperial cult, a structure that, from the middle years of Augustus' reign, often presided over one end of western provincial fora.[32]

For this structure and its location as for other features, the great exemplar was the Forum Romanum, teaching architects what the proper elements and forms ought to be. In Rome there was a senate house, a *curia*, at the right-hand upper corner as one faced the presiding temple; and similarly at Ruscino on the border in Gaul; again, at Conimbriga even before the town was officially enrolled in Roman political life and forms (it was a mere *oppidum* with *magistri* and a council of elders). As in some Italian towns of Augustan date, however, this important chamber might be no more than an extension at the back of the basilica, or off one end as at Clunia; or it might be represented by make-shifts within the building that have left no trace in stone.[33] In any case, a meeting place for the city councillors was as natural here as we have seen it to be natural at Leptis Magna.

In both Clunia and Conimbriga as on Romanized fora throughout Spain, the place of honor was reserved for a temple of the Roman style, high on its platform and with columns normally across the front alone. To what Beings should this be dedicated? One choice just described was Roma and Augustus. It competed for favor with the Capitoline triad. Jupiter, Juno, and Minerva might be received within a single building having three chambers or within three separate small temples, as at Baelo and, in Italy, at Brescia.[34] Another half-dozen Spanish *capitolia* have been identified with more or less probability, most of them of the second century B.C. Since the Capitoline cult is taken for granted in Vitruvius' recommendations for a proper forum (1.7.1) and in Caesar's model charter for the new town of Urso (caps. 70f.), surely some provision for the central element of Roman state religion must have been made in all of his or Augustus' colonies; but an altar not a temple might be judged appropriate.

Last to be mentioned in the city center are *macella*.[35] Such a building also was taken for granted in a town charter, that of Irni (cap. 19)—and why not? since it was so common a feature of urban Italy where the charter had been formed. Its

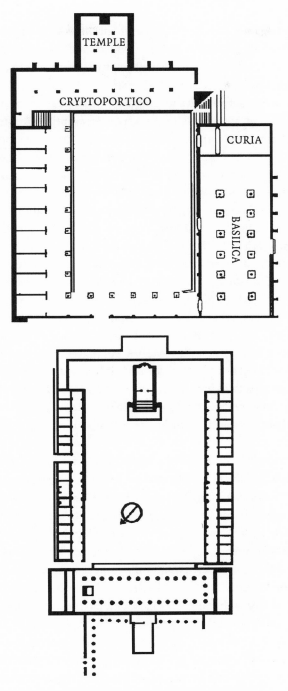

FIGURE 8. Augustan fora at Conimbriga and Clunia.

match has been found, above, at many a site in the eastern provinces as in the African. It served the general purpose of concentrating each certain common activity of the city in premises specially designed, according to a logic already emphasized as peculiarly Roman. *Macella* completed the group of basilica, *curia*, and pedestal temple, set around a rectangular porticoed space of particular proportions itself suited, says Vitruvius, to that quintessentially Roman purpose of staging bloody combats. Here, too, ideally, *kardo* and *decumanus* met, right in the city's mid-point, its navel; here were all the square corners and regulated determinations of the Roman way of life. At home in Italy, at Cosa, Luni, Minturnae, Ostia, and later-founded colonies down into the Augustan period, city centers and their chief buildings invite comparison with their imitations in Spain.

Scattered more loosely and according to terrain and convenience were other structures characteristic of that tradition: those needless declaratory arches already mentioned, to mark provincial boundaries; others for purely urban purposes. Also, aqueducts, by no means needless: one of them decorated by Agrippa with hundreds of pieces of statuary, another titled Aqua Augusta with elaborate decoration and advertisement on the city's coins, a third delivering water enough to supply a hundred fountains or three hundred houses, and a fourth reaching a couple of miles into the countryside to its source.[36] Major projects! As a characteristic part of the seal of Rome upon Spanish urbanism, these structures appear in the charter of Urso drafted by Caesar's order (cap. 99), where it is assumed the colony will wish to build its aqueduct at public expense, and will need to assert its authority in confiscating land for the necessary right of way.

Baths naturally followed. In Italy, facilities of the latter sort, at home in homes, then built for the public, were to be found in towns of any pretensions, and in Rome, where there were an incredible number of small commercial establishments, Agrippa constructed the first baths-building free for the general public, endowing and decorating it with a lavish hand.[37] In these decades the Roman abroad was already settled into the habit that later raised such monuments as Caracalla's or Diocletian's in the imperial capital. Testimony to the fact can be found in the charter of Irni, listed under the oversight of the municipal authorities along with temples, roads, and *macella*; and baths were among the comforts already offered in Augustan times to the citizens of Valencia, Baetulo, Conimbriga. . . . [38] At this last site, the handsome frescoes on the walls have survived at least in fragments, and some decoration with statuary may be assumed, too, on the model of the lavish exhibition in Agrippa's baths in Rome.

Roman entertainment found a home in race-tracks here and there, and amphitheaters, too—some put up in wood, most in stone. Italica's seated 25,000 and ranked fourth in size in the empire of the time.[39] At Gades, in some large facility of this sort, the younger Balbus, nephew of L. Cornelius, in 43 B.C. presented his native city with a gladiatorial show,[40] and the Urso charter of these same years (caps. 70f.) assigns such exhibitions, or alternatively, dramatic spectacles, to the office of *duumvir* and again, to the aediles, as a mixed municipal and personal expense in honor of Jupiter, Juno, and Minerva. They were to be staged either in the forum or circus.

This younger Balbus is a likely donor of a theater in Gades, unless it slightly predates the years of his gifts to the city (Strabo mentions them).[41] Baelo's theater was of the same date, that is, late Republican or a little later; Carthago Nova's, Augustan; Emerita's, the gift of Agrippa. Others, contemporary, total more than a dozen, of which Caesaraugusta could boast the largest, no doubt: it seated 6,000; but Corduba's was perhaps the most elegant, copying its architectural elements from the temple of Mars-the-Avenger in Rome, and doing so in marble shipped in from the emperor's quarries in Luna. Perhaps he had contributed to the costs of the project, designed as it was for a provincial capital.[42] Certainly a theater was an affair of great ostentation and expense; but the Urso charter (cap. 127) assumes the existence of such a facility. Cities so favored were almost without exception the sites of colonies, and of these latter, almost all had been founded by Caesar or Augustus. It is surprising how quickly the Marcellus-theater in Rome found its imitators in Spain.[43]

We here confront very substantial, complicated structures, all of them; still more, amphitheaters; and the groups of structures making up a proper Roman forum, the most so. The transformation wrought in urban Spain, beginning in the 40s and lasting for a generation—hardly more—is a quite remarkable phenomenon. Informing us of it, the relative abundance of archeological evidence serves to explain and fill in the gaps in our very incomplete picture of other provinces in the empire; for it is not to be assumed, *ex silentio*, that they were much less favored by the burst of energy displayed in the Iberian peninsula. There, in any case, no one would deny the effect wrought by that generation upon the visible scene in both the provincial capitals of Spain, at Emerita, Tarraco, and Corduba, and in quite modest cities like Baelo. What is more, the invisible scene within these edifices as we imagine them in use, daily taking in a stream of people from the surrounding territories and on festivals bursting with the crowds—this scene in the mind's eye shapes the behavior of visitors, makes them look about, stare, wonder, admire, and carry home the memory of what they had witnessed, for imitation.

Above all, surely it was the music they remembered. We know not a note of that, only overhearing snatches of conversation, as it were, about famous performers, or favorite work songs, or the like mentioned in various types of sources around the Mediterranean. All we can be sure of is the ubiquity of theaters, itself powerfully suggestive, where dramatic performances were, as we do know, half music and dance. Similarly at a lower level of entertainment: we have from Celsa in Spain, in mosaic form (Fig. 9), as from other provinces, a hundred testimonies to the popularity of board games, like checkers, cut or inscribed on the flagstones of public spaces for the idle poor or simply for bored people passing their time in amphitheaters or on the town square; but of the manner of play of these games we know nothing.[44] All that can be said, then, of such public places under the heading of "Romanization" is that they constituted so many classrooms where Roman leisure ways were taught; likewise in basilicas, giving their lessons in numbers, coins, laws, and language; likewise in temples teaching forms of cult.

Over-all, public buildings added instruction in Roman esthetics. Of this, the word "monumentalization" defines some central aspect, particularly marked in the latter half of Augustus' principate not only in the provinces but in Italy as well. It recurs in scholarly descriptions of city centers, associated with terracing, axiality, symmetry, and on occasion, sheer size (let us say, Emerita's temple, 142' × 75').[45] It applies to the rearranging of shops on the square so as to back on it, not open on it, thus leaving the internal porticoes free of strident chaffer and superannuated fish—so, at Emporiae or Baelo.[46] I have drawn attention to the enclosing of particular activities in particular buildings, as something characteristic of the Roman intent; and, beyond macella or public latrines, one could add from a later author (Frontinus, Contr. agr. 55.8f.) the ordinary provision of a Potter's Field in the suburbs. Ugly things should be beyond the pale.

Esthetics in a formal sense were governed by what was familiar and admired in Italy, especially in the imperial capital. The major temples on the Forum Romanum invited imitation; less specifically, Italian traditions in street grids, fora, baths, covered markets, theaters, and so forth, in instances noted above. Marble came into fashion in Italy, where one of Caesar's officers had opened up the quarries at Luni and Augustus had taken them over and begun to exploit them on a gigantic scale. Everyone knows of his "boast that he found Rome a brick city and left it marble."[47] In imitation, then, Spanish cities clad their public buildings in that gleaming stone, on occasion imported from Greece, as in the column capitals of the theater's stage back-drop at Carthago Nova, with their details and proportions just like those of Rome's temple of Mars-the-

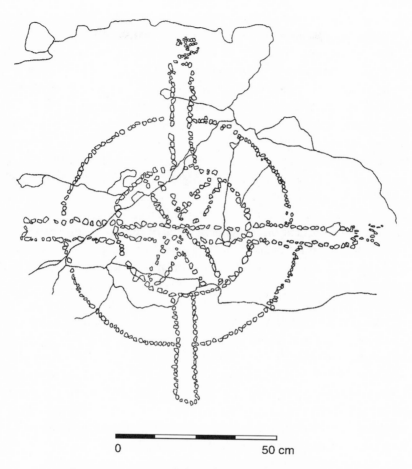

0   50 cm

FIGURE 9. A mosaic board game in a Celsa home.

Avenger; or architects in smaller towns used stucco or faux-marble, local light-colored substitutes.[48] But variations in such matters of decorative treatment from one site to another or from one decade to another belong to the history of Roman architecture in general. My own concern is only with the question, Was what we see in Spain, Roman or indigenous in inspiration? As to the sudden increase in Roman influence in Augustus' time, whatever the details, there can be no dispute.

It is demonstrable at a level beneath the obvious. Mention was made of the Vitruvian proportions of a proper forum. These, needing a great clear space at the urban center, could not normally be observed; but they often could be where individual buildings were planned. I reserve until later the evidence to be drawn from private houses and from Gaul; but I recall the Conimbriga forum, length and width in the proportion of three to two, as the authority specified (5.1.1f.), measured out according to the Roman foot and with no odd little lengths left over: the crypt wall of five feet, not five plus a few inches, the pillar-intervals two and a half with nothing left over, and so forth for the elements of the frieze, architrave, columns, and capitals.[49] Underlying these measurements, the foot was used as a base unit in multiples of which everything else was reckoned: a *modulus*, as Vitruvius calls it, using this term and method throughout his work, for example at 1.2.2, *quantitas autem est modulorum*. In its architectural application, "module" was his invention. The general method of course has been seen prevailing in centuriation, with everything expressed in *actus*; and in a town like Emporiae or La Caridad the city blocks (*insulae*) might be so reckoned.[50] In buildings with columns (which would include almost all that were public), the module would normally be the intercolumniation (the distance between the center point of two columns, used for example in the Belo *capitolium* or the temple at Emporiae);[51] or it could be the column base, which Vitruvius prefers at 3.2f., when he describes how to put up a temple and incidentally takes his models from Rome's of the 40s and 30s B.C. In Saguntum's *capitolium* on the forum, the three separate chapels are in the ratio 3:4:3, and a tenth of the interior dimension of the whole (28.5') serves as the base module, the walls being 2x in thickness, the exterior width being 14x, and the structure over-all being comparable to the *capitolium* at Luni.[52] Again, in the Vitruvian theater of Clunia, the bowl and stage are designed according to a simple geometry in the normal manner of architectural sketches.[53] Such disciplined design practices were not within the reach of builders in Spanish cities before the Romans came.

To go deeper into detail, into the native style of wall-building: dry stone or mud brick or adobe over a stone core prevailed in the earlier Spain, or sometimes wooden walls; little use of squared stone.[54] Then the characteristic Roman use of cement begins to appear in the archeological record in isolated locations, and so more frequently as the second century turns into the first, along with *opus reticulatum* even in funerary monuments, and the burst of building, the "Bauboom" as German scholars call it, gets under way. A characteristic structure is the elaborate mausoleum in the suburbs of Carthago Nova, commissioned at a mid-Augustan date by a second-generation Roman citizen, Titus Didius. Its design closely resembles what could be seen near Rome or in Campania, at Aquileia, or for that matter in southern France (chap. 4, at Glanum, the "Julii" monument).[55] The less urbanized regions, however, were slow to learn.

Some persistence of native practices in designing and decorating built structures seems altogether predictable even in the act of trying to imitate the Roman.[56] Very usefully for my purposes, it identifies the actors as non-Romans
eager to master foreign ways. The evidence for rather more competent imitation
is nevertheless overwhelming in the more carefully handled parts of the more
prosperous cities of Augustus' time—no need to recall the illustrations of this
offered above and scattered through the notes. In explanation, here and there,
the presence of artisans and planners directly drawn from Italy seems clear.[57]

3. The people responsible for change

These patrons and their agents in change who now enter the discussion need to
be further introduced, though they cannot be very fully typed or identified.
Among the people who initiated things, the most obvious characteristic was
certainly wealth. At the little town of Conimbriga, for illustration, the cost of
the Augustan building program has been estimated at half a million sesterces,
at a time when three or four sesterces constituted a day's wage for a laborer.[58]
That great total, for what it is worth, may be turned into six to eight million
dollars (in the year 2000, for whatever that translation may some day be
worth). Corresponding expenditures on provincial capitals or any substantial
city would be much greater. Who could afford so much?

The first answer is of course the great commander in the tradition of Metellus or Scipio, earlier; so according to his biographer (Suet., *Caes.* 28.1) Caesar
"gave magnificent public works as adornments to the foremost cities of Spain"
as well as other provinces; and in the course of the contest for the peninsula he
recalled to the citizens of Hispalis the favors he had shown them, *beneficia*, in
earlier years (*Bell. Hisp.* 42). Whatever the extent of these or of others to other
cities, now lost from the record, no doubt Augustus surpassed it. He spent
much more time in Spain, where he was not perpetually involved in war, either,
and he enjoyed a vastly greater length of term in a position of supremacy. He and
(by his nomination, we may be sure) members of his family took on local magistracies involving them in great acts of generosity. Though surviving evidence
allows only a few projects to be assigned to this imperial group, many more may
be assumed without any specific text in proof.[59]

Agrippa, also, was active and generous. Through his marriage he came into
possession of great riches and increased them many times thanks to his role in
the outcome of the civil wars. He could pay for a theater at Emerita; and an honorific marble relief in thanks to him sketches the outline of a city and the role he
must have played in its beautification and improvement.[60] On Gades' coins he

is saluted as Patron of the Township; Emporiae salutes him also in an inscription.[61]

A little beneath Agrippa we have a lower rank of authority signallized by *beneficia* to client cities: persons like governors, among them Cn. Domitius Calvinus. He had been set over the whole of the peninsula in 39–36. In his term in office he founded the colony at Emporiae. It addressed him as Patron. Likewise a successor in the office in 34–33, again a *patronus*.[62]

Like these great men, many local magnates, too, who earned special thanks from their cities were of Roman or Italian origin. Their connections and opportunities naturally helped them make their fortunes. A conspicuous exception, however, prepares the way for others of his kind: of indigenous origin, L. Cornelius Balbus. He earned citizenship from Pompey for his loyal service in war, taking his name from a second patron he encountered in Spain, attaching himself then to Caesar when Caesar was serving first as quaestor in the province and later as propraetor, with Balbus as his Commander of Engineers.[63] Known as "Caesar's intimate friend," he was able to win great favors for his home-town. It duly named him its patron; by Augustus' favor he was named consul. He had proved himself of that type that every conqueror embraces, the indispensable native—on occasion, collaborator or Quisling. Another we know of, useful to the Pompeian cause in Lusitania, was a certain Caecilius Niger, a native;[64] and eastern equivalents were pointed out in the first chapter, above.

Such types of course flourished most in disturbed times. Like Augustus himself, they were the creatures of those times; so was their wealth. Roman commanders and historians alike, so particularly proud, or proudly particular, about the exact number of towns they sacked and of wagon-loads of coin brought home from foreign enemies, have little to say about the profits of a civil war. Winners emerge with wealth to spare seemingly by magic. But they do emerge. In Augustus' time, touched by such disturbances in so many parts, inevitably they were many and prominent around the empire.

They gave much of their winnings to public causes. That was a response to monied prominence expressive of Hellenistic values, already emphasized in other chapters—a response of great importance, too, in explaining the progress of urban development in the western areas, Italy included.

In Italy, we have the charter given to Tarentum at the time of its resettlement (perhaps with veterans) at some date unknown between the 70s and the 40s, possibly under Caesar's direction. It provided due authority, to any magistrate who "*wishes*, to construct, to dig, to change, to build, or to pave roads, ditches, or sewers for the public welfare;"[65] and a second text of the same period, in Caesar's *Civil Wars* (1.15.2), describes how the later-famous T. Labienus "had founded the town [of Cingulum near Ancona] and equipped it with public buildings out of his own pocket." Together, the two testimonies show an ethic at work, a Roman version of that *philotimia* already noticed especially in eastern contexts. But there is a third testimony cited above in my first chapter: Suetonius in his description of wonderful improvements wrought in the capital under Augustus (*Aug.* 29) accounts for many of them by the emperor's leadership: "he encouraged everyone to the extent of his resources to make the city splendid with new or renovated or beautified public works." We think especially of Agrippa's response.

Shall we say, then, that the Regime remade the capital, the State expressed itself in stone? Can we not recognize ideology at work when we see it, calling to mind those architectural triumphs of regimes in Russia, Italy, and Germany still so oppressively to be seen today? But of course these analogies are anachronistic, they shed no light on Augustus' time. His great building followed in a long series of earlier grand acts by others which he wished only to emulate through his own coadjutors, a line that had nothing to do with the State or ideology, rather with the individual and his claims as such. That is what he insists on in a fourth text, his *Accomplishments* so carefully pondered and universally published, in the sections given to his public projects.

As Paul Veyne writes,

> We have speculated too much about the audience Augustus was addressing in his self-glorification. Was it for the populace that he listed his *euergesiai?* But the *Res Gestae* was reproduced throughout the empire. Why then not to this provincial public? Or perhaps a patchwork, for different readerships? These are idle questions arising from the fundamental mistake of interpreting the glorification of sovereign majesty as ideology. If Augustus speaks of the largesses he has provided for the city of Rome, this is not propaganda. The *Res Gestae* is not a document like a propaganda poster—it is a monument carved for the heavens to see, nothing more; and for all time.[66]

And Veyne goes on to derive this urge from eastern traditions grafted on to Roman self-advertisement in the search for acclaim and high standing. A fifth testimony fits well with his interpretation, though on a smaller scale: Cicero's declaration that he had bought himself a millionaire's mansion in the best part of town "to gain a little standing," *ad aliquam dignitatem pervenire.* It cost him many times as much as all of Conimbriga's monumentalization, but the capital had its own scale of expenditures.[67]

In Italy, then, and not only in Rome, we have Augustus financing civic improvements just as we have his predecessors, a generation before he was even born, doing just the same for the other cities they themselves chose to favor, in a sharply increasing surge of euergetism;[68] and beyond Italy, we have Herod and Ptolemy, not to mention various names in Sparta or Leptis Magna, taking advantage of their access to wealth to express their triumphant powers on a glorious huge scale while bowing from time to time in the direction of the man who had put that wealth within their reach—the autocrat at the center of their world.

Turning to Spain and a final testimony: the charter given to Urso (cap. 77) exactly repeats that of Tarentum, regarding any magistrate who "wishes, to construct, to dig, to change, to build, or to pave roads, ditches, or sewers for the public welfare." It even requires magistrates (cap. 71) to pay out from their own pocket not less than 2,000 sesterces in their year in office, toward the expenses of public entertainment. To such an extent had cities come to depend on philo-timia and euergetism. Other Spanish towns felt their benefits, offered by civic leaders in Emporiae, Tarraco, and so forth.[69]

As a specific instance, the nephew and namesake of L. Cornelius Balbus may serve best. The uncle had represented a first generation in the Romanizing process: not a spectator, rather, a participant. His nephew represented a second generation, already over-ripe. While Gades benefited from his monumental riches which enabled him to re-do a whole quarter of the city and construct a proper harbor, the sources of his wealth could hardly bear inspection.[70] He excused all that by describing himself in his very crimes as "just like Caesar." In 43, before slipping off from Spain to a safer haven in Mauretania, he put on a splendid show featuring the idol of the local stage and a specially composed drama on his own achievements, followed by exhibitions of gladiatorial combat. The correct fourteen rows of front seats at these spectacles were reserved for equestrian citizens, young Balbus of course prominent among them. An account of the whole event and its impresario was passed on to Cicero by his friend C. Asinius Pollio. In every aspect—not only in the grandest arrogance, avarice, display, and euergetism, but in the choice of entertainments and punctilio—his conduct could hardly be more perfectly Roman.

In airily characterizing his "thefts and robberies" as no different from Caesar's (the quoted words are those of Pollio), Balbus was not far wrong, perhaps. "Winner take all," nothing new about that—nor any wonder that he should enjoy the glory of his sudden winnings in conspicuous displays. But it was in a Roman cause that he and his like had fought (whichever side they were on), and with Roman rivals they had competed for distinction. From that rivalry flowed the consequence: a manner of enjoying the spoils of victory that should be peculiarly Roman, or Hellenistic. Hence, much of the grand euergetism that embellished Spanish cities, now clothing themselves in marble like Rome itself.

The lessons learned by the indigenous population in civic behavior, so evident in Balbus' behavior and well characterized by Veyne, was one highly important aspect of Romanization in Spain as elsewhere. A second closely connected to its operation regulated the relations of different ranks in society, through patronage. Patronage secured the needed connections between unfulfilled cities and new-sprung millionaires. Just as Balbus the uncle had risen so far in the world thanks to Pompey and Cornelius Lentulus Crus and Caesar, stepping eagerly upward in the train of successive commanders, so had others. Where advantage lay, where cities must seek it, seemed quite plain: Caesar had *beneficia* to spare, Augustus still more; everyone applied to them.

In June of 45 B.C., when the supporters of Pompey's cause had been cornered near Ilerda, fraternizing with Caesar's men led to talks about surrender. It was the Pompeian officers who did the talking, but (BC 1.74) "the same thing was done by the Spanish chieftains, *principes*, whom they had called to them to keep in their camp as hostages; and these sought out any individuals they knew who were their guest-friends, *hospites*, and who might recommend them to Caesar." The scene brings life to those *tabulae patronatus* and mentions of *hospitium* which have survived in bronze form—life and accommodation also to the Roman traditions, not all that different.

Another little scene, carefully contrived, illustrates again how the system worked and was recalled some twenty years later by Augustus in his autobiography, on which in turn Nikolaos of Damascus drew a few years after that:[71] Caesar, being triumphant over all his enemies after the battle of Munda and engaged in tidying up the aftermath of the fighting, held court in Carthago Nova, drawing to his presence all petitioners and problems.

Many had come to him, either for the sake of judicial proceedings, about which they had some measure of doubt in the case of some people, or for the sake of of political administration, and some to receive the rewards for their acts of bravery. He met many people about these affairs, and many of the tribal leaders came to him. Even the Saguntines, oppressed by very great charges against them and needing his help, fled to Caesar. He [Augustus] represented these men and, since he defended them very well in open court before Caesar, he delivered them from their charges and sent them home rejoicing, singing his praises to all and sundry, and calling him saviour. Then many men came to him needing his patronage, since he was of very great value, and some he freed from their charges, for others he asked boons or he raised them to magistracies.

The Roman system of patronage was thus put on display—if there had been anyone present among the Spaniards who was not already well schooled in its rules.

The Saguntines had enjoyed the patronage of the Fabii since the second century (there was no rule against their having more than one patron, Fabius or Augustus or whoever it might be); Pollio, Cicero' friend quoted just above, was governor in Spain in the 40s and so we may assume was chosen as patron by towns there; in any case, his son was chosen, afterward; and Agrippa as patron of many towns has been mentioned above, along with various governors, great senators, and the like.[72] So the lessons had been long imparted.

Where the Roman presence was less felt, in the northwest, the indigenous custom prevailed of drawing two parties into mutual protection and friendship. It is translated in one representative document as in hospitium fidem clientelamque. The fact that it is inscribed on a little bronze plate in the form of a pig, and the names of the contracting parties, Amparamus, Caraegius, and so forth, give it a very un-Roman quality; the spelling is faulty, too; but the wording belongs entirely to Roman custom. Even the date is by consuls. A slightly earlier example involves a younger son of Pollio, consul in 8 B.C., intimate of Augustus, married to Agrippa's daughter. The family had old Spanish connections and is here tied to the civitas Lougeiorum among the Astures in the northwest. The same community in another text calls itself Lougeii castellani, inhabitants of a strong-place; their negotiators are Silvanus son of Cloutos and Nobbius son of Adamus, identifying themselves not in the Roman manner and only one of them with a partially Roman name. A little earlier still among these bronze contracts is one written in Celtiberian script. Gradual accommodation to Roman ways, themselves already attested in Plautus, can thus be sensed in the Spanish series across time. Romans for their part welcomed it since it so easily fitted in with their own ideas.[73]

With the same flexibility they welcomed the tradition of loyalty unto death, sworn by warriors to their leader, devotio Iberica. Of this, Pompey and others had made use in recruiting their armies.[74] Later, it eased the way toward that general oath taken by all the population to Augustus' cause, sworn not only in Italy before Actium and much later attested at Gangra in Paphlagonia (chap. 1, above), but exacted from the Spanish province as well. The text inscribed on bronze for display in public, of the same date as Gangra but with differences in formula according to western or eastern traditions, bound the civilian population to the emperor and his princes, forever to support and fight for them if needed.[75] Taking the oath would constitute one more lesson in how the Romans conceived of and articulated power, and drew into the ceremony no doubt a large part of the whole population.

4. The formal articulation of change

It is striking that in all of the Augustan examples of patronage-contracts (*tabulae patronatus*, as they are called) the petitioners are peregrine, that is, non-Roman, communities; striking, also, are the outlandish names of the signatories to these as to other protestations of good Roman *fides*. "Outlandish" of course expresses only the Roman point of view. In Spain, it would be more properly the conquerors who deserved the term. Natives, however, can be seen taking on that latter point of view through the act of assuming names and offices with something Roman about them—an act expressive of a positive wish to change, without the formal preliminary of a Roman charter or citizenship.

As to their names: among scores of thousands of Latin inscriptions from Spain, Augustan or earlier ones can hardly account for a twentieth, if that. The lack of a usable quantity thus precludes anything but the most obvious truths. Even these, however, need to be brought out, given the importance of the subject; for how one decided to call oneself or one's child was a choice not made lightly.

The consul Balbus who got his name from a Cornelius and his citizenship from Pompey illustrates how the two procedures were separable, as indeed Cicero also makes clear in his speech defending the nephew in court.[76] That said, it becomes harder to say further, just what the relative frequency of Spaniards calling themselves Cornelius or Iulius must mean. Were they descended from clients of one of the Cornelius Scipio clan, several of whom were active in Spain at one time or another? From these they received citizenship? And similarly, Iulii were promoted by Caesar or Augustus? Or did some or most of them simply give it out to their community that they had added a Roman element to their names, and then subsequently dropped the indigenous element altogether? The authorities were certainly unable to police the matter in detail—as we are unable today to draw broad conclusions from what amount only to specific cases.

Given the very limited number of inscriptions datable before the turn of the era, it is also impossible to determine what percentage of indigenous families chose a new name for themselves. The Celtiberian persist into later centuries;

change was slow and imperfect; and predictably it went on faster among the wealthier and the more urban parts of the population. As to its rate and mode of operation, however, all that seems certain are the decisive effects of Augustus' reign.[77]

Not certain but probable, and certainly to be most expected in Augustus' time, is the acquiring of a Roman name by the natives of a city made over into a colony.[78] Despite agreement that such a process made sense, no one can say just how it may have operated. Suppose, however, that a hundred men from the indigenous elite in each of seventy-five centers of a Caesarian or Augustan charter were included in the act, taking on new names and citizenship together and sharing both with their close family—the results would have real significance. After all, among veteran settlers themselves in any given colony, there is no reason to think the elite (ex-officers, mostly) would amount to more than that same number eligible for the local senate. Directorates of any community in the ancient world were always narrow. In colonies, by my conjecture, they had been doubled. The resulting mixed elite would constitute the agents of change more generally. As such, fortunately for the historian, they do leave some mark in the epigraphic record.

Troublesome questions remain about the sharing out of Roman citizenship. With all their technicalities they sound like an interrogation in a nightmare. Did not the process of Romanization advance more rapidly in Roman *coloniae* than in those with so-called Latin rights, and more still than in all *oppida* and some *municipia?*—since *oppida* must be "Latin," like some *municipia*, admitting peregrines to Roman citizenship only as they were elected to magistracies? Might not *oppida* be "Latin" but carry on with traditional native magistracies? And might not a city be redefined at any time so as to be no longer a colony but a municipality?—this latter, the status preferred by Augustus?[79]

To the extent that these distinctions in urban status all fell within the bounds of Roman practice and involved no imitation in indigenous communities, they have in fact little relevance for my inquiry. The questions (all to be answered Yes) require no answer at all. They deal with differences which were at home in Italy, simply replicated overseas. Nevertheless, they did play a part in determining how much of an urban population, including former peregrines, would be fully Roman under the law and therefore would feel its full effects. Take, for example, the evident assumption in full Roman-citizen communities, that Roman nomenclature was normal; for, in order to be counted as a citizen or to be enrolled as a juror, a man must have a praenomen, nomen, and cognomen.[80] Granted, not all Roman citizens in Italy, let alone in the provinces, could show the full *tria nomina*; the law or expectation was not strictly enforced; but in Latin-right cities it did not apply to peregrine residents at all. Similarly with the names and numbers of magistrates: they exhibit a few departures from Roman norms in Roman colonies, but the constitutions of indigenous communities offer quite numerous departures in Augustus' time—along with unintentionally odd imitations of Roman titles as well. In the latter, we may see at least the wish to seem Roman.[81]

In general it seems likely that peregrine elites when they were folded into veteran colonies would most feel the pressure to act and think like a Roman; less so, peregrines attaining Roman citizenship through magistracies; less still, non-elite peregrines, and least of all, those who lived all or most of their lives in the country. True, this is guesswork. The difficulty the historian faces here as always is that of quantification: of measuring in any way just how much observed or disregarded were the various pressures or stimuli toward change that can indeed be noted under the heading of city status. Without quantification, historical significance can't be measured. Which is not to deny, of course, in the very long term, the certain and unquestionable results of pressures and stimuli eventually, and their significance in the history of the West.

In the face of problems in the evidence, there are still some usable odds and ends. Anecdotally, as it were, they suggest degrees of urgency, interest, or strength of motive. In Saguntum late in Augustus' principate the authorities piously renewed the inscription cut some generations earlier, thanking P. Cornelius Scipio Africanus, "consul and triumphator, for the recovering of the city in the Second Punic War." Similarly in Italica, generations after the event, an inscription was renewed that thanked L. Aemilius Paullus Macedonicus for his decorating of the city with trophies. And in a third city, thanks were inscribed "to Ti. Sempronius Gracchus, founder of Iliturgi."[82] Such was the reverence accorded to early ties with old Roman heroes, proposed in local senates for memorialization, and duly voted.

Other old-Roman institutions, too, were carefully preserved: at Saguntum (and nowhere else outside of Rome itself) the priesthood serving the ancient Roman war-god with their triple-beat war-dance, a college of Salii, danced still in Augustus' time and for decades more to come; at Emerita or Caesaraugusta, the Roman ritual furrow cut around the circuit of the city at its founding was recalled on civic coin issues, as, at Urso, the actual furrow continued to serve as a functioning boundary (charter, cap. 73). Hispalis' coins declared the name it had taken in Augustus' time, *colonia Romula*, Romulus and Remus were recalled on those of Italica, and there near the *capitolium* a relief was displayed showing

Faustulus and the legendary she-wolf suckling the twins; the same totem animal appeared on the reverse of Ilerda's coins with Augustus' head on the obverse; and Italica, again, instituted a cult of the Guardian Spirit of Rome, with Augustus' permission.[83] In all these evocations, the importance of the truly Roman past is surely demonstrated among the provincials, principally in colonies but not only there.

In contrast, Caesar on one occasion angrily confronted an audience opposed to everything truly Roman, as he saw it: opposition that was "barbarous." In fact, their crime had been that of supporting the wrong side in a civil war. Nevertheless, he flung the word in the face of the assembled citizens of Hispalis—this, not long before Cicero congratulated the people of Gades on having been cleansed in their manners and habits of all "barbarity" thanks to Caesar's code of laws recently established among them at their own request.[84] The code, thus instituted, offered the cure to what they must have felt was an uncomfortable deficiency—a cure and participation in the fame associated with Rome's Romulus, Scipio Africanus, and ancient warrior priesthoods. The two passages show what the Roman leadership thought, and how freely they expressed their ideas; they suggest also what Caesar judged would be the values of the general population of Hispalis, and how he might play on their sensibilities. In Gades as everywhere else brought under a Roman urban constitution, there is no hint of opposition to the empire or its representatives.

To return, now, to the point of departure two or three pages earlier, where it was asked, What was the attitude of peregrines toward rules and customs pressed on them by an urban constitution of Roman type?—even without any direct evidence, the answer seems reasonably clear. They were accepted willingly. The conclusion helps to explain progress in acculturation, since official pressure was not and could not be very strong. The Roman authorities lacked significant means of day-to-day enforcement, and were, besides, by their philosophy of rule, tolerant of variant laws and traditions.[85] Any changes in way of life according to charter were thus (but incidentally had to be) voluntary.

Adoption of the conquerors' form of nomenclature was instanced, above. Expectation of this was spelt out on the bronze tablets posted publicly at Urso in 44 B.C. Citizens there could also read about the titles, numbers, support staff, and duties of magistrates, all familiar in Italy; about the size of the local senate, when and how it should meet and vote, and so forth. However, beyond these matters of governmental form, a great deal more received mention in passing: the rhythm of the work-week marked off by markets every eighth day in the forum, quite on the Italian model;[86] the arranging of society in clear-cut ranks of slaves, freedmen, persons rich enough to count as equestrian and enjoy special seating, and even more special seating for municipal office-holders and Roman senators;[87] also, special relationships, of patron; also (using Caesar's model charter of 45 or 44 B.C., the so-called *Tabula Heracleensis*, to fill up the missing portions of the Urso tablets) of legal guardian.[88] Guardianships may be followed into the charters inscribed two or three generations after Augustus, representing, however, little that was novel in that later time. They supply only or mostly details to be assumed in the missing sections of earlier charters. The master text is that of Irni, near Hispalis. Here, *patria potestas* and the operation of manumission with the encumbrance of duties owed to the former master are assumed; also, pauses in municipal business during harvest weeks, in traditional Italian fashion.[89] Such matters represent the intersection of public and private life, in a manner unavoidable even for a resident who had no interest in or business with government and who might be, like many in Irni, a non-Roman.

Quite clearly, too, religion was a point of intersection. On this, the Spanish charters have much to say, but again, my concern is less with the replication of Italian custom among settlers of Italian origin in Spain, than with non-Romans. These latter, willy nilly, found themselves in a city with Roman cults ministered to by priests of Roman title in temples of Roman style on the forum, enforcing Roman taboos community-wide, just (says the charter) as may be found "in every colony"; and the generalizing intent of Caesar here may be supposed also in Augustus' model charter, the existence of which has been argued from the degree of homogeneity in the whole corpus of municipal constitutions of and after his day.[90] As observers of all these rites and rules, the indigenous population could hardly fail to become in some degree religiously observant in Romanized terms.

In Augustus' time emperor worship was born, and of that cult, too, charters naturally took account. Communities would assemble for feasts and celebrations according to a calendar of special meaning to the great commander, the red-letter days of his career which were described in my first chapter. Caesar had been responsible for the addition of a small number of festivals to the Roman state list, but Augustus for many more.[91] It was in fact while he was staying in Tarraco in the winter of 26/25 B.C. and using it as his headquarters that a mission from the east had sought him out, asking that he accept public cult; and with this moment, everything had begun, at least in the west. To Tarraco, primacy in the rituals of veneration was a source of great pride; the new-built altar was shown on its coin issues. On imperial festal days its *flamen* would preside over distributions of oil for the baths, a procession from the altar to the theater just outside of town, dramatic performances, gladiatorial combats in the amphitheater.[92] Similar altars were dedicated at sites in the northwest some years later; then another, twenty years later; and so on, seven that we know of, and not all in colonies or otherwise obviously Romanized centers. Indicating the popularity of the cult, Tacitus (Ann. 1.78.1) records that in A.D. 15, directly after the emperor's death, "a temple was erected to Augustus in the colony Tarraco at the request of the natives (Hispanenses)," by which, he goes on to say, "an example was set for all the provinces."

The uniformity sought in the regulation of public life in colonies and municipalities of the 40s B.C. down to the end of Augustus' principate becomes quite apparent, thanks to the texts surviving on bronze. Their testimony may be invoked in picturing the effects of urbanizing efforts over the same years elsewhere in the empire—for it must be clear by now that each region contributes its own different dossier of evidence, with its own profile, regarding the process and its cultural effects. The Spanish contribution is an urban one, unique in the large number of sites reconstituted by act of Caesar or Augustus, unique in the survival of so much information about their constitutions, and unique in the architectural changes they underwent, showing just where and how their characteristic activities were housed. As show-cases of a culture, imitated in the way discerned by Tacitus, their eventual effect on the life of all the peninsula could not fail to be decisive.

5. Arts, letters, private life

The imperial cult inspired and channeled creative energies in ways already indicated, especially inspiring the construction of temples.[93] As at Leptis or elsewhere in the empire, theaters in Spain followed the model of Pompey's in Rome with a chapel toward the rear of the bowl, the cavea: and these provided for an altar, a little shrine, or a dedicated gallery of imperial portraits. One or the other can be detected in the theater design at Carthago Nova or in an inscription from Hispalis referring to the display of statues for veneration, whether of the emperor or of some other member of his family. Italy afforded parallels to these arrangements; parallels could be found in the theaters of many other provinces, too. At Tarraco, the gallery was magnified into a portico backing on the theater's rear, to memorialize the whole range of the imperial family.[94] For the same purposes, naturally, fora were used (at Emerita, Italica, Saguntum, Ruscino . . .); in other public spaces and in smaller centers, busts or full-length portraits of Caesar, Augustus, Livia, the grandson-princes.[95] The sharp increase in sculpture which marked the 40s B.C. forward into Augustus' middle years, and then again to advertise his intended successors toward the end of his reign, introduced Roman art to a wide audience, in effect, anyone who set foot in the central areas of a city.

From this followed imitation in the honoring of private individuals, though ordinarily in connection with some office they had held. Allocation of public space for this was carefully controlled by the city authorities, assuring respect for the position in society of the individuals so honored, for their euergetism, and for the art they commissioned.[96] Statues *taught* all these things. That is what makes some mention of them important to my general purpose, quite apart from whatever relevance they may have for the history of art in its already Roman flow. To the modes prevailing and changing in Rome and Italy they responded quickly and sensitively in both men's and women's portraits, in the evident determination to be as perfectly Roman as possible; therefore, drawing on the skills of the very best sculptors available. Imperial portraits naturally exerted the deepest influence, suppressing earlier Republican styles. Statuary of any sort had been a rarity in the peninsula before Augustus; but then it became common in a rush; so teaching through art was widely diffused.[97] Indigenous styles persisted, but not far into Augustus' principate and in out-of-the-way places, even there, touched by the imported. Examples in the northwest—huge crude granite dolls holding round shields over their abdomens—run from the second century B.C. down to Augustus, ending with Latin inscriptions on the shields.[98] Too little of such indigenous work survives, unluckily, to allow much understanding of how and when it resisted outside influences, and then succumbed.

Among the imported influences were works of relief in stone. One such at Emerita with Agrippa in the act of sacrificing has been mentioned, above. Respectful of ritual procedures and symbols traditional in Rome, it closely echoes the Ara Pacis. Tarraco's altar to Augustus was mentioned too, on which the reliefs included the honors voted to Augustus by the senate: a *corona civica* and *clipeus virtutis*.[99] The two symbols have been noted in north African works of Augustan art and will reappear in the next chapter. Rome's Mars-Ultor temple enjoyed great éclat and its features, including the carving of its distinctive Corinthian columns, were often recalled in provincial art and architecture: the influence of these models can be seen in the capitals carved for the theater at Carthago Nova.[100]

It was thoroughly Italian to decorate public baths with art of all sorts, and Spain provides at least one Augustan example. Its walls were painted in simple

patterns; but frescoes of any sort in public buildings are rare from this early period, rare even in private homes.[101] Enough to have pointed to the origins of an
art fully developing some decades later.

Simple black and white lines, volutes, or floral patterns are not uncommon
in mosaics on the floors of private houses, *opus signinum*. They too begin in the
second century but only become at all common as the first goes along.[102] Some
have names with or without other words spelt out in tesserae. I show a pretty example from Ilici datable to the third quarter of the first century B.C. The names
on it are Acos and Ailacos, Iberian, and more, illegible, all in Latin script.[103]
A generation earlier, inland and to the south at the hilltop site called La Caridad, another private house floor has the insciption LIKINETE EKIAR USERK-
ERTEKEU, taken to mean (in Iberian) "Licine's work, of Osicerda."[104] The
house in which this ornamented the entrance to the dining room took up an entire block, more than ten thousand square feet, with sixteen rooms and mosaics
on the floors of a number of them. Its plan was typically Italian, atrium and all,
such as can be found (generally of later date) at Emporiae, Belo, Bilbilis, and
so on.

Too early to fit within the chronological limits of my study, Likine is nevertheless too useful to leave out, personifying as he does the transition from one
way of life to another that specially interests me. The name is imperfectly Roman; the language on display in the grandest room of the residence, indigenous, and presumably what was spoken there daily. By itself, the house declares
the same mixed ways: in its walls, of a purely native technique, adobe or mud
brick sometimes. It does so through the modest use of squared stone. The over-
all plan is laid out in modules, eight on a side, the three rooms along each side in
a series of modules 2–4–2, and the atrium in the middle measuring 1 × 2 modules (all, with slight deviations—see Fig. 16 in chapter 4). The architect had
been trained in Italian fashion, then; but the household lived close to the land,
with fragments of dozens of sickles, hoes, pitchforks, and the like scattered
about in every room.[105]

Other homes in the broad Ebro valley bring the story down into Augustus'
time. They have been excavated at Celsa and elsewhere. If they have an open
space in their midst, it is not a regularly shaped atrium with impluvium; and the
floor may be of beaten earth or plain plaster, reflecting native building styles;
but then, there may after all be a Tuscan atrium, there may be geometric fresco
patterns on the walls or proper fancy paintings, a paved floor also with black-
and-white mosaic design, and a tile roof of Italian style, *tegulae* and *imbrices*. At
various points in the building design the Roman foot as measurement may be

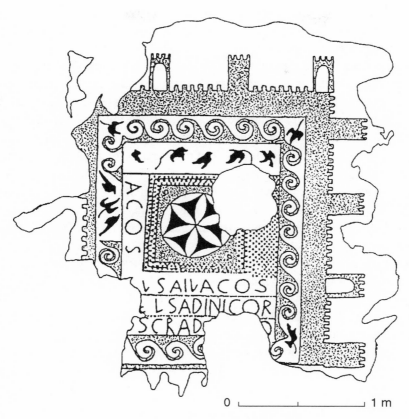

FIGURE 10. The mosaic of Ilici.

easily noticed. At Emporiae, houses with atria are 120 Roman feet on a side, ex-actly one *actus*.[106]

Such elements as these, all entailing such skills and expense as must make a house, penetrated only slowly into the urban scene over the course of the first century B.C., and very little at all into rural homes. In some areas, notably around Emerita, in fact there were very few villas; rich men must have lived right in town and left the countryside to itself.[107] In contrast, in town or country, items of civilization that cost less than a house show up quite early: especially Italian pottery. It makes its way into the peninsula from north to south, Empo-riae to Gades, becoming more than a rarity by the turn of the first century B.C. in the area of its early entrance; but, in Baetica, only well down into Augustan times.[108] Native pottery held its own for a long time.[109]

Strabo notices an un-Mediterranian peculiarity about some of the mountain folk above the Tagus valley in his day: they still drank beer.[110] To judge from amphorae found in the peninsula, if not from Strabo's silence itself, everyone else had been converted to a taste for wine. Other changes in diet may be read in the pottery shapes of the first century[111] and in the style of dining, in the *tablinum* of private houses. There the natives at least of the upperclasses could pass for Romans. On feast days they would wear togas, no more unbearable in Baetica's summers than in Calabria's; or the lighter type of pallium. Strabo's sources of information told him that all the people of the south were completely converted to Roman ways, which would hardly have been said if they still dressed in traditional costumes. Indeed he says that the population of the chief centers in the central and southern parts were called "Toga-wearers."[112]

Roman dinners came in many sizes and guises. A grand occasion hosted by Q. Caecilius Metellus Pius may illustrate the acme. In the banquet hall, "robotic Victories gave out gold trophies and wreaths to the guests," no doubt including the host, to mark his recent successes on the field, "and choruses of boys and women sang Victory chants"; and he later stimulated the efforts of Cordovan poets to hymn his achievements. They recited their verse in a manner derisively described as "rather broad-sounding and foreign." Cicero is their critic. Perhaps the orator had no first-hand report but, for humor's sake, spoke from his experience of listening to Spanish ambassadors in the senate: they were so hard to understand they needed interpreters.[113] The fact remains, however, that you could actually find native Latin poets in Baetica in 74 B.C., just as you could find some reasonably broad-based knowledge of Latin versification, even of Vergil, in late Republican to late Augustan times in Saguntum or Carthago Nova—on epitaphs, thus in some sense addressed to the casual passer-by.[114]

The epigraphic habit in itself caught on at about the same time in Spain as in Italy, though to less effect, given the difference in language distribution, producing, as Armin Stylow terms it, "una auténtica explosión epigráfica" in Augustus' time.[115] It naturally took place in the colonies first and most detectibly, therefore in centers where the persons most likely to consider their concerns of general interest were Italian-born—to boast about, as winners of some high honor, or to mourn, as survivors of the beloved dead. Still earlier inscriptions in Greek or (Celt)iberian are very rare, the habit itself was Roman.

On stone, Iberian continued in use for a while on epitaphs across the general area around Tarraco, along with Latin, but nothing post-Augustan. In the northwest, *tabulae patronatus* in that language were mentioned, above. They were soon joined by Latin, before becoming exclusively Latin before the turn of the era; and there are Spanish bilingual inscriptions of other categories, funerary and so forth, some in Iberian only.[116] Coins begin back in the second century with Iberian legends, even where the weights are on a Roman standard, and are joined by Latin as well and then by Latin only, and end up with no Iberian at all later than the 40s B.C. So much for the various categories of evidence, rapidly surveyed: they fit well with what Strabo says of the southern population, that people there had quite forgotten their traditional language.[117] By then, it is safe to assume that all private legal documents were in Latin.[118]

This is a quite remarkable linguistic transformation when one stops to consider it. It is remarkable even if one allows for the undoubted distortions that result from the predominance of the urban scene. To explain how it came about, the points of contact between the two dominant linguistic groups need to be distinguished. They were several; but a start may be made with those characterized by the most obvious imperative: in the army, to understand orders, and in civilian life, to understand the law. During the wars of Augustus' time recruits were raised among native-speakers for auxiliary units and subsequently discharged as veterans, many of them with the gift of Roman citizenship. In peacetime, they enjoyed enhanced wealth and prestige.[119] Really, nothing more can be said about them, however, as agents of acculturation, except that they certainly played a significant role.

Language learnt in order to handle the consequences in law of one's own or others' actions is also a part of the picture which lies beyond much further definition. In standard charters, plainly the position of magistrate would require Latin, and it would be very nearly essential to the duties of a town senate or jury panel.[120] In short, the entire leadership of any town with the least size or ambition must master the master-tongue from at least Caesar's latter days forward.

Then there is the account in Plutarch's life of Sertorius (14.2), that that rebel Roman leader in the 70s B.C. "assembled in Osca, a substantial city, the boys of the highest birth, where he assigned them teachers of Greek and Roman studies . . . , and their fathers were wonderfully pleased to see their boys going to school in their purple-trimmed costume." A generation later, Caesar could address the general populace of Hispalis in the assumption that they would all understand what he said (Bell. Hisp. 42). The passage was used for another purpose, above. Here, it confirms the picture of major linguistic change achieved in selected areas.

Some confirmation lies in the kind of Latin that established itself in the peninsula. It was a bit old-fashioned and touched by rusticity and plebeian plainness.[121] Comparison of later words in Spanish with lexical choices in Cato the Elder, Lucilius, and other sources for Old Latin, produce *trapetum* = trapiche = [oil-]-mill, *mustacei* = mostacho(n) = sweetmeat, *rostrum* (lang)'rostro = face, *gumia* = gomia = glutton, and so on, all of a vocabulary that one might expect to find in the second or first century among conscripts off the Italian countryside. It seems exactly reasonable. The likes of Cicero from the imperial capital, grandly characterizing all Spanish folk like all Gauls as *barbari* and sneering at their accents, were hardly fit intruments of mass instruction. No, ordinary people encountered as retail or wholesale merchants or as veterans, turned into modest or substantial landowners, served the purpose much more naturally. On the part of the peregrine population, the inducements likewise were ordinary, in the course of daily life; and they taught themselves, orally, I would suppose, only incidentally learning how to write and spell. To establish Latin, however, as the language of the masses must require a critical mass of native Latin-speakers, and that in turn was attained only in Augustus' time.

At the end, the more well-to-do among the native inhabitants, when they arranged their funeral monuments and buried their dead, showed themselves quite conscious of Roman models. The environs of the larger cities display what is most tastefully Italianate on a lavish scale, and the rush of art into these memorial settings belongs exactly to Augustus' lifetime, exactly along the lines one could see in Pompeii or along the first mile or so of the Via Appia. The classes a little lower, however, speaking *en famille*, spoke also with their traditional accent for a much longer time. The reluctance to abandon their native language, indication of descent, form of tomb, or decoration on a tombstone persisted far into the most thoroughly Roman centuries.[122]

IV GAUL

1. What the Romans found

The inhabitants of the Iberian peninsula, our sources agree, were a thoroughly warlike and untamed folk when the Romans entered their world, and remained so in many areas still into the first century B.C.;[1] and it may be assumed that the eventual peace re-made their way of life in some of its most central characteristics; but just what their customs were that they had then to give up, surviving evidence doesn't make very clear. In Gaul, on the other hand, pre-Roman life is better attested and the consequences of pacification can be a little better imagined.

I should say, however, here at the outset of the chapter, that Gaul as one whole expanse of various terrains and peoples cannot be very accurately fitted into general statements. Armorica=Brittany had its own culture, Aquitania another, and the southern coastal strip which the Romans called simply "Province" and in the course of time "Narbonensis," enjoyed a quite distinct degree of urbanization and peaceful settlement from a period long before any that I am concerned with. I only turn to its history later on.

That warning given, and turning now to the regions beyond Provincia: a Greek traveller, Poseidonios, reported in the 80s B.C. on the civilization he had encountered in central Gaul, and his description fits well with scattered archeological finds in that region and elsewhere, too.

He says little about the mass of the population whose engagement in subsistence farming and whose buildings and artifacts of wood or other perishable materials have left few traces in the earth—only, that they drank beer because they were too poor to drink wine, except as their betters might provide it at feasts.[2]

As to these latter occasions: they were in the gift of the aristocracy, who (of course, as they always do) monopolize the historical record. They loved display, it was of the essence of their position. They greedily gathered in a hugely disproportionate amount of all that their world could provide, and gave it out again to impress the populace and so to recruit young warriors, whom they added to their following. They supported them in peacetime with smaller daily feasts, where a closely watched ranking by superiority in arms was asserted in occasional duels and challenges and deaths in the presence of the other guests. They drank a great deal, wine with a little water or (gross, to a Greek observer) unmixed. The arms carried at these evenings and the utensils for drinking ("ceramic or silver jars like spouted cups . . . trenchers of these materials or of bronze . . . , wine imported from Italy or from the territory of Massilia," distributed along with gold and silver, as Poseidonios tells us) were all very striking. Other observers specially note the gold ornaments, too, worn around the men's necks, and show-off gold decoration on their wrists or fingers or costume.

They made their home in hill-top clusters of houses, sometimes large and populous, oppida, or in villages, vici. Occasionally their big rural dwellings apart are mentioned. In the environs of population centers they had their cult centers and their cemeteries; and in the latter, the richer burials show Italian pottery including distinctive "ACO" cups from Italy and bronze imports, both, of good or the very best quality; also lots of containers for wine, bronze strainers usual in wine-service, spears, and swords. The latter weapons continue to be found occasionally in burials far down into Augustus' reign, most likely permitted to the owners through their having served in auxiliary units of the imperial army.[3] The growing predominance of unwarlike luxuries, however—bronze candelabras, mirrors, olive-oil lamps, and perfume bottles—mark a transition to Roman ways, until, in the last decades before the turn of the era, the population developed its own productive capacities in at least wine and fine ceramics.[4] But that is a matter for a later page.

Their luxuries the aristocracy paid for with a part of their riches. Beyond jewelry and precious-metal objects of every sort, they took in and lavishly gave out gold and silver coins, which had entered their world from the south. In the south, to facilitate trade, the intermediaries had first used Greek currency, then their own based on the Greek, changing to a Roman standard for silver around the turn of the first century, and adding bronze issues a little later. In the rest of Gaul, however, local rulers used coins less in service to commerce than for display and reward, with an obvious preference for gold. This they minted themselves, stamped with their names. Native silver was limited to mints in the Rhone valley. Both coinages are found overwhelmingly in oppida.[5] By the 80s B.C., an occasional tribal capital as such, a civitas, began to mint, and, from the 50s, the demands of war drew them all into the action—the product being

much debased, and on a Roman standard to prevail against the *denarii* released
by Caesar and his armies. Roman *denarii* soon won out; by mid-century native
production of gold came to an end forever; native silver issues lasted only
to Augustus' middle years, supplanted by the yield of his mint first at Ne-
mausus=Nîmes, then at Lugdunum.[6] At the end of his reign even bronze small
change from Gallic mints ceased altogether.[7]

The obverse of coins issued in the 40s advertised great Roman commanders,
Octavian=Augustus included, and so encouraged the drift of native issues likewise into Roman numismatic conventions: so they show a Minerva, for example, or a wolf surmounted by ROMA, or proclaim themselves EX S. C. without, of
course, the mint workers knowing what those authoritative initials actually
stood for.[8] The rapprochement brings forward the Roman commanders as
"heads," with the names of their Gallic supporters on the reverse, or Romanized natives like Q. Iulius Togirix on coins of Sequanian territory, a Roman citizen by gift of Caesar, one assumes; and other chiefs who supported Caesar issue
silver with their names but Latin legends and on a Roman standard.[9] Toward all
these developments, the policy of the Romans, now masters, was one of toler-
ance: whatever (within reason) the Gauls chose to put on their currency was
quite accepted, in the same easy manner shown to other subject provinces. In
this important, prominent, public part of their civilization the Gauls thus just
gently came to resemble their masters.[10] So it would appear.

Romans had naturally sought allies from the population. Those favored in
Republican times took pride in their promotion and spelt it out, not very well,
on stone: Couitos=Quintus, lekatos=*legatus*.[11] Those favored by Caesar fill the
pages of his commentaries on the Gallic wars with their Celtic nomenclature
and Roman loyalty. He sometimes explains that loyalty from its origin, when he
lays warrior leaders under obligation to him through his *beneficia* (5.27) or re-
ceives them into his *fides* (e.g. 2.14 or 6.4) through the intervention of some
older-established client "who enjoyed his good will," *apud Caesarem gratia* (6.12,
cf. 1.20)—exactly as the young Augustus was seen to enjoy it at Tarraco, in the
previous chapter. The knitting of ties of influence, the opening of paths to ambition through the Roman way, were all acted out in this changeful period of
Gaul's history to an impressionable audience; all readily made sense and
brought in converts in war as, later, in peace. To everyone's mutual advantage.

But Gallic currency, as it was just reviewed, and with whatever obscurities
and heterogeneity, tells a more complicated story. The aristocracy can indeed be
seen taking on Roman names, citizenship, privileges and even some degree of
power, on Roman terms; they rise in the world, as some of them would certainly

have said with satisfaction; but they lost, besides their independence, any control over their own coinage, not only its weights but its physical appearance, art, and symbols. Among the latter is the warrior himself with a sword in one hand and a severed head in the other—this, for example, among the silver found at Alesia and minted in payment, no doubt, for all those warriors and their vassals there assembled against Caesar.[12] Indeed, why not this image? Among this people, severed heads on coins were "sacred . . . , a dominant motif in Celtic art." And swords that defined a way of life and the means of ascendancy within it were in some sense also sacred.

Of their precious swords, the chiefs who advertised themselves on the warrior coins at Alesia, DVBNOCOV-DVBNOREX and so forth, were stripped by the victorious Romans; so (to pick up again the subject of aristocratic grave-goods) they generally ceased to carry them or to be buried with arms.[13] Life and its values as they had lived it made no sense in the *pax Romana*.

And as to severed heads: these are portrayed on coins (as was said) and attached to the eaves of houses or in niches for display; found also at cult centers evidently as offerings. Two sites are well known: one of them at Gournay among the Bellovaci in Belgic Gaul, levelled in the 60s B.C., the other a dozen miles northeast of Amiens, levelled in Augustan times.[14] They appear to supply confirmation of accounts of human sacrifice in Caesar (BG 6.16), Strabo (4.4.5), Diodorus (5.29), and a good handful of other writers, among whom some information derives from Poseidonios, some belongs to Augustus' time.[15] The poet Lucan imagines Caesar on a campaign of shrine-destruction, the shrines being sacred groves of oaks and other dark trees; and Augustus forbade Roman citizens to practice the Druids' religion. Of this ban, some archeological trace has perhaps been found.[16] Since, however, no outside observer reports human sacrifices of his own knowledge, it has been supposed they were a rarity (as they were also among the Romans); and accounts of them misunderstood the undeniable exhibit of severed heads, shorn from the enemy dead as American Indians shore off scalps, or perhaps taken from the dead of one's own kin after decease.[17] Whether this, the more probable view, is right or wrong, and to what extent the conquerors are likely to have gone to war with the gods in order to prevent a ritual they found too savage, in any case the exhibits were thus given up along with at least the public role of Gallic Druids.

And Strabo says (4.1.5), without indication of any force applied although vicariously triumphant, "coming under Roman dominion, the barbarians living beyond [Massiliote lands] became more and more tame as time went on, and instead of carrying on war have by now [in Augustus' middle years] turned to civil institutions, πολιτεία, and agriculture."

As to Druids, they had over the centuries supplied Gauls and Celts in general with a sort of ideational superstructure. They had served as guardians and interpreters of oral history and tradition; but their leadership had a political dimension which Caesar was not about to tolerate.[18] The threat they were perceived to represent and the shocking savagery attributed to their teachings led in subsequent reigns to their outlawry.

Other deep changes began in Augustus' time in Gaul's polytheism. "Poly-" indeed it was, a confusion of literally hundreds of different divine names surviving in inscriptions, worshipped in ways quite strange to Roman observers. Shrines were not constructed in cities; they had no roofs over them, they presented no carven representation to the devout. Many were simply at some place with little or no construction: springs and lakes especially; also groves of trees. If they were built things, they were not rectangular but round and exhibited other peculiar features; and animal offerings, including dogs and horses! were deposited in pits or trenches, not burnt on altars.[19] There seemed to be nothing comprehensible about the Gauls' religion.

To grasp it and to change it presented the Romans with two quite different challenges. Change in fact they left to the natives. It proceeded at its own pace, never approaching completeness. Early phases in the Three Gauls, "Long-haired" as distinct from the Province, can be seen for example at Gournay: there, re-ordering of the facilities for worship proceeded quite spontaneously, from their third-century oval form, to a square, and from mere pits and posts marking the edges to stone footings. The process was completed in the 40s B.C., probably with a roof added as the finishing touch as at other shrines of the last half of the first century.[20] Sites to show what was going on in this period are few, compared to the richness of evidence for the first two centuries A.D.; but stone can be seen replacing wood, roofs replacing open courts, altars replacing offering-pits, and rites themselves growing simpler and more conversationally addressed to the gods. The general drift is toward a pantheon of beings who look like people, live in handsome houses, and respond in ways intelligible to their petitioners. Along this path, by Augustus' death, clearly a start had been made.

The precise composition of the Gallic pantheon was another matter, puzzling to the Romans and, as they thought, important to understand. While approach from a modern western point of view has often tried to find in it god-stories like Greek myths, a sort of theology, the Romans were content with simpler concerns: by what names did these gods go, and what could they do for you? Caesar in his war-commentaries digresses to describe the extreme piety of the Gauls, shown "above all, to Mercury. . . . After this deity come Apollo, Mars, Jupiter and Minerva" (6.17); and he continues, to indicate what area of life each superintends.

He obviously offers his own particular choice of names for individual divine beings, according to some perceived correspondence with the Roman in their activities and oversight, war or trade or healing. It is not likely that he got much help in detecting equivalences from their stone portraits. In times past, the Gauls indeed had laughed at the very idea of a divine being shaped like a mortal, and their shrines remained for the most part aniconic, or, in Augustus' time under the influence of practices to the south, represented only by shapeless stones and logs. But a hundred miles north of Lyon, a few miles from Beaune, at Mavilly, native sculptors in a half-Roman style had carved on a great pillar a full set of eight figures to serve pilgrims to the local sacred springs: Jupiter with his thunderbolt in one hand, sceptre in the other, Neptune below him holding a fish and with a good Gallic torque around his neck, Mars torque-ed, too, and so on. Acculturation had certainly begun; but "the deities of the pillar are those of the country; they correspond only very imperfectly to the Roman."[21]

A word more on Mars in this work of art: it is not only his torque that betrays the Gallic warrior, but his coat of mail as well, and his hexagonal shield decorated with spirals. At his right side is a ram's-headed serpent twined around a staff of some sort, a creature found in reliefs elsewhere, a favorite at lake- and spring-shrines, sometimes with a fish-tail, suggesting both a watery and a subterranean home. It is, after all, at a spring that his portrait was on display; so he is more than a war-god, evidently. In his multiplicity he is typical of his tradition. There were simply too many sides or attributes that might describe him, too many powers or characteristics, local variants or features of a particular site or worship, of his as of many Gallic cults; they could not all be matched with some one Roman equivalent. Hence endless confusion, as the modern viewer must see it. What Tacitus called "the Roman interpretation," when he describes how a German tribe explained their gods (*Germ.* 43), could not be tidy or, often, even intelligible.

The confusion is of course reflected most directly in nomenclature: so "Mars" among the Gauls may be tacked on to a local deity ("Leherennus Mars," for example), eventually promoted to the front position ("Mars Leherennus"), and at last given sole billing as simply "Mars" alone. There are dozens of such

"Mars," suggesting in writing and across time what difficulties a sculptor might encounter in finding the right terms for a translation; and in the virtual absence of any written record for this Augustan period or earlier, it is the sculptor alone who must speak to us. Hence the interest of portrayals of favorites like Mercury, Silvanus, and so forth.[22]

Silvanus-iconography had its own special complexities, the details of which throw no further light on the process or rate of acculturation; but they introduce Sucellus. Perhaps he was the Dispater from whom, as Caesar was told (6.18), all Gauls declared themselves descended. With Sucellus, too, Silvanus was often confused. In the Three Gauls, the evidence for both comes mostly from the Rhone-Saône valleys (area also of the Mavilly pillar). They served as the chief highway northward from the Province.[23] Sucellus is most often represented in the short Gallic tunic, sometimes with trousers, rarely unclothed, holding a long-handled sledge-hammer.[24] In a bronze figurine from Vienna=Vienne now in a Baltimore collection (Fig. 11), while the hammer has disappeared, tiny miniatures radiate from his head. The date of the piece is best set in the closing years of Augustus, perhaps a little later.

What is worth noticing is, first, the region in which the work turned up, just where it should have, so to speak: that is, on the northward highway tying the more advanced arts and acculturation of the southern province to the markets of the north, where Sucellus-worship was most manifestly popular. Furthermore: the artist drew in expert fashion from a very well known representation of a mature male deity, as the native image of Sucellus required, namely Zeus—the fourth-century Zeus of Leochares, often adapted, from the early Empire on, to various divine personifications in Italy and the western provinces by the addition of various attributes. In sum, we have in the figurine a completely classical rendition of an idea identifiably Gallic: Sucellus, "the sole native god to have figured in a long series of bronzes obedient to classical norms, . . . while still retaining his personality. He well represents the Gallic national deity as Caesar saw him."

Between Vienne where this figurine was found and Mavilly with its pillar-reliefs of eight gods lay the principal city of the west, Lyon, and a famous shrine. That was the stupendous complex dedicated to the cult of Roma and Augustus. Its interest here lies not in its features so obviously Roman—the marvel of engineering that was its 150-foot terrace, the height of its pair of columns, the symbolism of the laurel wreaths borne by winged Victories surmounting them, and the oak-leaf wreath on the great altar—not even the day, August 1st, chosen for the annual festivals held there. It was rather the fact that it was in the form of a

FIGURE 11. Sucellus.

portico and lay to the front of a sacred grove, truly Gallic in these essential features; and the provincial high priest at its initiation in 12 B.C., facing Tiberius Claudius Drusus, was Gaius Iulius Vercondaridubnus.[25] With men like Togirix, he represented one more new Roman citizen half-way won to the civilization of his masters.

2. Re-ordering Gaul on an urban basis

Lyon was the key element in the administrative framework devised by Augustus for the three new provinces. Each of them had a capital (Paris and Bordeaux as well as Lyon) with subdivisions centered according to Roman style in cities, *civitates*, sixty or sixty-four in number, representing a generous selection out of the one hundred or so tribes that Caesar had confronted. Lyon, however, serving as imperial mint-center for the gold of all the west and as the place of meeting of delegates from all the *civitates* annually, clearly stood out; and it was the starting point, historically, of the Gallic road system, too. On this, as on a strong armature, all of them depended; and on this, Agrippa had made a beginning in 39 B.C.[26] The work went on throughout the course of this first and his second term of government in Gaul, a decade later, extending the project due west to Poitiers, north to Trier, northwest to Boulogne, and south to the Province, in four great branches. While there had naturally been bridges and roads before he began, he and Augustus added and improved on a grand scale, with corresponding effects on the economy. Whole towns were quickly or gradually lost to the light of history because they lay at an awkward distance from the network, or, to the contrary, were created from scratch or grew and flourished because they were tied in to it. It was a matter of policy here as in Spain to encourage urban development in lowland areas, even to require hilltop centers to be given up, and it is a sign of the novelty of Agrippa's and Augustus' measures that the great majority of *civitates* chosen for capitals appear nowhere in the earlier record left by Poseidonios or Caesar. The many that bear the emperor's name in one form or another (Augustodunum, and so on) are a further sign of the effect; so, too, the name given to the trunk leading out of Tropaeum Augusti=La Turbie into the Province: the Via Iulia Augusta.[27] A grand plan thus remade the map for all time.

Lyon: there at the juncture of the two great rivers, L. Munatius Plancus, governor of all Three Gauls, had been authorized by the senate in 43 B.C. to establish a colony. It was perhaps intended to receive the founder's veteran troops but expressly, also, Roman citizens who had been settled at Vienne in 45 B.C. and subsequently driven out by the surrounding native population. From the start,

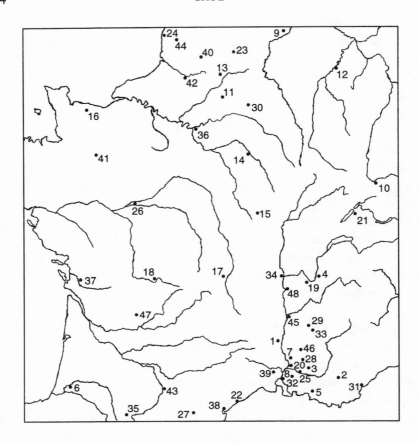

FIGURE 12.   Caesarian and Augustan urbanization in Gaul

THE ORIGINS OF THE CITIES:

c=colony;   C=Caesarian;

R=full Roman;   T=triumviral, ordinarily meaning

L=Latin-right;   Octavian;

per.=peregrine;   A=Augustan

1 Alba Augusta Helviorum=*Albe*
(LcA)

2 Alebaece Reiorum
Apollinarium=*Riez* (LcA)

3 Apta Iulia=*Apte* (LcT)

4 Aquae Augustae Tarbellicae=*Aix-les-Bains* (RcA)

5 Aquae Sextiae Salluviorum=*Aix-en-Provence* (LcA)

6 Aquae=*Dax* (LcA?)

7 col.Iulia Firma Secundanorum
Arausio=*Orange* (LcT, RcA)

8 col.Iulia Paterna Arelate
Sextanorum=*Arles* (RcC)

its streets were drawn on the familiar grid-plan. In connection with Augustus' presence in 27 B.C. to hold a general census, it was made the point of deposit of all resulting records. It received from the emperor one or both of its early aqueducts, a walled circuit (if that was not from its founding), a new forum to replace the one laid out by Plancus, a theater, and an amphitheater, or at least the begin-

---

9 Atuatuca Tungrorum=*Tongres* (Roman camp becomes town, Aug.)

10 Augusta Raurica=*Augst* (RcT)

11 Augusta Suessionum=*Soissons* (new, replaces Noviodunum, Aug.)

12 Augusta Treverorum=*Trier* (per.cA)

13 Augusta Viromanduorum=St. Quentin (per.cA)

14 Augustobona=*Troyes* (per.cA)

15 Augustodunum=*Autun* (LcA)

16 Augustodurum=*Bayeux* (per.cA)

17 Augustonemetum=*Clermont-Ferrand* (per.cA)

18 Augustoritum Lemovicum=*Limoges* (per.cA)

19 Augustum=*Aoste* (?per.cA)

20 Avennio=*Avignon* (LcA)

21 Aventicum=*Avenches* (new, Aug.)

22 Iulia Baeterrae Septimanorum=*Béziers* (RcT)

23 Bagacum=*Bavai* (new, Aug.)

24 Bononia=*Boulogne*=Gesoriacum (amplified, Aug.)

25 Cabelio=*Cavaillon* (LcT)

26 Caesarodunum=*Tours* (new, Aug.)

27 Carcaso=*Carcassonne* (LcT)

28 col.Iulia Meminorum Augusta Carpentorate=*Carpentras* (LcA)

29 Dea Augusta Vocontiorum=*Die* (new, Aug.)

30 Durocortorum=*Reims* (new, Aug.)

31 Forum Iulii=*Fréjus* (RcT)

32 Glanum=*Saint-Rémy-en-Provence* (LcA?)

33 Lucus Augusti=*Luc-en-Diois* (LcC)

34 Copia Felix Munatia Lugdunum=*Lyon* (RcT)

35 Lugdunum Convenarum=*Saint-Bertrand-de-Comminges* (LcT)

36 Lutetia Parisiorum=*Paris* (new, Aug.)

37 MediolanumSantonum=*Saintes* (new, Aug.)

38 Narbo Martius Decimanorum=*Narbonne* (Rc118 B.C.; vets.,C)

39 Nemausus=*Nîmes* (LcT)

40 Nemetacum=*Arras* (amplified, Aug.)

41 Iulia EquestrisNoviodunum=*Nyon* (RcC)

42 Samarobriva=*Amiens* (new, Aug.)

43 Tolosa=*Toulouse* (LcA?)

44 Turnacum=*Tournai* (new, Aug.)

45 Valentia=*Valence* (RcC)

46 Vasio Voccontiorum=*Vaison-la-Romaine* (LC)

47 Vesunna=*Périgueux* (new, Aug.)

48 Vienna=*Vienne* (LcC, RcA)

nings of one. Not to mention the provincial cult center or the interesting early signs of pottery production, harbinger of much manufacturing power in the west generally. Both items were mentioned above.[28] From having been nothing more than the site of a modest Roman encampment, the Gallic capital had burst into full Roman flower in little more than a generation.

Processes of urban development were of course not limited to Lyon. A larger picture appears on the map (Fig. 12). Like other maps in previous chapters it identifies most urban centers where some formal step is known to have been taken toward Roman forms. My list would be much shorter if doubtful items were excluded, but it must do at least for purposes of illustration.[29]

Some centers won designation as a *civitas*-capital, but with what further approximation to a Roman urban model, there is no saying; and some appear under a "Julian" or "Augustan" title without there being any sign of their reorganization by the Roman authorities. They had, perhaps, requested approval for re-naming themselves. It seems likely, however, that the major *civitas*-capitals received Latin rights. In the Province, of some seventy-five centers to which Caesar had granted this level of privilege, Augustus reduced a majority to dependence on a select twenty-odd, though without the losers necessarily forfeiting access to Roman citizenship through their local elections. More generously, near the end of his reign, he extended to every citizen of the Province the right to stand for office in Rome itself, surely a dramatic gesture of incorporation.[30]

My concern for the moment, however, is chiefly with the Three Gauls. So far as concerns their governmental structure, there were no *municipia* among them, but otherwise no general rule or uniformity. Even in urban centers calling themselves colonies there were (as in Italy, of course, and other regions of the empire) anomalies in title, number, and assigned duties of magistrates: Mediolanum = Saintes with its *vergobret* (the first incumbent having a Roman citizen son, C. Iulius Ricoveriugus), while other towns had their *gutuater* or their (Latin but irregular) *praetor* in charge.[31] Still, it seems safe to assume that the majority of the *civitas*-capitals and all but a few of the sites on my map were, by the end of the reign, governed by elected officials in pairs with titles matching what Augustus might have found in Italy: ordinarily *duumviri* with aediles, sometimes *quattuorviri*. The choice among these titles was no sure sign of full or merely Latin rights, nor was it consistently observed by a given city. What counted, rather, was the fact of the whole land being assigned to superintendence by elected officials based in urban centers and conducting affairs in Latin. To find so much as this in any of fifty or seventy-five points of power and influence scattered across the Three Gauls represented a very great change.

Some physical, visible change ordinarily accompanied the institutional. In Caesar's day agglomerations of people were defined for defense by a palisaded ring or ditch, within which streets went where they pleased and construction relied principally on wood with adobe or mud-brick for variation, and little cut stone (dry).[32] Roman rule alone could impose a grid, on occasion using the line of Agrippa's highways for orientation (as in Spanish examples).[33] A built city wall was rare: one at Vienne, perhaps a second at Augustodunum under the auspices of the emperor.[34] Signs of centuriation in the Three Gauls are rare, too.[35] Augustus, making four trips to Gaul expressive of an abiding interest in the area, built an amphitheater at Senlis=Augustomagus, a theater at Limoges, a Janus-temple at Augustodunum; and, at the latter city, two aqueducts perhaps date to his reign.[36] The use of tile roofs or cement in building is very rare; so-called "petit appareil" stone walls, rare; mosaic floors, the same; likewise, column capitals on the model of those in Rome.[37]

The impression conveyed by the architectural picture is consistent: where the Roman authorities could intervene with corvée-demands and major funding, much was possible; much, too, was needed. Consider only the estimate of eleven million quite uniform blocks of stone to be cut for the walls around Vienne.[38] Engineering expertise was needed to lay down city-center plans where a free hand could be exercised over a new site: at Augusta Raurica, for one, where *kardo* and *decumanus* crossed at an altar in front of the chief temple, itself neatly disposed in one city block facing another open that served as a forum. The two-insulae disposition of space was applied also at Lutetia, Iulia Equestris, Lugdunum Convenarum, and Aventicum.[39] There are reasons in each case to suppose help from the army. At Forum Segusiavorum some thirty miles west of Lyon, it seems more likely that civilian architects followed a model common in northern Italy (below, Fig. 14), complete with *curia* and three-aisled basilica; but it wasn't laid out until the early years of the first century A.D.[40]

As to domestic architecture, again, Italian design is sometimes obvious, and the hand of Italian architects, themselves or their Gallic students from the Province, must be suspected. The ambition to live in a Roman house expressed itself at the tribal capital, Bibracte, before the conquest and in Lyon a decade or so after its founding; but the techniques and materials of construction remained quite primitive.[41]

Where could the money come from for anything on a grander scale, earlier? For public projects, attempts were made to attract the favor of the imperial family by nominating them as patrons or otherwise honoring them.[42] Better, resort to a local elite. They must be not only rich and eager to live in a Roman fashion, themselves, but ready to give to others, euergetic. The impulse must derive from a value-system of Italian origin, immigrant or imitated; the wealth, from land. Army payrolls spent locally of course made available cash from beyond the Three Gauls, but to the benefit only of camp environs and middlemen along the Rhone-Sâone line of communication;[43] it was really farming on which prosperity must depend, in the hands of a businesslike class with ambitions for the urban center in their midst.

The particular favor enjoyed by time-expired recruits from Italy would place them in positions of leadership in military colonies; but of these, in the Three Gauls, there were only Iulia Equestris=Nyon, Lugdunum=Lyon, and Augusta Raurica=Augst; and the first of the three received a mix of indigenous ex-cavalrymen and native civilians.[44] What must rather do the job were the natives everywhere choosing to live in towns on their rents—income drawn from large, profitable farms of the regular Italian villa-type, such as can be seen at Baeterrae in the Province but also in the northwest. The processes of urbanization described above, particularly the assignment of Latin rights, must, and did, bring about the active participation of such men as these.[45]

In trying to imagine how the aristocracy took on the values and roles of urban civilization of a more or less Italian sort, there is some obvious help in the sheer number of Iulii to be found in the epigraphic record over the first few generations post-conquest. They advertised their citizenship in their names; or rather, most did, and some usurped the appearance, thus at least showing their loyalty. In every region they are more easily found than Valerii or citizens of any other Roman *nomen*, proof of the generosity with which Caesar and his adopted son rewarded any native who had helped them. Theirs was the period crucial to the development of a demographic base for acculturation.

In the early 50s B.C. Caesar made use of a C. Valerius Procillus, described below. Then in the 40s B.C. (BC 3.59) we hear of two brothers of an eastern Gallic tribe "who had long held the very first position in their *civitas*, men of remarkable bravery whose outstanding and most valiant support Caesar had enjoyed throughout the Gallic wars. On these, for these reasons, he had bestowed the highest offices in their homes, had arranged for them to be chosen for the senate in advance of the usual sequence, had assigned to them lands in Gaul taken from his enemies along with large cash rewards, and had made them, from poor, rich men." Similar success stories are likely to explain the wealth of C. Iulius Rufus of Mediolanum, donor to his city of a splendid arch, whose father was less Roman but perhaps no less rich, C. Iulius Otuaneunus, son of C. Iulius Gedemon, son of Epotsorovidus. Otuaneunus had represented Mediolanum as priest of the imperial cult at the gathering each year in Lyon. Four generations thus sufficed to rise from an untouched "barbarism," as Romans would have termed it. Choice of the right side in the 50s had brought Roman citizenship; then provincial honors; then, growing under Augustus and achieved in A.D. 19, the ambition to place the proper tria nomina on stone.[46] Disturbed times presented the best of opportunities to a warrior-people hardly able to foresee how differently their children would measure success.

3. The Province Narbonensis

Turning now to the south, other stories illustrate the phenomena seen in the north, but do so in a little more detail. The pre-conquest native elite seem all to have owed their position to their services in war, receiving their reward in land in areas centuriated and at the disposal of the conquerors, sometimes with citizenship added to the gift. Even post-conquest, Rome continued for a time to acknowledge and in some sense lean on small tribal rulers such as Loukotiknos or Rigantikos whose names appear on their bronze coin-issues; but they remain mere names.[47] An occasional figure emerges in clearer outline: in Pompey's day, a family of the Vocontii northeast of Arausio, while in the earlier 50s Caesar made use of C. Valerius Procillus, son of C. Valerius Caburus who had received the citizenship from C. Valerius Flaccus, Roman commander in Gaul a generation earlier. The son, whose brother C. Valerius Donnotaurus was the Helvian chief, is described as almost a member of Caesar's household, "a young man of outstanding courage and civilization," humanitas; and a second son in the later 50s, as it appears, C. Valerius Donnotaurus son of Caburus, headed the Helvii.[48] A third generation in this family would typically assume a more obviously Roman cognomen than Procillus; but they can't be traced beyond the second.[49]

At Glanum on the so-called Monument of the Iulii (to which I return, below) three men of the family pay honor to the founder of the line, C. Iulius, depicted in the frieze toga-clad with the Tiber in the background, while Victoria reads aloud from a document—the scene, receipt of Roman citizenship in Rome for valor in battle, under Caesar or Octavian. The grandsons erected the memorial in the 20s B.C. They are Sextus, Lucius, and Marcus Iulius.[50] As another illustration: at Aquae Sextiae=Aix, the tomb of the Domitii was built at the end of Augustus' principate or a little later, where a father, mother, and son are remembered. The son rose to equestrian rank, the first of his city known to have done so. As the Roman patron to whom these local Domitii owed their citizenship, probability favors L. Domitius Ahenobarbus, Gallic governor in 50/49.[51]

In the Province even more clearly than in the Three Gauls the basis of such wealth as equestrians could boast must have exactly resembled the Italian. Long-term profits came from the land. As in northeastern Spain, one can see where new methods allowed difficult terrain to be opened up for agriculture that paid. Wet boggy areas could be drained, with improvement to local health; centuriation fixed the size and shape of fields and encouraged Roman methods, or at the least discouraged an uneconomic degree of transhumance.[52] A wise man, however, would also keep an eye open for such other investment opportunities as might arise in a modestly urbanized, long-settled territory with access to transport by water.

By Augustus' time there was not very much that the Province had to learn in these matters, whether from native enterprise or from Italian businessmen whose ubiquity Cicero described for an audience in Rome (*Pro Font.* 5.11). Olei-culture was a serious business at least in some areas by the start of the first century B.C.; before long, viticulture also, to compete with the Italian exports—though, around Massilia, not before the 20s B.C.[53] The best evidence comes from Baeterrae's territory, more than three thousand square kilometers of it. Here, wine was an important product already at Augustus' birth, and at his death one can count more than a hundred villas, *fundi*, in operation.

In the intervening time, much rural property had changed hands with the creation of a colony for Caesar's veterans of the Seventh Legion. Farming plots had been assigned through centuriation; but it is worth noting that a third or so of these new and very generous estates, spread evenly over all the territory, were owned by native Gauls.[54] Place was perhaps left for them only because there was little needed for veterans: the latter had been sent to only five locations (Baeterrae, plus Arausio for Caesar's Second, Arelate for his Sixth, Forum Iulii for the Eighth, and Narbo for the Tenth), and in depleted numbers. The total infusion to the Province can't be estimated above five thousand. Against that, fourteen Latin colonies through their elections added an annual quota to the citizenship rolls. Roman nomenclature thus spread rapidly; the huge proportion of Iulii alone suggests generous gifts of citizenship in Augustus' time. Just as in the Three Gauls, demographic facts provide a natural background to the proud family monuments just described, especially the one at Glanum.[55]

Augustus' general survey of all Gaul for purposes of inventory, meaning taxation, had the effects on agriculture indicated a page earlier; but it served also to diminish preexisting political loyalties by disregarding their traditional boundaries. As a consequence of choosing the wrong side in the civil wars, Massilia lost a piece of its territory to Aquae Sextiae; Nemausus had a native population assigned to it as tributary (the Arecomici); and, for the benefit of Arausio, land was taken from one tribe and another was forced to make do with less desirable areas. Thus they weren't wiped off the map, but they suffered.[56] As the Romans made evident by their arrangements in the Three Gauls, they wanted not too many, and not too undernourished urban centers as administrative intermediaries between themselves and the rural masses, to be responsible. Surely they applied the same unsentimental reasonableness, unrecorded, in instances other than the three just mentioned.

Where redistribution was to take effect because of veteran settlements or censusing—although there are traces of pre-Roman cadastration, Greek or Gallic, here and there in the Province—the Romans used their own familiar methods. Examples are especially plain to aerial photography at Baeterrae, Narbo, and Arausio; but there are traces, or more, at Forum Domitii, Tolosa, and Valentia, Arelate, Nemausus, Aquae Sextiae—some of which were surveyed more than once, and five, in the 40s and 30s B.C. The great coast road marked the edge and direction of centuriation here and there; and here and there, boundary stones were set up to divide the territory of one city from another's.[57] There was to be no excuse for armed disputes in the *pax Romana*.

As circumstances allowed, meaning, where prior urban growth did not prevent, the Roman authorities must be credited for obviously major urban projects. Determination of a *kardo* and *decumanus* to cross at the city center, perhaps determining centuriation outside (as at Arausio), was a first step toward the orthogonal grid of streets detectible at Forum Iulii, Nemausus, or Baeterrae.[58] These were all colonies. Nemausus received its six kilometers of ramparts from Augustus in 16/15 B.C. (an inscription credits him with the gates, too)— throughout, of good Roman cement construction with an *actus* used as the inter-tower module.[59] Arausio's walls exhibit some characteristic Italian design features, too; and an Augustan wall encircled Arelate and Forum Iulii, probably also Aquae Sextiae.[60] An indication was given, above, of the demand for stone for Vienna's circuit; so it is no surprise that new quarries had to be opened up near Glanum and another close to Nemausus, the former supplementing still others opened up around Lyon for that city's needs. At the modern St. Beate in the Pyrenees, a large marble quarry was opened to serve Lugdunum Convenarum.[61]

Augustus' very important role in construction comes as no surprise, considering the years in separate sojourns that he gave to Gaul, and in comparison with the euergetism shown by him toward other provinces. There is no saying what proportion of this activity was grandly spontaneous—like his presenting

Nemausus with a place of worship to a local deity, in 25 B.C., or Agrippa's gift of a temple to a favorite Glanum god—and what was otherwise elicited by honors and petitions directed at the emperor or members of his family from municipal senates.[62] There was always local ambition, too, stimulated, we may suppose, by the pervasive sunlight of the first principate. As an illustration from a tiny town near Montpellier we have a laconic inscription declaring that the not-very-Roman-sounding "Sex. Vetto and C. Pedo, aediles, directed the repair of the road and the ornamental basin, *lacus*, according to the Council's decree" (*CIL* 12.4190). The editors give it a date between the end of the Republic and the early Empire. Later illustrations of the process here at work are easy to find.

General treatments of the Province today see a particularly energetic character in Augustus' time, a "building-boom" such as scholars detect in Spain too (above).[63] For my purposes the concentration of it on the city not the country-side, on public not private display, is in itself something quite Roman. Then there is the mix of traditions to be noted, and the particular means by which the imported could be effectuated—turned into stone that survives and dominates in the evidence, or into less enduring materials as well.

A survey of this building activity conveniently begins with its gross features: city walls, already mentioned, and aqueducts, including the spectacular one fifty miles long, borne across the Gard to serve the baths of Nemausus (Agrippan? mid-first century A.D.?).[64] Augustan aqueducts are noted at Narbo, Mediolanum, or Forum Iulii supplying, of course, public baths which survive (Lugdunum Convenarum, Mediolanum) or must be assumed. In one instance we know the army was at work, in others, sometimes to be assumed. Where baths are known but no aqueduct (Glanum, Vaison), the latter or some ample arrangement of supply must be assumed.[65] And the usual series of chambers can be noted in the better-preserved designs for one's delightful progress through water of different temperatures, surrounded by one's neighbors in the relative luxury of mosaics and statuary and rub-downs. A very important part of the day was thus given over by the sons of Vercingetorix to the solvent pleasures of the master race.

Pleasure dictated the construction of theaters and amphitheaters, though both served cult purposes as well. Theaters for traditional rites are often encountered in rural areas throughout Gaul, with modifications of design that evidently suited Gallic needs; amphitheaters served the imperial cult, as city charters indicate, where gladiatorial exhibitions on imperial anniversaries are to be paid for by the city and its magistrates and where other aspects of the liturgy are to be acted out.[66] At Nemausus, apparently at Arausio also, a theater formed a part of a sanctuary to Augustus.[67] Just what else went on in these places of entertainment is nowhere indicated. The Province's theaters had a special track on the stage for curtains to slide on, not found elsewhere; but there is no reason to think they rolled back to reveal anything other than the standard fare seen equally in Italy or Spain. It certainly was enjoyed by the masses, with corresponding glory and gratitude to be won by the millionaire citizens who underwrote the building costs. Their reward was that excellent invention, privileged seating "among decurions and senators."[68]

Toward the edge of the city of Nemausus overlooking its forum a different sort of structure was built in 26/25 B.C.: an altar at the famous water shrine, serving the imperial cult very suitably. Indeed, it was more than that; for Nemausus bore the name of its patron, a water god; and altars, in preference to temples, met the taste of the time or of the first emperor: Tarraco's in the same year comes to mind, other Spanish sites, Lyon in 12 B.C., the Ara Ubiorum near Cologne (Tac., *Ann.* 1.39.1), and various examples in the east.[69] The Nemausus shrine was soon wonderfully amplified as a proper Augusteum.

But altars for this cult were ordinarily more centrally located. In Arelate, apparently in the middle of the forum, one was set up in the same year as Nemausus'; and at Nemausus a temple was added, specifically dedicated to the princes: this, the Maison Carrée.[70] Two imperial cult temples at Glanum were built of about the same date as the altars at Tarraco, Arles, and Nemausus; podium temples of good Roman style have been identified, dubiously, as Capitolia.[71] What can be learned from the number and prominence of all such points of public worship is, simply, how much the citizenry of the time themselves must have learned, through participating in the festivals and ceremonies that found here their physical focus, all, quite alien.

At Narbo, arrangements for the emperor's cult were laid down in the 20s B.C., perhaps dictated by himself, and published on a bronze tablet affixed to an altar. It prescribed a liturgy in line with what was traditional for the worship of Jupiter in Rome.[72] Private cult acts are attested from the same years and the witness of inscriptions and celebrations continues thereafter down to the end of Augustus' principate when (A.D. 11) the general populace set up an altar with a bronze tablet on it in the forum.[73] On it was engraved their thanks for his recent intervention in a local dispute, along with the terms of the establishment of an association dedicated to the cult of his Divine Spirit, his *numen*. Provision was made for annual festivals on his birthday and other anniversaries of his career henceforward. It concluded the enunciation of rules by referring to those of Diana-cult in Rome as a model in cases of doubt. Together, the two texts show how

Roman rites came to be known, followed, and acted out to the whole city, at its very center; but the rules and the story of the process in other Provincial cities, doubtless very similar, is lost.

Sucellus' worshippers were especially many in the Province, where, as in the Three Gauls, he was conceived of along the same lines as Silvanus. He may stand for the hundred distinct deities and more whose names crop up in Provincial votive inscriptions of the period of the Empire. Augustus' and Agrippa's favoring of them with temple-construction has been mentioned, and one instance fronts on the grand avenue of Glanum (Fig. 13, inscribed with Agrippa's name, the temple of Valetudo, standing for a healing god under a Roman name).[74] Yet they are joined by Roman gods, even on the forum. Several towns of the Province had their Capitolia; and others built their temples to indigenous deities but on a podium, Roman fashion.[75]

Glanum in the 20s B.C. underwent radical, grand reconstruction which brought together near the town center many of the architectural features so far mentioned: orthogonality, though lost on the west side, and a clustering of everything thought of as importantly public.[76] Religion presided at one end of the forum, administration (in the three-aisled basilica) at the other. Along both flanks of the open space lay shops, their remains barely detectible. Over-all, it approximated to the tripartite forum which was the Romans' favored and which is so often identifiable in Spain (Fig. 8). From the northwestern corner of Italy, I show for comparison an example at Augusta Bagiennorum, and another also of Augustan date in the northeast of the Province at Feurs=Forum Segusiavorum.[77]

The same three forum elements can be seen at Arelate, Lugdunum Convenarum, Augusta Raurica . . . both in the Province and in the Three Gauls. The rapidity with which so many city centers emerged throughout this vast area, redone and all on Italian models, even in construction techniques, is very striking. It is often remarked on. So, too, the sheer labor required for the effects achieved: terracing on a grand scale, tons and tons of earth moved, huge expanses raised on vaulted substructures, cryptoporticoes at Forum Segusiavorum, Narbo, Arelate. . . . [78] Yet of course that Roman reasonableness already invoked in explanation of forum design—plain sense responding to prior arrangements or impossibility of terrain—never aimed at perfect uniformity, nor ever achieved it.

Smaller structures in the Province include those types favored in Italy: a curia opening off the basilica at Forum Segusiavorum, Glanum, Alesia (or Clunia);[79] or again, macella at Narbo and Lugdunum Convenarum.[80] The latter building (Fig. 15) is one of the grandest markets in the Roman west, its floor decorated

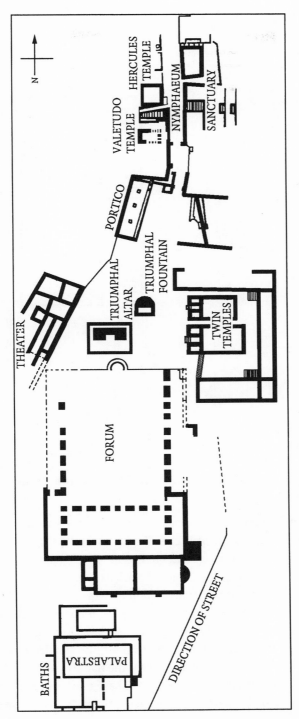

FIGURE 13. The Augustan forum at Glanum.

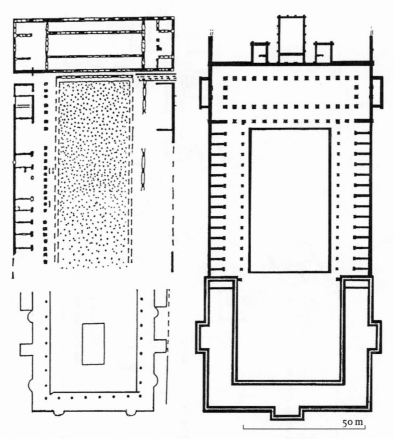

FIGURE 14. Fora of Augusta Bagiennorum and Forum Segusiavorum.

with black and white mosaics, a square marble basin set in the middle, and a pair of kiosks just like those at Lepcis Magna. Most *macella* had only a single round tholos in the center, as at Pompeii (Fig. 4).

Just as public and private building in Spanish cities betrays Italian planning even when the materials of construction don't (chap. 3 at nn. 49ff.), so does the architecture of the Province. The *insula*- and *actus*-modules used in Lutetia's and other northern cities' grid and in Nemausus' walls were mentioned above; add, in the aqueduct of Nemausus, the Pont du Gard, the smaller arches of which have a width used in multiples of 3 and 4 for the flanking and major spans and again, in sixes, for the major arch height.[81] These may have been measures of convenience, making large-scale layout easier; but practiced planners for pro-

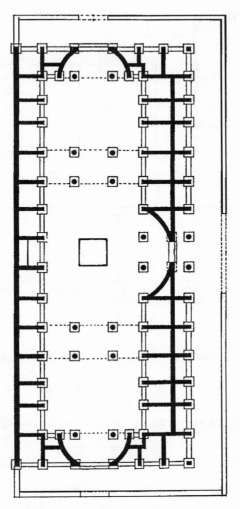

FIGURE 15. *Macellum* near the forum of Lugdunum Convenarum.

jects also followed what Vitruvius (6.3.5) calls the method of proportions, *ratio
symmetriarum*. The architect should begin with the choice of a base measurement dictated, again, by convenience, but applied according to esthetic conventions. Vitruvius spells them out according to his art. For illustration: the particular passage just cited flows into prescriptions for residential design, room by
room. How they might be used, more or less accurately, may be seen in Fig. 16,
top, or better, in the House of the Dolphin at Vasio = Vaison. Here the architect
takes the column diameter of one and two thirds Roman feet as the module con-

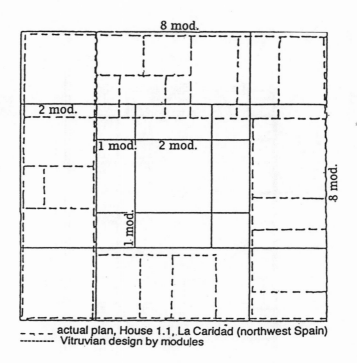

8 mod.

2 mod.

1 mod. 2 mod.

1 mod.

8 mod.

- - - - actual plan, House 1.1, La Caridad (northwest Spain)
-------- Vitruvian design by modules

90

20

10

30

5

60

5 X module of 1 3/4 Roman feet

0   10

15

Forum of Glanum, first phase, 20s BC

FIGURE 16. "House of Likine" (La Caridad, Spain); Glanum's forum.

trolling all the dimensions of the central peristyle court.[82] In the same way, multiples in the Pont-du-Gard answer to esthetic demands; so does the design of Augustus' Trophy at the modern La Turbie. The diameter of the Trophy's central core dictates everything else, width and elevation alike. Another instance of the ratio in city-center design appears in Glanum (Fig. 16, bottom), where the whole forum grows, as it were, from a module of 52 cm (one and three quarters Roman feet), dictating the diameter of the columns, five of which determine the interaxial dimension for the porticoes, ten for the colonnade, and so forth. Similarly, the forum of Forum Segusiavorum, where the module is a fifth of an actus (48 feet) determining the forum width (5x), cryptoportico length, lateral porticoes, temple enclosure, basilica width and length, and so forth.[83]

The main road for which Agrippa was responsible, running west from Lyon, cut across this structure and gave it and the city center their orientation. The work of army engineers is certain for the road, naturally to be assumed for the layout of the city center. The apparent sophistication of design is not surprising. Was not Vitruvius at one time employed in service to Caesar's army? For his likes (he was no Greek freedman, after all) such an appointment was rather a plum, something reasonably to be aimed at by an ambitious man of talents— very much the way Da Vinci or Michelangelo might be employed in the design of devices and structures of war.[84]

Domestic architecture of an Italian character in the provinces is nowhere better known than at Vasio; but even adding what is known at Glanum, Baeterrae, or Forum Iulii, the sampling from the south remains too small to convey much beyond the fact of a great deal of Italian influence evident in houses of Augustus' time, even before. Their character speaks in the baths facilities, wall paintings, mosaics, tile roofs, cement construction faced with small stones ("petit appareil"), and their whole ground plan. It has been noticed that wall paintings of Pompeian type (so-called Second and Third styles) can be found at a large number of sites from the 50s on into the 20s, but those sites are native, not Roman colonial; and the fact is suggestive.[85] All such information is very helpful, without, however, yielding a sense of proportion; and, for all the Roman-ness of the scene, houses may have touches of the Hellenistic about them or display-niches for skulls in good Gallic fashion.[86] At most the evidence fits with what is known of acculturation under other headings: towns that could, at a minimum, boast of veteran settlers, Latin rights, and a charter prescribing governmental form, must have their share of citizens living in houses of the same master civilization. As the prevalence of this minimum became established in Augustus' time, so too did the prevalence of Roman house-styles.

4. Artists and patrons

For the Romanized elite, there must be a Romanized ending. What was observed in Spain can still be observed in the Province as well: remains of rich tombs in the outskirts of towns, notable from Augustan times on: "organized in a hierarchy of mausolea, groups of chambers and individual graves, marked by headstones . . . the great mausolea came to serve as landmarks."[87] Among the most prominent must be counted that of the Iulii referred to above. Its derivation from models attested in Umbria (Sestino) and Cisalpina (Mantova) appears in a comparison with late Republican and early Augustan examples, individual elements of which find their parallels further scattered over the period and peninsula (Fig. 17).[88] The most obviously striking thing about the Glanum monument, however, is not its thoroughly derivative character, bought by a Gallic family, but its complexity. The question occurs at once, How ever did it get there?

The constituent parts and influences of the structure are not so much my concern as the feasibility of producing such a thing in the Province. The two usual explanations, or a mixture of the two, require Italian architects and stonecutters, or those local ones somehow trained or guided by Italian templates and drawings. Somehow the manner of cutting the volutes and so forth must be made to say whose hand it was at work, from what shop and team, of what land of birth, and what was the origin of the sculptural ideas.

On the Monument, the ideas for a frieze are traced back to analogs in Italy, thence to the Hellenistic world. They appear to indicate the heroic actions of the founder of the family fortunes at Actium, through reference to legendary eastern wars (an Amazonomachy) and a marine setting (a water-deity present). Composition in the 20s B.C. favors that. Or his services in war were rendered a little earlier, to Caesar.[89] Whatever the case, the communication of the ideas is, to say the least, indirect. Nature in the form of common-sense would suggest something altogether different; but nature is not art. Art had to be taught by someone who knew it to those who did not. It can only have been a stone-cutter recommended by some third person with a name, some member of the select, who said, If you would like to honor your family as I honored mine in my proper fashion, speak to So-and-So. And the Iulii would apply to him, and he would suggest what would best meet their objective: namely, to confer honor without the possibility of any misjudgement. Fashion must be Italian. Whether by birth or second hand, So-and-So could convincingly promise an imitation in the best manner. I return to the point, below.

Sometimes the mastery of Italian models is hard to explain except as the

0

5 m

Left, the Monument of the
Iulii at Glanum; above, the
Sestino tomb (upper story);
at right, the Mantuan tomb.

FIGURE 17. The Monument of the Iulii and Italian models.

product of an immigrant from the very scene of the model—as in Nemausus, to judge from the perfect fit between some of the column-capitals and those of the much-copied Temple of Mars-the-Avenger in Rome. Yet perhaps the explanation underestimates the powers of local talent to work from drawings or plaster models or from a miniature stone model of an entire building like the one discovered in Ostia. Vitruvius (1.15) speaks, too, of using scale drawings.[90] Where ground plans and elevations were concerned (1.2.2), of course imitation from drawings would be easy, compared to the imitation of free forms in three dimensions required for reliefs, capitals, and similar decorative elements. Reference has been made at various points above, to the copying of Italian fora, theaters, and so forth, in their broad outlines.

Here and there, the operation of one hand has been detected at several points, even on projects in different towns;[91] or conversely, the decoration of a single building betrays several levels of skill, where exact imitation was certainly intended but not achieved. A good case is the Corinthian column capitals on the Maison Carrée, on which three different levels of skill surely representing three different teams of stone-cutters were at work.[92] That whole building was of course an exercise in really careful imitation of a Roman model, the new temple of Apollo in the capital. The latter, celebrating the god's special favor toward Augustus at Actium, had been dedicated in October of 28 B.C.; on its Provincial copy, all care was lavished.

In 27 B.C. the senate had voted to hang a shield in its *curia*, bearing the words, "For the salvation of his fellow citizens." This famous object was widely celebrated. The proofs have been seen in Africa and Spain;[93] they are seen also in the Province, witness the beautiful replica in Arelate dated 26 B.C.[94] Similarly, the Altar of Peace, erected (13–9 B.C.) in Rome's Field of Mars: its elements were imitated around the empire, and not neglected in the Province. Its vine scrolls and acanthus leaves are seen not only on the Maison Carrée but on the headstones of the city's cemeteries as well.[95] However, among all the elements of the best new style, none was more obvious to the eye than the lavish use of marble, cynosure of Augustan construction in the imperial capital. War's profits paid for it there, the new Carrara quarries were freshly open, and every city had to put on a new suit of clothes in the best fashion, exactly as the ladies of the provincial elite observed the style of hairdressing most in vogue on the Palatine. A number of grand big gleaming edifices attest to the fact in Arelate, Arausio, Augustodunum, Vienna, Lugdunum, Nemausus. . . . At Narbo, the "Capitolium" in its time had built into it a variety of unusual marble elements, recalling those found in the St. Tropez shipwreck, the latter bringing from Italy "roughed-out columns, capitals, and other architectural members of the same material; and since these are unparalleled elsewhere in Gaul or Spain, there can be little doubt that this is a shipment to Narbonne that never reached its destination."[96]

Imitation was eager, so much is evident. The money was there, to be gauged from the cost of the materials and the size of construction projects. Speed in imitation is an indication, too. I call attention to the delay of less than a year in the displaying of Augustus' honorific shield in replica at Arelate; but events in construction can't often be dated exactly, so the general impression of rapid response to Roman influence must lean on evidence from other arts and practices: hair-styles and coin-types, for example, and wall painting. The so-called Second Style of Pompeii (which stands for central Italian more generally) developed into the Third through a transitional phase detectible at very nearly the same time, certainly within a decade, in the Province as in central Italy itself— so say the frescoes of a rich house some fifty miles west of Tolosa.[97]

This fact needs to be set against the temptation to infer a push from the center in explanation of all the copying, that is, the Romanization, that so plainly went on in the provinces of Augustus' time. For "push" read "propaganda," for "center" read "regime," and the next word out is "ideology." No term is more prominent in recent treatments of Augustan art and architecture, importing quite anachronistic assumptions, quite unsupported by evidence, into the discussion. The emperor had no interest at all in how people decorated the walls of their homes. What explains the rapidity of imitation was pull, not push.

Approval or admiration or envy, any of those lovely things that could be won from one's community through an appearance of Roman-ness, not to mention the approval of influential people more truly Roman than one's self, is not in question. "Imitation is the sincerest flattery," true enough, amply illustrated in various anecdotes and testimonies already referred to. To compel imitation, however, could only make plain its insincerity. As one might expect, then, no attempt at compulsion on Augustus' part can be adduced; nor of course had he the means for it. The limit to his powers—surprising to a modern observer— can be easily shown; the limit also to his wish to compel, or to the existence of anything one could call a program.[98] Yet, in the euergetic style that had become Roman and was in due course inculcated among populations unacquainted with this engine of civilization, Augustus built and decorated in the Province; Agrippa built and decorated; no doubt other magnates of Augustan times did so as well. Their intent was not, however, to communicate a message of any sort that could be called ideological. They wanted only to advertise their personal greaterness, their *maiestas*.

Beyond the sheer size of the Augustan "building-boom," with all its fora and aqueducts and so forth, the decorative character of its arts has been seen as ideological, a message in itself. Augustus was a plain home-body, he loved his wife and wanted no loose morals in his court; he felt a nostalgic veneration for his people's ancient lore and rituals, simpler but better; he championed their traditional dress; he wanted no uncontrolled flooding in of new citizens, meaning freed Greeks; he preferred apparent simplicity in his own and other's public acts, even of self-celebration. Of these characteristics of his, were he in charge of taste and vigorous to use it as an instrument of communication, the esthetics of his time might be expected to offer some reflection. And in fact, he did so use it, so it has been argued: he pushed, and it was thus from the center of the empire that the impulse reached out to shape the art that can be seen, for example, in the Province.99

Among the decorative arts, take for illustration that Third Style of painting, so promptly popular in Gaul. There is no disputing that its origins lay at the center, in Rome, establishing new fashions. "It is hardly coincidental that these changes took place simultaneously with Augustus' efforts to bring about a 'moral turnaround.' . . . The painters who developed the new style were apparently trying to give expression not only to a changed aesthetic taste, but the new system of values. This is most evident in the moral implications of the imagery."100 So art expresses ideology, such is the conclusion or assumption. But it is not easy to see the connection between the emperor's social conservatism and the Third Style. What is seen there is rather an art of retreat and serenity, sought in simple scenes and ornamentation. It originated in the vision of one particularly gifted painter. His work appears to have attracted the patronage not of the emperor but of his daughter, by no means noted for her moral qualities, and her husband. The likelihood rather confuses the picture! Yet there is no mistaking the reflection of the Third Style in the Altar of Peace.101 Whence it might be inferred that, whatever values Augustus might have held to and believed in, he never thought to express them in vine scrolls and rustic idylls. The artist chosen for the Altar got the job because his work was admired as art.

Court art, beauty bought by the aristocracy of Rome, of course included everything they touched: the weave of their clothing, the music of their private celebrations, their furniture, the vessels they ate and drank from. Of the latter, some little survives. If the frescoist favored by Julia is unknown, by name, at least, and the sculptor of the Altar, yet Marcus Perennius' atelier we can identify behind the most remarkable of ceramic output from Arretium in Tuscany. Proudly and conveniently, he put his signature-stamp on his pieces. In the earliest days of so-called Arretine ware, stamped with relief decoration, his product stands out. It can be recognized in sherds from all over the empire; and it partic- ipates powerfully in the development of taste. Paul Zanker, who has advanced the understanding of this period so greatly, does not neglect ceramic art and its usefulness as a mirror to reflect artistic taste of the closing decades B.C.: it may, he says, reflect taste in so small an act as a preference for the image of Au- gustus' Victoria or *clipeus virtutis* "instead of one with a chariot race or an erotic scene."[102]

Some of Perennius' most beautiful products, however, show how miscon- strued this choice really was. In fact, there was no choice needed: you could have an erotic scene, and you could have at the same time the most perfect Neo-Attic, simple, serene, Augustan style—not that the specimen given in Fig. 18 is ade- quate through a line drawing to suggest how perfect indeed are the successive scenes of love that run around this bowl (from Bilbilis in Spain). Several stamps employed in their reproduction survive from Arretium itself. "It was one of the Perennius workshop's most common themes of decoration"; a number of stamps to produce slight variations survive, and sherds from bowls made by the stamps, all "of great delicacy, avoiding anything gross or obscene . . . , inspired by Hellenistic models termed 'noble'," and in "a manner cooly restrained, smooth and elegant, . . . of late Augustan classicism," placing it "among the finest examples of Perennius' kilns."[103] Plainly, erotic art and what we may call high art were entirely compatible, one with the other, in the minds of the most discriminating purchasers, first in Rome and then in the provinces (Spain, Ger- many . . .).

"Great Hellenistic relief-work" in precious metals, "court silver" (as it is termed), offers images identical with those in clay. They help further to indicate the high place in Roman society enjoyed by this taste and its patrons. From such reliefs indeed *terra sigillata* drew some of its stamps or their inspiration.[104] Among the best examples are the silver cup found just beyond the empire's borders to the northwest, showing scenes of male homosexual intercourse— whether of Alexandrian or Capuan manufacture, in any case datable to the last fifteen years of the first century B.C.[105] They belong naturally with the other erotic art just reviewed, and support further the same inference: that there was no ideological quality to style, whether in wall-painting, marble reliefs like the Ara Pacis, Arretine ware, or precious-metal sculpture, any more than in archi- tectural decoration; therefore there is no reason to suppose a push from the cen- ter to inculcate the style and with it some supposed "message."

That said, it remains to explain, if possible, just how someone who wanted a

FIGURE 18. *Terra-sigillata* relief from Perennius' shop.

family memorial, an ornamental public fountain, a chapel with frescoes and reliefs, or any similar expensive piece of decorative art or architecture went about
commissioning the work. My concern is with the provinces and their acculturation, true; and the evidence comes from Rome; yet it cannot be imagined that a
provincial patron for a Roman style would pursue his aim in any way very different from a patron in the imperial capital.

It is a conversation, naturally, that needs to be overheard, between two men,
customer and purveyor. About the former, from Augustus' time, we are in-
formed by Vitruvius and Cicero. The former would like to be read by every educated person, but he generally addresses himself to fellow-professionals, indicating that patrons need not receive any instruction, just the finished product;
and of course it should be well suited to who they are.[106] Let them beware of
thinking they know how to advise the professional! Let them beware of listening (notice, not proposing their preferences) to some incompetent or faddist
decorator! Then there's Cicero, always in a great hurry to make this or that new
residence yet more rich and striking, so as to *épater* his visitors, reporting on a
passage with his architect Cyrus (*Att.* 2.3.2 of 60 B.C.). He, Cicero, had remarked that the design of the windows made them look awfully big; whereupon
Cyrus explained and defended their size in technical terms that Cicero found
ridiculous but accepted. He himself was no expert. Elsewhere he seems more
concerned with costs. He buys things he hasn't seen and has them shipped to
him, just like the Province customers for articles of luxury found in shipwrecks

off the southern coasts.[107] So, in sum, anyone he hired who had confidence in his own taste and skill would be left pretty much to his own devices (within budget), as Vitruvius' patrons also would not be expected to express any but the most general opinions about the design they were buying.

To express more would require a background of knowledge not quite suitable to a patron. A gentleman would instinctively observe the distance between his connoisseurship (if he could claim so much), and the command of the skills needed to earn a living with them. The distance was socioeconomic, first and last. Should he decide for some reason to acquire a menial's degree of skill (as one Roman did, we know), he should work only a few hours a day, wearing the insignia of citizenship, his toga (imagine painting in a toga!) even up on his scaffolding, and ever mindful of his *gravitas*.[108] Ordinarily, painters and architects belonged to a class quite distinct from that of a patron, a Roman; and he would want to keep it that way. They were overwhelmingly Greeks in Augustus' time, tainted with defeat and servitude, however glorious the inheritance they purveyed.[109] A curious relationship.

In trying to understand it, only a few useable oddments of testimony can be cited (yet they are not very often looked at). Instead, understanding is generally sought through this or that reconstruction, plausible to the extent that the past was like the present. Yet it really was not.

Conveniently, we have a long essay on what appears to be more truly comparable material, from the Renaissance, presented by someone preeminently qualified to explain it, Creighton Gilbert. Focusing on a period of roughly a century and regarding works in intarsia, tapestry, and precious metals as well as the more familiar bronze, marble, and painting, he collects what can be known—of course, vastly more than any collection that might be attempted for antiquity—on the initial shaping of art works. To the familiar pair of actors in the process, patron and artist, he adds from the evidence another pair of importance: the agent or broker who knows where good work may be had, and the adviser or humanist who may be called on for his knowledge of literature and its conventions, whether secular or sacred. The four actors can be seen doing what defines them in scores of preliminary situations, revealed in more or less detail through contracts, letters, and histories.

Initiative lies with the person who issues the commission. He or she, Julius II or Isabella d'Este, or by contrast sometimes representatives of a church who are quite ignorant of art, first seek a qualified person. They make plain in the search their chief concern: they want a work that will be seen with approval or admiration by the audience their actions are addressed to, and so will draw approval or admiration to themselves as the persons responsible: in short, win them "honor." This word that Gilbert uses to encapsulate this relationship and its perceptions is not difficult to find in his sources: for example, the price for a commission must be pretty high, or "it would not be sufficient for our honor. . . . Things like this, done for honor, should be such that they induce that response or one should drop them, for otherwise one gets only shame from them."[110]

To find the right man for the job, general report may point the way: So-and-So's altarpiece is the talk of the town, or the talk of some other town even grander, or on display to general applause in such and such a palace; or resort may be had to a person known to be knowledgeable in the arts, familar with reputations and prices and value for one's money. He is the agent; and a great lord will be in touch with several such.[111] As to what is to be produced, the patron may occasionally have not only clear but quite detailed ideas; but that is rare; and they may have to be abandoned because they seem too constraining or clumsy to the artist. He has his own ideas on how to fulfill some very general suggestion (let it be a Pietà, a battle, the patron and family at worship). But he may feel the need to elevate and complicate his work; so he applies to the fourth party in art-production, who may be called the Ideas-person. "Asked what Justice is," to be represented in his painting of that title, Mantegna answers, "I established 'Justice' when painting, in a certain way. He who can do everything [the pope] ordered it. Since I am a sort of painter who pays particular attention even to the last touches, and had always heard various things about Justice itself, I therefore thought the philosophers ought to be consulted"—and for that reason Mantegna tried them out, with indifferent success.[112] Or again, as Alberti says of well-instructed artists, "Let them cultivate the enjoyment of poets and orators, for these have many adornments in common with painters, and abundant knowledge of many things; they will help a great deal toward composing the narrative. . . . We praise in reading it the description of the Calumny, as Lucian told it, which was painted by Apelles"—and there follows a description of the depiction of that vice in symbolic form, along with Envy, Penitence, Truth, and so forth. Except in the broadest terms, then, the message of the final work is unlikely to be anything the patron intended from the start, communicated to the world through the artist's normal conventions. Sophisticated symbolic intent doesn't exist;[113] it is idle to look for it; or if it does exist, it is something shaped by the artist and presented in a language familiar to his fellows and advisers, but needing to be explained to the patron. By contrast, what the patron wants to get across is of the simplest: We are very great persons, able to command the best.

With this relation and its workings, the relation of Augustan court circles with the artists and architects of that time may be compared. The two seem to me a very good match, even down to the existence in Greece of a broker to assist Cicero's friend Atticus, or in Rome, of "humanists," meaning, poets and other litterateurs, ready to tell a painter just what a Victory looked like or what legendary or mythological figures could best stand for this or that dramatic action. He would then take up his brush, later explaining it all to his patron. To expect any ideology to emerge from this setting hardly makes sense; equally unlikely, that a governmental ukase could have imposed it.

5. Public versus private

Where we can most naturally expect to find a message expressed through art is in an honorific arch. A number of these serving no other purpose were erected in the Province (as in other parts of the empire in Augustus' time).[114] Their message was simple: that the person or persons signallized was or had done something wonderful, most often martial. They had an obvious political tradition and significance, being for that reason brought under his control by Augustus.[115] Best known is the example at Glanum. Its four relief panels each show a female figure next to a male captive, the latter plainly a Gaul.[116] Accentuated by displays of captured arms, the images of the arch recall sculptured trophies (as well as the famous Pergamene depictions of captured Gauls); they exalt some great victory—Caesar's over the Three Gauls or perhaps Augustus' or Agrippa's over Aquitania, the Salassi, or an Alpine people.[117] Strange, to see such advertisement of their humiliation, in a Gallic monument; but then, the tribes had been at war with each other off and on since time began. The trumpeting of their conquest, which was Rome's, in Hellenistic terms, is certainly as Romanized a statement as one could wish. There was a second war monument nearby in Glanum, a water-shrine with sculptures, strewn with the sculptured arms of the defeated. At Lugdunum Convenarum, an arch even displayed an eagle, triumphant Jupiter's.[118]

It has been suggested that the Glanum Arch was intended as a platform for statues of the princes, a part of the effort to make their names and faces known to the empire.[119] Arches commonly did bear sculptured figures on top. Stone portraits of Augustus' line were of course political statements. The accuracy of their Roman-ness will be emphasized in the chapter to follow. They included

Caesar (even his celebrated ancestor, Marius), Augustus himself, Livia, Agrippa, and those various younger figures on whom Augustus concentrated his favor, until they died: the princes Gaius and Lucius in particular. Like arches, portraits of the imperial family couldn't be set up at a venture. Position, size (if more than life), presumably also quality where possible, the emperor wanted to control. The sense of that can be read in the decree regulating the imperial cult at Narbo, including the priests' right to erect statues or other representations of the emperor at public expense, and of themselves, at their own.[120] What was public was subject to a special discipline.

Mention was made, however, of departures from Roman models even in very important buildings, as different hands, more or less practiced, showed what they could do. Specialists in art and architectural history are at one in seeing quite a range of skill and accuracy;[121] but they agree also in detecting the determination by local stone-cutters and architects to do things their own way, to achieve or maintain some degree of independence whether traditional in the region or the creation of the individual. A nice touch of the sort was added by a ceramicist who shaped the acroterion on the temple of Good Health at Glanum: a palmette with powerfully swinging curves, in the Hellenistic style popular in Italy, serving as frame to a goddess' head. Around her neck is—a torque![122] The deity worshipped under his Latin name Valetudo was a local one, almost Glanum's private protector, and some little un-Roman-ness was therefore suitable, at least permissible.

Here in the Province, the adoption of imported decorative elements into shrine- and temple-designs, as also changes toward ground-plans of Italian style, went forward slowly, though some decades in advance of what has been noted above in the Three Gauls. The earliest example of a temple with a cella and ambulatory around it, made of brick and with columns around the ambulatory, dates to the 40s B.C. near Tolosa—a style halfway approaching Roman— while the Gallic square center or cella persists.[123] Persistence in this and other aspects of the indigenous religion is in fact easy to demonstrate, as easy as the slow progress of Romanization; but what is by no means easy is the measuring of these opposing tides chronologically. Specifically of Augustus' time, there is little to be said.

A part of the problem lies in the relative poverty of epigraphic material. It was only in the latter decades of Augustus' time that the habit took hold in Rome and Italy itself, soon to produce a great rise in the quantum of historical evidence. People in the Province imitated those of the empire's center with not very much delay, but on a quite insignificant scale. The earliest inscriptions in the public sphere record the dedication of a replica of the Shield (26 B.C.) voted to Augustus, hung in an Augusteum, and of a shrine at Nemausus in 25 B.C., one dedicated to Augustus. Their early date is explained by their character not only as public but imperial. By his scattering so many milestones along his new roads, bearing more than the bare mile-number, and by other new frequent uses of inscriptions, especially on public buildings, Augustus' practice is the most obvious explanation for the spread of the habit into Gaul, so it has been argued.[124] In any case, by the turn of the era it had begun its real history.

With inscriptions begin also the history of French. That is, Latin must be seen first to establish itself, and in a form which can be explained as ancestral to the modern language. Literary texts indicate only that Latin was commonly spoken (and the fact unusual enough to need comment) among the population at the Rhone mouth toward the end of the first century B.C.; and it was spoken along with Greek and Celtic in the Massilia area; but to the north, Romans needed interpreters, so even did Irenaeus in Antonine times.[125] An ever-increasing command of Latin along with the native tongue must be assumed, and the prominent position, too, of that small percentage of the Province's population that had come in from Italy as traders or colonists. Inscriptions are crucial in showing, beyond the literary texts, that it was not literary Latin that formed the basis of Gallic Latinity, or, for that matter, the basis of Latinity in other western and northern areas. Rather, it was spoken Latin of a middle-class character.[126]

Among inscribed texts, of special usefulness are those scratched on wasters around the kilns of Condatomagus=La Graufesenque, illustrating the kind of selective bilingualism that may be assumed as increasingly common. Where native conscripts to the army must learn one set of words and expressions to do what was expected of them, and stone-cutters another, and so forth, so likewise did the potters in western Narbonensis. They needed to know Latin=Roman dating, numbers, accounting terms, ceramic manufacturing terms (of course), and a scattering of other words in addition to some grasp of grammar.[127] The mid-first century A.D. date of this material makes it both inapplicable to my study, and useful, since it shows how little Latin had penetrated to working-class levels at so late date, as well as the circumstances in which it penetrated at all.

The potters' free handling of Latin matches what they did with a variety of familiar motifs of the art of late Augustan times and on: seen, for example, in almost unrecognizable distortions of Bellerophon and Hercules or of the wolf and Roman twins (Fig. 19).[128] The composers of the former show their ignorance; they have not mastered the master civilization; but the latter design must

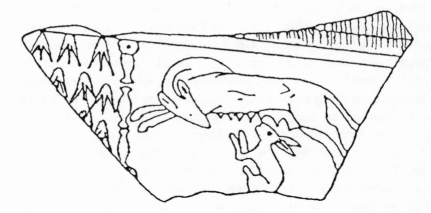

FIGURE 19. A variation on a theme in Gallic *terra sigillata*.

surely be read as mischievous. In any case its creator took for granted that he was sharing his joke with a world that knew the myth of the twins—to that extent, Romanized. To a field archeologist, nothing is more instantly recognizable as Roman than *terra sigillata*, to the eye (with its characteristic bright reds and tomato colors) or to the feel (with its slick surface that sheds the dirt from which it is recovered); and this extraordinarily distinctive ware turned out to be just what the western markets wanted, from the moment of its serious production in Italy toward 30 B.C. A taste for better pottery had been prepared by Gallic importation of Italian wares in the previous generation, in turn teaching the local craftsmen of the Province to shape their own accordingly.[129] Imitation through borrowed stamps, in two small production sites at Lyon, was mentioned, above, too; then these latter lost their market share and other production sites started up to the west and especially in the Province, at La Graufesenque. This, in brief, is the background to the Perennius sherd and the wolf-and-rabbit.

The significance of pottery, however, reaches well beyond these two illustrations. From La Graufesenque, once under way toward the end of Augustus' time, an estimated million vessels a year were turned out (and over the span of the site's history, some six hundred million); so the development was big business.[130] Moreover, as something rightly described as "demi-luxe," *terra sigillata* appealed to a wide segment of society, witness its presence in the most lavishly decorated homes, yet, in others, patched when broken because a replacement could not easily be afforded. It brought to the table something quite novel, introduced most likely to the western Gallic market by Roman soldiers in the 20s B.C. and to the northern also by troop concentrations up there that were more or less permanent, and constituted a major market.[131] Yes, but even with no introduction from Italian-born customers, the product would have spread. Its intrinsic appeal is apparent; and that, rather than any centralized sales strategy, most likely explains the attraction of potters westward out of Italy, beyond Lyon, and so to a handful of other sites in Gaul, recruiting indigenous skilled labor as they moved.[132]

Among the products of Italian type produced at La Graufesenque, unlike anything traditional, are cooking and eating vessels clearly used for a certain menu. The Gauls, having been first taught to like wine, came to like Italian staple foods: stews, soupy sauces poured over crêpes. It is explained as *moretum*, what Italian peasants took as their main food. Eating and cooking vessels from Mallorca, at a Roman colony of the latter second century, suit only an Italian diet, and, in the same shape, they suit the legions on the Rhine a few generations later. From these outposts the shapes and diet together spread around.[133]

Spooning up these imported concoctions, the Gauls may be imagined doing it in clothes of an Italian cut—not up to the standard of Rome or Milan, Valentino or Armani, nor very often the toga even in Augustus' time, but at least not those ridiculous trousers of their forefathers. *Bracae* were the mark of barbarism, abandoned after the conquest (and what a remarkable fact that is, when you think of it); gradually disused, too, the traditional long-sleeved tunic, among men. Women's dress changed little and more slowly.[134]

And to this Italianate domestic scene, last, the Romans added the domestic cat.[135]

V REPLICATION

1. The means

Some generations before Augustus, a very great Roman achievement took its place not in the usual history books (it is barely recorded by Livy) but in the capital. It was, or is, the public storage barn called the Porticus Aemilia. Parts survive. Designed to receive comestibles on a capital scale, it measured two hundred feet by sixteen hundred and fifty, with two stories, divided into some two hundred chambers.[1] Nothing like it had ever been seen for sheer size, and practicality. As the second century went on, the limitless powers of construction here demonstrated were demonstrated in other Roman storage barns as well, though none so big as the Aemilian; they were demonstrated elsewhere in Italy again and yet again, most spectacularly in the footings of gigantic structures like the terracing of Palestrina or of temples at Tivoli or Tarracina.

There was a trick to such building: foundations and vaults and other parts not meant to show could all be done in plain poured concrete. You needed carpenters to build the forms that would contain and shape the pouring till it cured; then you took away the forms and their supports and moved them down the line, or up the wall, to repeat the process. There was nothing terribly complicated about it. Under proper direction, a little-trained work-force would do.[2]

The trick lay in the forms—but of course not only there. Concrete itself was essential. This was the material that set Roman architecture apart from Greek, liberating it for its most characteristic achievements. Combining mortar with stones, as big as two fists or just chips that needed little or no shaping, *opus caementicium* proved infinitely adaptable to any project at hand. And cheap. For at least the gross elements of major projects, "observing how soon the quarrymen would cut half a ton of *Spawls* [that is, chips] from an unformed block," who would go to the trouble of ashlar?[3] And the bare concrete could always be made more pleasing to the eye, and better protected against moisture, too, if it was faced with small stones unshaped ("petit appareil") or shaped only on the side that showed, or with segments of brick, in a random over-all arrangement or in a net pattern, *opus reticulatum*. For *opus reticulatum*, stones in the desired arrangement toward the outer sides of a wall, to a height of several layers, would be set in mortar as the wall rose, so as to make small forms themselves, between which the core-space was then filled in more roughly, and smoothed off, and the process repeated. This had become the technique of choice in Augustus' time, used even on his mausoleum, the Theater of Marcellus, and so on.[4]

Such simple economical methods were soon learnt. With or without admixture of traditional building techniques, they appear in a great deal of public construction already noticed in eastern and western provinces alike. They explain the terracing on vaults that transfigured the center of so many cities. In the late 40s B.C., Narbo got a cryptoportico tucked into sloping ground near the forum with 126 chambers along three hundred feet of vaulted aisles; and not long after Augustus' death, in Vienna, a storage barn almost double the size of the Aemilian was constructed—double, that is, assuming it had no second story (but it probably did).[5]

Terms used by scholars to describe the techniques of construction outlined here make plain their particular character: "industrialization," "mass production," capable of endless mechanical repetition because in their essence they consisted of quite simple forms—*Roman* forms.

In an extended sense, lines and holes on pavement could serve as a form (Fig. 9), by the rules of which the hands and calculations of game-players were governed. Wherever such a thing was drawn and put to use, bystanders learned how to become Roman. The ball-court constructed for the people of Nemausus by prince Gaius served the same purpose, inviting them to a set activity and thus shaping their behavior.[6] Baths-buildings with their tripartite plan afforded a form into which life itself was poured, and cured; theaters in which everyone knew who was who and where he was supposed to sit inculcated distinct ideas about social place, quite aside from ideas of entertainment. And so forth—not excluding the form of bronze tablets conspicuously displayed "at eye level and in a much-frequented part of the city" (as the standard phrasing so often insisted).

Texts like those defining a constitution for Spanish cities were certainly prominent by the hundreds, even if they don't survive, spread across the provinces in Augustus' time. They were first at home in Italy, shaped there in their teachings and requirements, carefully considered by due authority as to necessary content and wording, publicized from the 40s B.C. if not earlier, and repeated without any very significant modification thereafter for the benefit of one urban center after another, again and again. It is a safe guess that almost all of the places marked on the maps of the four preceding chapters had such a text on the wall of their finest temple, perhaps rather in the basilica, but in any case where no one could miss it. Once its essential content had been more or less decided on, early in Augustus' time, the imposing of it on a fresh population was as easy as putting up work-forms for a wall; pouring the population into it was as quickly done; and the hardening of their habits of at least partial conformity could be expected to yield an equally durable set of institutions: prescribing nomenclature, guardianships, social ranks, religious ceremonies, and so on and so forth, all, thoroughly Roman. There was no need to re-invent them each time.

We in our modern world might expect some force to be applied to produce conformity. The masters of the provinces could call up their legions ad lib. and compel obedience to a charter, could they not? But there is never a hint that this was even thought of.

Still, the legions did play some part. They built major highways serving as armatures on which might depend a dozen, indirectly a hundred, urban centers needing access to each other for commerce and growth. Spain, Gaul, and the most habitable parts of the province of Africa, equipped with such gigantic structures laid down across their whole expanse, took on the look of Italy. In Augustus' time, Italy's network was long familiar, a characteristic of its civilization. The width of the roadway, depth of stone, and delimitation in Roman miles were all so well known, they could be laid down in the provinces with perfect confidence and ease. Once in place, the indigenous populations took advantage of them to develop their economy.

The legions proved useful in other tasks of civil engineering. Many clear instances have turned up in the previous chapters,[7] along with others less clear, where an army role must be inferred from surviving construction. Does the crossing of *kardo* and *decumanus* at some provincial city's center, and the arrangement of the open space and surrounding municipal offices, replicate the headquarters-area at the center of a camp? There are differences; but the plan of Barcino or Forum Segusiavorum (Fig. 14) must surely recall Italian Republican colonies like Ostia or the later Augusta Bagiennorum, laid out by army surveyors.[8] For the imperial authorities set over a province, legionary legate or governor, the only experts at hand to help in preparing some center for its share of responsibility were attached to the Commanders of Engineers, *praefecti fabrum*. So Vitruvius had served outside of Italy. Others like him have appeared in construction roles, above. The forum-form they imposed serves my purpose equally well whether derived from camps or ordinary Italian town centers, so long as it is clear that it was ready and waiting for implementation—that it shows Romans' capacity to transfer designs ready-made from their homeland to the lands they conquered. There was certainly a call for their help in the Augustan "building-boom."

No need, perhaps, to rehearse the role they played in surveying the lands set aside for the use of veteran settlers. It does need to be said again, however, that the form of squares of twenty *actus* pressed down on the land by centuriation marked it forever as Roman, and redistributed the farming population in a manner to change their farming practices. Land reclamation and sedentarization followed.[9] At the same time everyone came under the authority of the town in their midst, according to a pattern of responsibility at home in Italy; or rather, they or at least the richest persons among them took their place in the town's *curia* to exercise that responsibility, presided over by magistrates just like those to be found in Italian municipalities and just as the town's charter prescribed. The *curia* was a form, the basilica where magistrates held court was one other; so was the forum for public assemblies, perhaps equipped with a replica of Rome's rostra, even of the Roman forum's Marsyas statue, and dignified by a great podium temple at one end. Assemblies would be held according to form, that is, with preliminary Roman rites in the temple or at an altar in front of it. Indeed, the more fully Roman centers, *coloniae*, were marked out from their very inception by a priest's plowing of a sacred furrow, depicted on the coins of Emerita or Philippi, for example, according to the same rites that had initiated Rome itself; and from that moment forward, if there was any doubt just how a cult should be conducted, questions could be directed to the capital, to find out what was the custom, the form, at the shrine of Diana or of some other appropriate deity. Provision that this be done was written up on bronze in the charter "at eye level and in a much-frequented part of the city."

Toward the end of a remarkable book, Lopez Paz takes into one single vision the Roman city surrounded by its centuriated lands: "The entirety of this huge structure, the territory of the Roman community, realized itself in something changeless over time, destined to endure, stable, eliminating all conflict that might destroy it." It was "the ideal community but not utopian," Roman not Greek; and, everywhere, its exact specifications, their permanence, and their advertisement for future reference were of particular concern to Augustus. It was he who proclaimed by edict just what should be the width of border-roads around *centuriae* and how corner-*termini* should be set up and inscribed; he who arranged that site-plans and allotments should be registered and preserved.

Much of the map of one area of assignment in the provinces is still before us, once posted in public to remind people exactly who owned what, near what inscribed boundary-stone—this, the well known marble plan of Arausio.[10]

Even in quite remote areas in Augustan times the application of the Romans' Standard Operating Procedure is described: "their soldiers were wintering there [near the Rhine] and towns were being formed: the barbarians were adapting themselves to orderly Roman ways and were becoming accustomed to holding markets and peaceful assemblies" (Dio 56.18.2f.). Evident in the passage is the need as yet unsatisfied for a built assembly place, a forum with a comitium, and a built market-hall, a macellum; but the future would supply these; for it was a particular characteristic of a Romanized urban center, even in Corinth or Antioch, that it should have accommodations in stone for the activities thought to define a city.

The design of them needn't depend on the moment's inspiration. There were forms easily followed from handbooks. Vitruvius' is only the most pretentious and complete. Something much simpler could have dictated the plans of private houses and fora (Fig. 16), capitolia or theaters, aqueducts or tropaia.[11] All of these structures could be laid out according to modules in prescribed ratios; all accustomed the eye to the Roman aesthetic, for all had in sight the corresponding structures of Italy, often, of the center of Rome itself. The decorative elements of the temples of Apollo and of Mars-the-Avenger were particularly favored for imitation. One had only to ask for a drawing or plaster cast to copy, as local architects and stone-cutters can be shown to have done in many provinces.

Nothing, however, taught the Italian aesthetic more ubiquitously than Italian pottery. In one variety or another it could be found everywhere, within the reach of people of almost every level of wealth. It is too much to say that its characteristic shapes, suited to the Italian diet, served as a form to impose that diet. No, lessons under that heading worked through other means; but the new appetites would certainly be accommodated by Italian shapes. As to the decoration, from Arretium = Arezzo in Tuscany (still today a center of ceramic production) flowed a stream of the most striking wares marked, from early Augustan times on (abut 30 B.C.), by reliefs, many of them of the highest quality. Terra sigillata relied on a simple trick: a hollow form, a baked clay matrix, in the inner walls of which had been impressed reliefs by stamps; and the matrix was then cooked to be hard; and a soft clay vessel could be placed inside the matrix and its sides pressed out into the matrix-walls so as to take on the reliefs; whereupon, as it dried and lost bulk, it could be removed from the matrix to be fired without damage to either, and the matrix re-used indefinitely. Many matrices and stamps have been found both at Arretium and in the western provinces. The stamps could be applied in any arrangement ad lib. (Fig. 19).[12] In the preceding chapter an indication was given of the extraordinary flow of finished vessels from only one, though by far the most active, cluster of little workshops in the Province in Augustus' time. "Mass production" thanks to mechanical replication of designs is the obvious term by which to describe this whole business. Its principles could be applied wherever the rewards of efficiency of manufacture were evident: for example, in meeting the great demand for an entirely different kind of vessel, crude large amphorae required for oil-export from Spain. The Spanish kilns turned out "large numbers of surprisingly uniform bulbous containers."[13] Another example is the mass production of terracotta figurines by mould to sell to pilgrims at a Gallic shrine, or the identical bronze figurines of Aphrodite and Asclepius from scattered western sites.[14] Moulds, again, or forms.

No one would expect that stone sculptures of some undeniable artistry might be standardized and mass-produced. Explanation of the process may best begin with the mass-produced: portraits of the imperial family in quite remarkable numbers. They are found in army camps, carried around with the troops; in places of imperial cult, most naturally, after the mid-20s B.C.; in or near theaters, sometimes in special galleries; and on fora. Those more than life-size are of the emperor.[15] Beginning in the east in the 40s B.C., the wish of the greatest Romans to present themselves in portraits to the people had taken hold, producing rare Antony's (but many were destroyed), a thin scattering of Caesar's (some thirty survive), but a very great number of Augustus's. Though a majority of the more than 250 of the latter that survive do so without context, some seventy can be traced to Italy (the most) and the rest, to all regions. On the assumption that every least city in the empire that might think itself worthy of the name would have wanted some public advertisement of its proper loyalty to be set up in more than one choice location, Augustus-portraits must have numbered above twenty thousand by the end of his reign. With others in proportion for the various princes, the total spread over a generation or so is a match for the output of La Graufesenque. It is undeniably mass production.

From this effort, Romanization resulted intangibly, as the identity of supreme power took on a specific human shape in poses and costumes that were specific to the civilization of the masters of the world. That is, provincial populations were taught a political lesson of the most obvious importance, and, along with it, lessons in art and image. The rapid approximation of portraits of

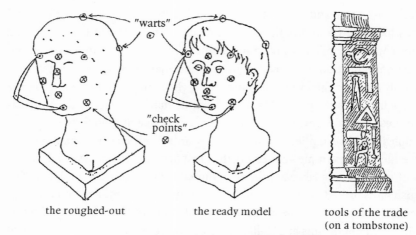

the roughed-out   the ready model   tools of the trade
                                                  (on a tombstone)

FIGURE 20. Copying-methods for statuary.

private individuals in Spain, and of a native king in Africa, to the face and expression of the emperor, has been noticed.[16] Provincials were taught the habit
of advertisement itself through statues set up in public, along with lessons in
the epigraphic habit. In these various respects, then, the output of carved stone
and its ubiquitous display deserves a place in these pages.

But by what trick could mass production be achieved in this marble art?
Michael Pfanner has drawn attention to what he calls "warts" or, in the modern
craftsman's language, "puntelli," to be noticed on a number of not quite finished pieces of Roman sculpture—notably, on a full-length barbarian destined
for a monument in Rome a century after Augustus, but found unused on the
Field of Mars.[17] On this work there are two dozen little protuberances left after
the surrounding stone had all been cut away to the proper figure. They must correspond to their like, of plaster, temporarily and identically situated and attached to a now-lost model of which the barbarian was a copy. The sculptor
decided what would be the most convenient points on his model by which
to measure with calipers a matching distance, in three dimensions, on the
roughed-out block of stone he had before him. Preliminary roughing-out he
could do by eye, but more accuracy was attainable through his calipers, and the
greater the number of "warts," the more perfect the outcome. Modern methods
explain "warts" left on dozens of pieces of ancient statuary. Slight variations in
technique and instruments can be added to the picture of the stone-cutters at
work; and the extraordinary accuracy they could attain can be demonstrated by
comparing the profiles of Augustus-heads of the several most famous, fre-

quently copied styles, of Prima Porta and so forth.[18] These latter derived from models, or in my metaphor, from "forms," most often made available in plaster casts for reproduction, the process beginning in the Carrara quarries that the emperor controlled and being completed on site in Emerita or Caesarea-in-Pisidia. The patterns of distribution of the result indicate the surprising speed with which the work could be done. "Roman imperial culture," Pfanner concludes, "had become a mass culture."

He is not the first to have been struck by the sculptural evidence that rather abruptly appears in the 20s B.C., transforming the character of public areas in cities everywhere. The trick of replication, not unknown in Hellenistic times and therefore no Roman invention, was nevertheless applied on an altogether new and Roman scale, exactly like the trick of concrete wall-building. In architecture, too, so far as it was official and public, a special degree of standardization was pointed out, above. At Tarraco, standardization was applied even to private individuals' votive portraiture set up in the city's principal shrine—a place semi-public. The replication of bronze statuary to meet private demand, having nothing to do with political correctness and everything to do with being Roman, established itself at the same time. It too used "warts" and favored reproductions of the best known classics in the art.[19] That such classics were also Greek made them no less Roman.

2. The opportunity

It was of course essential that replication should be physically possible on a scale to respond to demand, whether in art or pottery or typical comestibles, chiefly olive oil and wine. Otherwise, no historically significant acculturation could take place. Yes, but every reader of the more classical detective stories knows from their last chapter, when the dark mystery is explained under three headings, there must be not only *means* but *opportunity* as well (with *motive* first and last of all).

In the earlier decades of Augustus' time, while war was threatened or actively waged, the antagonists must seek everywhere for support. For example, in Massilia. Wooed by both Pompey and Caesar with rich favors, its people were in no hurry to end their courtship: they declared it absolutely beyond their intellectual powers to tell who was in the right. Or in Baetica, Pompey lavished his *beneficia* on the chief cities, and Caesar mentally added up those favors and estimated their danger to his cause, and topped them.[20] What was promised in pressing circumstances had to be delivered afterwards, for years. A usual award was some reassignment of taxes or direct gift of plunder taken from other parties.

To all such, there must be some limit. Better by far were generous gifts of charters and citizenship. These cost no one anything and could be indulged in so long as they did not too much offend public opinion in Italy. A shower of gifts to provincial communities set in in the 50s B.C. and continued into the 40s and beyond. As a result, long before the end of Augustus' reign, in the Province there was no one left outside the boundaries of some chartered city—all of southern Gaul could fairly be called "Latinized"—while southern Spain was treated almost equally well.[21] Similarly, in large areas of north Africa and parts of northwestern Greece. It was owing to the opportunity of civil strife that the process of partial or complete incorporation into the Roman state should have been offered to those who wanted it, on a scale unmatched in any previous time.

Then, too, it was only by the opportunity or accident of war that several dozen legions came together at Philippi and, at Actium, dozens again with huge naval forces to support them, while still other troops were serving at the same time in other theaters; and something had to be done with them all when the fighting was over. Victorious commanders could maintain their position only by postwar demobilization, which had to be seen as generous, or at least acceptable, and not too long delayed by further campaigning against external enemies. The salience of the problem is clear in Augustus' *Achievements*, where he gives an early paragraph (3) and some monumental sestertius-totals to his handling of it. Resettlement in Italy was what the men wanted. Much along this line was achieved. But seizing land there involved a political cost and buying it at a fair price, a prohibitive cost in money. There was a third possibility: to settle the men overseas. Even then, their farms had often to be purchased, not confiscated. As against the 600 million sesterces Augustus had to spend in Italy, he paid out 260 in compensation to provincials. Italian land was certainly more expensive per acre. To bring up the total cost of provincial land to 260 millions, we must suppose that a very substantial proportion of the 300,000 veterans whom he re-settled were sent overseas. That would fit with the total of perhaps sixty colonies attributed to him, if each received 1,500–2,000 men. As many again must be added, from Caesar's and the Triumvirs' colonies, earlier, at some forty sites, counting, too, a huge number of civilians from Rome dispatched by the dictator to Carthage and elsewhere.[22]

Both the beneficiaries of these policies and the form in which they were settled proved effective instruments of acculturation, though by no means sufficient in themselves to explain the process that interests me. Among movements of people in ancient history, nothing compares with these more than 200,000 veterans and scores of thousands of civilians set down in successive waves at well over a hundred points of colonization, with close to a hundred other, mostly pre-existing centers newly chartered in a Roman fashion. Mighty changes! and over the course only of a generation.

Had there been no such changes. . . . To imagine the provinces instead untouched makes us confront the import of what was actually done. Plain statistics—or call them approximations—indicate its scale. At the same time, it is well to remember that areas in southern Gaul and southern Spain, where Roman culture was already familiar at Augustus' birth, at his death still retained much of their non-Roman character, while in the east, in most of its aspects, imported Roman culture faded out after two or three generations.

So far as Romanization resulted, sheer numbers played a very important part; but the particular quality of the settlers made a difference, too. It was a matter of opportunity, here again. The vast majority of them were legionaries, used to hanging together, to acting for a common end, and they had special skills applicable to community projects.[23] Even where, as in "Old" Africa, some were scattered among villages in little clusters, they were assured of a dominant position by reason both of their civic status and the relatively generous acreage of land they were assigned; and where, in the great western areas of the empire, there was the most changing to be done toward those city-centered Roman-Hellenistic customs and institutions, Roman warriors even at rest counted for something.

This last point surely should be given a good deal of weight. Positions of leadership among the Celtiberi or Helvetii, the respect accorded to an opinion or a choice, had been generally won through war. Contemporary sources make that plain.[24] Now by the verdict of war the victors, whether Roman or peregrine collaborators, had been declared; in terms of native values they had won the right to lead and to be heard. This right remained to them even in peace, or especially so, since warriors of the old style were now forbidden to flaunt their swords and spears and soon ceased even to be buried with them. In their place were "ACO" cups and Arretine.

To afford such civilian collectibles cost money. It was opportune that much became available for free expenditure in the course of civil strife. The losers are not heard of, only the winners. These latter, however, if they enjoyed some local prominence to begin with, found themselves competed for by Roman leaders just like their comunities, with the opportunity similarly to offer their *officia* for *beneficia*. In the confusion of the times, by means and methods they could excuse as no different from their leaders', they might hope for sudden wealth, and can be seen applying it to the purchase of prestige through conspicuous consumption and largesses, little different in Roman terms than in indigenous. They built aqueducts and theaters, they put on gladiatorial games. A fair number of individuals of the sort have been instanced in earlier chapters.[25] Had they been in any doubt that lavish public giving would serve their ambitions, Caesar and Augustus set an example—the latter over a very long period and with very obvious help from Agrippa. To add up the amounts spent by Augustus and Agrippa in the west, by some extrapolation from their attested acts of patronage, is surely to understand a great deal about the "building-boom" of the period; and it was crucial to their means, and at the center of their opportunity, that the wealth of Egypt had fallen to the victor at Actium. Civil war paid for much of that construction.

3. The motive

Comparison of the degree of acculturation achieved in these western regions, with that achieved in the east, suggests, however, how important was the intrinsic attractiveness of the Roman way of life seen through the eyes of the indigenous population. The point was made in the preceding chapter (at nn. 65ff.), with illustrations that could have been drawn from any province at all. Baths and wine and so forth recommended themselves to the senses without need of an introduction. They felt or they looked good.

It is thus possible to speak of a higher civilization, in conventional terms, in contact with a lower. Romans of Augustus' time had no hesitation in doing so, untroubled by cultural relativism and post-colonial guilt. They could use the term "barbarian" in a value-neutral sense of "native," true, but usually in a sense of more or less horrified denigration.[26] There are instances of the latter before a company of the natives themselves. To make quite tactless comments was one of the pleasures of *maiestas*. The natives would be taught, if it was not plain enough on its face, that they could better rise into the ranks of the master race by reforming themselves—by talking, dressing, looking, and in every way resembling Romans. They would and did respond as ambition directed. They *pulled* Roman civilization to them—to their homes, their families, their world.

It used to be supposed that acculturation was more a matter of push. Long after Augustus a pair of comments, one from Tacitus and the other from Pliny the Elder, articulated the Romans' *maiestas* in cultural terms: their heaven-sent mission was "to soften people's ways, *ritus molliret*, to bring the clashing wild speech of infinite different peoples to a common conversation through a common tongue, and to supply civilization, *humanitas*, to men, that all races might, in a word, belong to one single *patria*." So Pliny; and Tacitus described his father-in-law's "intention" as a governor in Britain "that people who lived in widely dispersed and primitive settlements and hence were naturally inclined to war should become accustomed to peace and quiet by the provision of amenities. Hence he gave encouragement to individuals and assistance to communities to build temples, fora, and Roman-style houses. He praised those that responded and censured the dilatory. Ambition for promotion, *honoris aemulatio*, took the place of compulsion. Further, he educated the sons of the leading men in the liberal arts. . . . Thus even our style of dress came into favour and the toga was everywhere to be seen. Gradually, too, they went astray into the allurements of evil ways, colonnades and warm baths and elegant banquets. The Britons, who had no experience of this, called it 'civilization,' *humanitas*, although it was a part of their enslavement."[27]

The general tendency to minimize these two passages seems to me correct.[28] Pliny is simply noting the fact that Latin is spreading. The pride he felt in the ascendancy of his own tongue makes him treat the phenomenon in grand terms, as something the very gods wanted (else, perhaps, they would have awarded the western half of the "known world," too, to the Greeks and their tongue). As for Tacitus' account, it might have more weight except for its singularity. There is no match for it elsewhere, in words, nor any indication of it indirectly in the actions of governors. They betray an interest only in making their jobs easier. That need not involve more than bringing down the native populations from elevated strong-places to the plains, facilitating communication, clarifying approved forms of local oligarchy, and making clear through routine publication of laws and imperial orders that a knowledge of Latin would be taken for granted. All these steps have indeed been readily discerned in all the provinces, especially in the west. They looked, quite rationally, to the end the Romans always had in mind, the realities of power. More than that was not on governors' minds, gratifying as that "more" might be, if it were imitation of their way of life, and generally to be smiled on as it was by Agricola.

For the period with which I am properly concerned, something not said may count for more. Strabo, describing the whole empire from his knowledge of it in the middle years of Augustus' principate, says nothing about acculturation. He saw the Romans' power exerted in administration and the spread of colonies in the east while, in the west, it was exerted in pacification by force of arms, and, here too, in colonizing and diffusing Latin and law. For him, the barbarism to be overcome was violent, savage behavior, not boorish ignorance or bad manners. It stood in the way of peace and prosperity, without such peace also requiring atrium houses, worship of the lares, or gladiatorial games in every town on every weekend, a vision at which Strabo would have shuddered.[29] His testimony thus fits well with the distinction made in the preceding chapter between the public and the private spheres. In the public sphere, the spread of citizenship, charters, law, and imperial cult was obviously initiated or at least encouraged by imperial authority. In that sense, they represented push, with cultural consequences already sufficiently emphasized—but yet, consequences not foreseen or cared about by the Romans.

It may qualify as push or pressure from the center of the empire, that the bellicosity of "barbarians" was seen as something in need of chastening. Barbarians weren't fit to govern themselves nor even able to draw due benefit from peace. It was for Romans to preside not only over law-courts but commerce as well. For the chastening needed, there was Caesar with illustrative passages in his works; for the handling of business and respect for law, Cicero; but Cicero's bland claims extend over the Greeks of the east as much as over the Gauls.[30] His testimony proves too much: he had in sight only materialistic exploitation. Add to the picture a little note: that in an inscription of Ephesus we see the Triumvirs in 43 B.C. providing large tax-exemptions for physicians and professors, not out of any reverence for the civilization they represented, surely, but because the Roman ruling class had personal need of such skills and extended their favor to the purveyors as to clients.[31]

The notion of an abstract "Rome" with a cultural mission has been often enough dismissed.[32] Of any individual, specific champion there is no sign. A claim is sometimes entered for Augustus—a claim implied in the detection of an "Augustan ideology" of undefined content, but somehow "moral." The message was read in the art. Risk here of Procrustean subjectivity, so as to force the past "to make sense," is obvious. To discount it, evidence was offered in the preceding chapter, showing the adoption of new styles across all genres without confusion of esthetics and ethics or any flowing of the one into the other (where, too, the quality or impact of the style has been variously interpreted).

It makes no sense, in the face of some centralized culture-push, that Augustan style should have been quite unobserved in the homeland, around the corner from Augustus, so to speak, but in quite déclassé localities, then and now—localities outside the capital, then, and today to be found in local Italian museums rarely visited by art historians.[33] What determined choice were local tastes, not imperial "ideology." They retained their independence because that independence was never challenged.

It was different in the provinces. The populations there knew their land was not Italy, nor their ways Roman regardless of their being "provincial." Above and beyond their taking on of Roman traits in the public sphere, then, they must do so to some significant degree in the private sphere as well. It was the eagerness particularly of the urban well-to-do, the pull of that rich class, that so greatly accelerated the process. For all the reasons often noted, the alien civilization was embraced: its speech, its dress, its leisure customs, its rituals of burial and commemoration, most particularly the value it placed on euergetism, and so on through a catalogue of borrowings. Sometimes what was borrowed seemed in itself better, sometimes a means rather of gaining some further good: favor among the powerful, community esteem. "It was a process that went on through imitation, by osmosis—assimilation of oneself in the knowledge that one could live better and more easily if one played the game by Roman rules."[34]

Notes

1. Horsfall (1996) 24 on bilingualism; on names = descent in the Rome area and south Italy, Leveau (1984) 154; further, MacMullen (1990) 179f.
2. On the likelihood of a gift of Greek sculpture to a Spanish city in 168 B.C. by Aemilius Paullus, see Rodriguez Hidalgo and Keay (1995) 399.
3. On the changes in Cisalpina obvious in art and architecture, and problems of taxonomy, "Romanization," or "Hellenization," see Denti (1989) 10; export ceramics, Hochuli-Gysel (1977) 119, 139, with post-Augustan Hellenization more deeply in Cisalpine export sculpture, Hatt (1970) 222.
4. On the identity perceived between what we would call civilization, meaning the higher form, and Greek ways in their classical form, see such assessments as those of Veyne (1979) passim, idem (1998) 17, Zanker (1991) 195f., Keay (1995) 299, M. Torelli in CAH, 10 ed. 2 (1996) 941, or Galinsky ibid. 362 and chap. 7 passim. Gruen (1992) concerns himself essentially with the third and second centuries, not the first. For the quotation, see Ad Q. frat. 1.1. 27, 29, of 60 B.C.
5. Petrochilos (1974) 24 on Augustus' command of Greek; on his encouragement of bilingualism and the carmina saecularia, Kienast (1982) 383f., noting also the creation of a public library in two sections.
6. Borbein (1975) 247 on the Ara Pacis; Furnée-van Zwet (1956) 4f. and Trillmich (1976) 40f., 43, on women's hair-dress.
7. Flacc. 19.
8. OGIS 532 = ILS 8781 of 6 B.C., sworn "before Zeus, Earth, Sun, all gods and goddesses and the Augustus Himself."
9. Magie (1950) 1.162f.; Loukopoulou (1996) 143f., Chalcidice; Ste. Croix (1981) 529; Hatzfeld (1919) 261, rarity of term conventus in the east; businessmen as individuals in triumviral and Augustan times, esp. at Corinth, with links to Italy, cf. Spawforth (1996) 170–73, good evidence in excellent pages; and, on Petra, Wilson (1966) 144 and Sherwin-White (1983) 202 n. 44, a large group in late Augustan times. On Narona, Brunt (1971) 220; post-Augustus, we have associations with curatores or a council, Hatzfeld (1919) 282.
10. E.g., Caes., BC 3.29; Dio 51.20.7; Hatzfeld (1919) 71, 102, 284; Wilson (1966) 129f.
11. Brunt (1971) 220, Dalmatian conventus.
12. For example, Ad Q. frat. 1.2.3, 10f., 14; Ad fam. 13.24; Hatzfeld (1919) 328f.; Rowland (1972) 456ff.; Saddington (1993) 93.

13. Jones (1971) 157f.; Dreizehnter (1975) 236.
14. Ste. Croix (1981) 524f., 530; Sherwin-White (1983) 229, 258; Wörrle (1988) 91f., with some earlier precedents for the novelty elsewhere in Greek lands.
15. Hatzfeld (1919) 59f., 70f., 85, 98, 100, 102f. (Pollio), 153, 295f., 306, 350ff.; Wilson (1966) 134, 148.
16. E.g., Hatzfeld (1919) 66, a Sempronius wins the children's boxing title; further, on *Rhomaioi* (prior to the Social War, more often called *Italikoi*) as ephebes and *neoi*, 70f., 86, 104, 304, and Wilson (1966) 129, 134; the interesting case of ephebes with "Romans" at Athens, numerous from ca. 120 until identifiable names peter out, all absorbed and Hellenized, three generations later, cf. Rizakis (1996) 17; further, finding in Rhodes a law forbidding the public use of Roman-form names, out of hostility to Rome, Hoët-van Cauwenberghe (1996) 233ff.; on intermarriage, Hatzfeld (1919) 294; on landowning, Magie (1950) 163; on Mussius and his like, Hatzfeld (1919) 65f. and Wilson (1966) 134.
17. Brunt (1971) 207, offered as a guess, but in line with Hatzfeld's and others'.
18. Nigdélis (1994) 215f. on M. Insteius in Macedonia, *imperator*, kinsman of Mark Antony, εὐεργέτης of Europus; IG 5, 1.374 of 18/12 B.C., bilingual (Latin honored by first place), the donor receiving citizenship from Augustus, C. Iulius Deximachus, after whom is named, I presume, a son of Eurykles, ibid. p. 307 and IG 3.801b; other statues, below, n. 90, or of Caesar heroized, at Sparta, F. S. Johansen (1967) 42; of Agrippa again, in Plassart (1926) 448 with notes, or of Augustus, cf. Hatzopoulos and Loukopoulou (1992) 79 lines 35ff., a statue paid for by a rich citizen of a Macedonian town "as an eternal memorial of Augustus' benefactions to all men"—the statue (ibid p. 80) identifiable with the colossal and cuirassed torso surviving. At Corinth, notice the statue of Augustus *capite velato*, in the Julian basilica, Niemeyer (1968) 82, and at Gythion, provision for statues to be set up in the theater of the emperor flanked by wife and son, with annual painted portraits to be supplied by magistrates for the rituals of the imperial cult, cf. Seyrig (1929) 85–88, perhaps more conveniently in Ehrenberg and Jones (1955) 88.
19. E.g. the Agrippiastai of Sparta, IG 5, 1.374, with their officers and celebrations; a voting tribe in Corinth called "Agrippia" and another "Vinicia," West (1931) 15; OGIS 458 = Ramsay (1895–97) 2.479 = Sherk (1969) 329f.; ibid. 257f.; and a good sampling in Seyrig (1929) 95 n. 4.
20. In Delos, Tchernia (1986) 71 (Apulian amphorae) and Morel (1986) 487, Italian black-slip ware; lamps, Pavolini (1990) 111; in Corinth, Engels (1990) 34 and Hayes (1973) 426f., 449, 461f. ("ACO" beakers), and passim; Troso (1991) 66, on P. Cornelius, whose product is found also in Athens and Palestine; and Morel (1986) 484, Pergamene ware of Italian influence.
21. Burnett et al. (1992) 1, 1, pp. 8, 21f., 24, 28f. and 53 (Augustus' Thessalian *diorthoma* of 27? B.C.), 245, 256, 368; 284, Antony's "fleet" issues seen as an attempt at achieving a single imperial coinage; Baldus (1987) 146 on Syrian coinage; Wilkes (1969) 47, 55, on App., *Illyr.* 28, taxes; and Crawford (1985) 252, 256. Roman *cistophori* had first been tried in 39 B.C., thereafter not till after Augustus; meanwhile, in 19–18 B.C. the coin issued from no less than 71 local eastern mints (Burnett 23). On the Roman-compatible bronze of Sparta (in the mid-30s?), "the earliest instance of romanization of a Greek civic coinage," see Kroll (1997) 142.

22. The sources I draw on are numerous, not worth naming in detail: principally RE (e.g. s.v. "Parentium"), Vittinghoff (1951), Bowersock (1965) 62ff., Levick (1967), Brunt (1971), Wilkes (1969), the *Princeton Encyclopedia* (1976), Burnett et al. (1992) 258ff., and Mitchell (1993) 1.76f. (Attaleia, etc.), 87f., 90. These are by no means always in agreement. I do not show a few small centers raised in title and responsibility from villages, found in Jones (1971) 93 (Sebaste), 162−64, and other cities reconstituted, Mitchell (1993) 1.76, 86f. (Tavium, Pessinus, Ancyra). For Buthrotum, see Rizakis (1990) 261, with ref. to Cicero' letters to Atticus; for Dyme, 260, 266, 268.

23. Engelmann and Knibbe (1989) 114f., *ius Italicum* in Alexander Troas; also for Dyrrhachium, Philippi, Dium, and Cassandreia, Brunt (1971) 598f.

24. Christol and Drew-Bear (1999) [pagination not available]; Levick (1967) 58, 73; but Moatti (1993) 37 for Augustus' contrary policy in the east, of returning their lands to temples. I have read much discussion of the number of persons settled in colonies, virtually all of it openly speculative. After note is taken of the majority of Caesarian and triumviral veterans drawn back to Italy (Keppie [1983] 50), and likewise Augustan veterans, there remain those of all leaders who, through re-enlistment, never lived for a final reward; and, as I assume this to be a substantial category, my estimated totals are lower than some scholars'. See further, below, chap. 2 n. 2, chap. 3 at n. 5, chap. 4 at n. 54.

25. The standard *IVviri* at Corinth (1966) 23, 26f.; *duoviri iuri*(!) *dicundo* on Corinth coins, Sherwin-White (1963) 92; Millar (1993) 279, Beirut; Levick (1967) 78, Lystra; Mitchell (1993) 88, in Bithynian cities, according to the Lex Pompeia, an age-minimum etc., also chief magistrates called *archontes* with a *protos archon*, and similar anomalies more fully known at Ancyra and Pessinus; pre-Augustan quaestors at Narona, Vittinghoff (1951) 125, and Augustan quaestors at Antioch, Levick (1967) 82, along with Greek-style *grammateis* and *gymnasiarchai* at Antioch, 73.

26. The proportion of original residents to Roman settlers seems to me impossible to estimate, though clearly in some cities they were many and the immigrants few, as Kienast (1982) says, p. 382. It is likewise impossible to say how regularly *peregrini* received citizenship. Kienast 402 n. 167, citing Patras as a known case, considers the possibility "anscheinend nicht selten," and Brunt (1971) 254f. says it is generally believed to have been bestowed on the upper strata of *peregrini*.

27. Levick (1967) 45, 76, 90; Rizakis (1997) 19ff. on the composition of the territories of Patras, Nicopolis, and Knossos.

28. *Dioikeiseis*=*conventus* (not to be confused with Roman citizen associations under the same name), Sherwin-White (1963) 93 and Jones (1971) 61.

29. Illustrations in MacMullen (1976) 86 with notes; a fine survey by Galsterer (1986), whose views can be slightly amplified by Sherwin-White (1963) 14f., 74f., Hatzfeld (1919) 319f., 324f., Wörrle (1988) 97, Millar (1993) 364 ("we would not know that we were in the Roman empire at all," to judge from the law applied in a Palestinian village in A.D. 55, balanced by some surprisingly different texts of a later date, p. 528), Biscardi (1993) 261ff., Gardner (1993) 187ff., Klingenberg (1993) 153, 174, and Kränzlein (1993) 186. Rights of Roman citizenship are usefully spelt out by Augustus in his letters to Seleukos of Rhosos, most of them conveniently translated in Johnson et al. (1961) 110f. On Egypt as a special case, see Galsterer (1986) 20f. and Hobson (1993), the evidence being largely too late for my purposes (showing, later, the fuller

penetration of Roman law than anywhere else; but, among a hundred petitions from Oxyrhynchus, "none that invokes the law is earlier than the third century," p. 203).

30. Johnson et al. (1961) 113, 123f.; or SEG 8.13=Riccobono et al. (1968–72) 1.415f., a notorious text regarding violation of sepulture, which Zulueta (1932) 185 dates to around the turn of the era, as does Visscher (1963) 161ff., 175, noticing the mix of legal traditions.

31. Caninius a protégé of Agrippa, then of Augustus, made procurator of Achaea, later IIvir quinquennalis of Corinth, Spawforth (1996) 173, 176. On Greek Antonii, e.g. Spawforth (1996) 170, 176; on the many homonyms of M. Insteius, likely a legatus-governor for Antony and then his fleet-wing commander, Nigdélis (1994) 219f. Antony's quaestor M. Barbatius Pollio explains some homonyms, too, Spawforth (1996) 170.

32. "The number of Roman colonists was small," says Kienast (1982) 382, adding, "Even these few colonies were of a strongly Greek character, most of them, from the start, whether because the settlers themselves were of Greek origin or because the former Greek citizens were sooner or later accepted into the new Roman colonies." Walbank (1997) 97 supposes that at Corinth the majority of the settlers were of Greek origin (and Strabo 8.23 says most settlers there were freedmen), as they would have been, so Brunt (1971) 252 says, at many other Caesarian foundations; cf. Wilkes (1969) 200, 231, on Dalmatia. Brunt offers some guesses (256, 263) for the total of Romans overseas, civilians and veterans in both east and west, which are perhaps not worth using for another guess at the strictly eastern portion.

33. Suet., Claud. 16.2, a splendidus vir Graeciaeque provinciae princeps, compare Dio 60.17.4f. of A.D. 43, where many other easterners by the same emperor are similarly punished, being "unworthy of citizenship"; on publicizing of law, notice the obvious preponderance of senatusconsulta and imperial and proconsular decrees and edicts, while statutes rarely received the same publicity, Crawford (1988) 127f.

34. Rizakis (1995) 374 on Macedonia, 377f. and 382 on quick fading away of Latin among immigrants; Schmitt (1983) 556f. and Millar (1993) 527 with the same term, on Beirut a "Sprachinsel"; MacMullen (1966) 3 and Schmitt 563 on Greek loanwords; Burnett et al. (1992) 1, 1.361, 650f., Beirut coins in Latin, cf. Corinth (1966) 18 n. 5; but Levick (1967) 131 is right to point out that Latin on coins does not prove Latin on the streets; Corinth (1966) 19f., inscriptions overwhelmingly Latin but in official texts under Augustus; and Levick (1967) 90, 130ff., and Rizakis (1995) 383 on the fate of Latin in the east generally, fading in colonies by Hadrian's day.

35. Christol and Drew-Bear (1995) 121, 126, 132; iidem (1999) [pagination not available] collecting a number of Latin inscriptions by Antioch's veteran colonists; Collas-Heddeland (1999) passim, with a passage quoted on nomikoi; and such bilingual official texts as the Res Gestae and the provincial edict of 9 B.C., below, n. 42.

36. Eadem (at the second page of what I have seen only in manuscript).

37. At Prusa, a tribe named after Antonius, Seyrig (1929) 95 n. 4; Corinth (1966) 23; Levick (1967) 78, the tribe "Romana"; 76, Roman vici-names at Antioch, also at Lystra; Millar (1993) 354f., Anthedon, etc.

38. Above, n. 13, on Pompey's Pontic cities; Strabo 14.664, Soloi; a sample of Sebaste-towns in Kienast (1982) 382 and of Caesarea's in RE s.v. "Anazarba" col. 2101, "Mazaca" col. 956, and Leveau (1984) 18.

39. Dreizehnter (1975) 239f. on Pompey's Pontic cities, Callu (1993) 125 on his Syrian ones and Caesar's with their new eras, all using their coins to advertise the change; Downey (1961) 157 and Burnett et al. (1992) 1, 1.24, Caesarian eras on Syrian coins.

40. In Republican times, a month Rhomaios at Pergamum, Mellor (1975) 161; RE s.v. "Anazarba" col. 2101 (19 B.C.); dating from Actium at Amisus etc., Callu (1993) 126f., or from refounding by Augustus, Mitchell (1993) 1.86; Grether (1946) 232, Mellor 161, and Samuel (1972) 183f., on Cyprus' calendar with months Livios, Octavios, Neronaios, etc.; in Egypt, the month Sebastos, Schwartz (1944) 266ff.

41. Snyder (1964) 153, 159; variations on Augustal days in Egypt, idem (1938) 198, 204, 229; other red-letter days of his ascendance, see Herz (1978) 1147, or Snyder (1940) 233, Gangra celebrates Augustus' pontificate day, the association of resident Romans leading the way.

42. The bilingual OGIS 458=Johnson et al. (1961) 119; a part also in Apamea Cibotus, CIL 3.2240; Samuel (1972) 174ff., 181f.; Price (1984) 54f.; and Hänlein-Schäfer (1985) 11. Local calendars were brought into workable synchrony with the Julian in 30 B.C.

43. Herz (1978) 1147, 1150f.; Sept. 23rd celebrated at Athens, Stamires (1957) 264; and the Paphlagonian oath, IGRR 3.137=Johnson et al. (1961) 127.

44. Moretti (1953) 150–67 passim, including games for the princes; cf. Sherk (1969) 257f., Sardian agones for a proconsul in early 1st century B.C.

45. Mellor (1975); above, n. 18; Millar (1993) 261 on Syria, briefly; Le Glay (1991) 118f. on Asian preliminaries; Hänlein-Schäfer (1985) 5f., 16; and Price (1984). The latter's insistence on such cult as being a means for Greeks "to represent to themselves" (or a like phrase) great figures without hurt to their own pride (pp. 25, 29f., 47, 52, 225f., rulers to be accepted by "the proudly autonomous Greek city") may be right, but remains a conjecture.

46. Mellor (1975) 80, 67, the Roma-cult by the date here of 45 B.C. having much earlier models. Cf. Dio 51.20.6, Romans at Nicaea in 29 may worship Roma and the deified Caesar.

47. OGIS 456=IGRR 4.39; Zanker (1988) 304ff.

48. J. and L. Robert (1980) 423ff.; iidem (1981) 426; Moretti (1980) 36ff.; Derow and Forrest (1982) 80 lines 26f., 86ff. (offering a 3rd-cent. date as another possibility).

49. Iliac Augustan coins with Aeneas and Anchises, Burnett et al. (1992) 1,1.391.

50. On Alexandria-day, see Snyder (1940) 231 or Herz (1978) 1147; on the Actian Games at Nikopolis, Moretti (1953) 150 or Rieks (1970) 111.

51. Merkelbach (1974) 192, an inscription of Naples where Olympia offers rules for the Augustus-games to be set up there.

52. Lv. 41.20, at Antioch, Robert (1940) 263f., and shows actual or wished-for in Delos among local Roman associations, to judge from frescoes; by Lucullus, ibid., Plut., Lucullus 23; also in the 50s B.C. in Laodicea in Phrygia and at Mylasa in the next decade, Cic., Att. 6.3.5 and Philipp. 6.5, the references in Robert (pp. 33, 241), with (p. 148) IGRR 3.527 at Lydai in Lycia near Cape Artemision of late Augustan date, gladiatorial shows with venationes also repeatedly offered not only in his own city but (in the restored text, rightly) in other Lycian cities, by a rich and prominent Roman citizen, head of the imperial cult in the province, descendant of a ?freedman of Caesar, C. Iulius Heliodorus, cf. Hicks (1889) 58; the evidence for anything pre-Augustan dismissed by Woolf (1994) 126 as only a whim of generals or, at Antiochus' capi-

tal, as "une fantasie royale . . . sans lendemain," in Robert's words. In Ancyra the evidence begins in a few years after Augustus' death, Mitchell (1993) 1.108, and (p. 111), like Robert and Leveau (1984) 203, Mitchell sees an essential link between it and emperor worship.

53. Vitruv. 5.1.1f.; on Herod's gladiatorial displays and *venationes* in Caesarea, for which Augustus sent him everything needed from his own supply, Jos., AJ 16.136–41, with an *amphitheatron* ready, BJ 1.415; another in Jerusalem, AJ 15.268–75, ready for games in 28 B.C., cf. Lämmer (1975) 97ff., 130–34 (the Caesarean games in 11 B.C.?); 99 (Samaria); 141 n. 20; and, correcting misinterpretation of the term *amphitheatron*, p. 117, 120ff., it was really what is called the hippodrome. By A.D. 70 there were facilities in many other Palestinian cities, BJ 7.24, 38, 95.

54. Downey (1961) 155f., from Malalas; Strabo 17.1.10, *amphitheatron* and *stadion*.

55. Engels (1990) 34.

56. Clavel-Lévêque and Smajda (1980) 34, the term *centuriatio* known only from the first quarter of the first century A.D.

57. *Centuriazione* (1993) 20; Attolini (1984) on Falbe; Attolini (1984a) 170f. Figs. 159f., the orientation of Padua and Pola apparently identical; Ramilli (1973) and Attolini (1984a) on Kandler, who published only in 1866.

58. Galsterer (1992) 415f., 419ff.; Calzolari (1993) 152; Walbank (1997) 125, at Corinth, a facility for *munera* perhaps not an amphitheater; Schubert (1996) 44, 70.

59. Schubert (1996) 26, Larissa as an example of pre-Roman cadastration; Lopez Paz (1994) 382, Patras in 16 B.C.; Walbank (1997) 102, Corinth of the late 40s B.C.; and Rizakis (1997) 26f.

60. Hinrichs (1989) 125 on Pannonia, adding (170) perhaps Beirut; Lopez Paz (1994) 368f., 382; Bradford (1957) 184 with Fig. 17 on Salona, 178ff. on Iader and Augustus *parens coloniae*, 175f. on Pola; on the latter, also Favory (1983) 130f., detecting a *iugerum*; on Iader and Parentium, Suic (1976) 98ff.; and Rizakis (1997) 26f., on Nicopolis.

61. Lopez Paz (1994) 107ff., 173f., 184, 165–203 passim.

62. Walbank (1997) 116; RE s.v. "Parentium" col. 1462l; and Suic (1976) 128, 130, city street grids, with 150f., Iader's forum.

63. Sherwin-White (1983) 156; Levick (1967) 38f., the Via Sebaste begun in 6 B.C.; Alföldy (1991) 301, CIL 3.6974, 12401a–c, etc.

64. CIL 11.6218f., at Fanum Fortunae, Augustus *murum dedit* in A.D. 9/10; Waelkens (1987) 100, Pisidia; CIL 5.525, Iader, *murum turresque fecit* in 33 B.C.; RE s.v. "Tergeste."

65. Downey (1961) 155; Bammer (1976–77) Beibl. 84; *Inschriften von Ephesos* (1981) 96, the bilingual of A.D. 4/14; Coulton (1987) 73; Kienast (1982) 359.

66. Yegül (1992) 57–63, on independent development of Roman and Greek baths in the 1st century; Farrington (1995) 45ff. on central Italian 1st century B.C. baths arrangements finding their way into Lycian baths by 1st century A.D.; Downey (1961) 155, 171, at Antioch by Caesar and by Agrippa; at Elaiussa-Sebaste, Keil and Wilhelm (1931) 222 and Dodge (1990) 112. Notice also Augustus' rebuilding of Paphos, much damaged (by quake?) in 20/19, Rieks (1970) 112.

67. MacMullen (1959) 226; Brunt (1974) 161, 173, and 183: "conceivably the cohort itself," *coh. Apulae*, of which the man was prefect, "was employed in the construction." On the architect, who died in Verona, cf. Donderer (1996) 202 on ILS 7729, with

(p. 153) another army *architekton* in Egypt in A.D. 18, and still another at work on colonizing in Italy in Triumviral times, Blume et al. (1967) 1.244 lines 5f. (*Liber coloniarum*). For Caesar's projects in Antioch, it is "clear that Caesar had in his suite Roman technicians (presumably military engineers, who had to possess many talents) capable of instituting building"—so, Downey (1961) 170.

68. Basilicas: Downey (1961) 155 and Roller (1998) 82f. on Antioch, datable in or soon after 47 B.C., and Alzinger (1972–75) Beibl. 250f. on Ephesus; also at Corinth, Ward-Perkins (1981) 258; the Italian-style basilica of the last quarter of the 1st century in Corinth, ibid. 256 and De Ruyt (1983) 264; Wilkes (1969) 207, 368; Ward-Perkins (1981) 314, 317 on Heliopolis, noting the column-capitals imitative of those of the Temple of Castor in Rome; another podium-temple with other Italian-type features at Antioch-in-Pisidia, Lyttelton (1987) 41f.

69. Walbank (1997) 112 Fig. 6, 116, and the Latin inscription, p. 121.

70. Gros (1996) 1.63; CIL 5.50=ILS 2229; RE s.v. "Pola" col. 1227 (E. Polaschek, 1951), suggesting a date soon after Actium, but that is a little early for Gros. For another Augustan arch, see example at Ephesos, Gros p. 84; Alzinger (1974) 1.34 and 2.14 Fig. 17.

71. Balty (1991) 456f., 562.

72. Woodward (1923–24) 131ff., 154; idem (1925–26) 204; F. S. Johansen (1967) 42; RE s.v. "Eurykles" col. 1330. Compare late Augustan imperial portrait statues (Augustus, Livia, Tiberius) at the Arsinoë amphitheater, Clavel (1970) 495ff.

73. Frézouls (1982) 388 (Antioch, Malal. 9.279, 288) and 416f.

74. De Ruyt (1983) 140, 158ff., 246, 252ff.

75. Thompson (1987) 4ff., marble-paved with a fountain-house, and the supposition that the temple of ca. 20 B.C. to Augustus on the Acropolis recognized his gifts to the city, Hoff (1994) 110.

76. De Ruyt (1983) 226f. on SIG 2.783, and 264, Mantinea, and 57, on Corinth's market with 50 shops; Ward-Perkins (1981) 258; West (1931) 102f., 124, a *macellum piscarium*.

77. Marble used as facing throughout the late Augustan theater at Sparta, Woodward (1924–25); below, in Herod's buildings; paving at Antioch-in-Pisidia, Lyttelton (1987) 41; marble generally, Dodge (1990) 109f.; at Corinth, Ward-Perkins (1981) 258; at Athens, Thompson (1987) 6.

78. Brick used in *bouleuteria*, Balty (1991) 562; at Sparta, Woodward (1925–26) 179 and Dodge (1987) 107; concrete at Ephesus, Alzinger (1972–75) Beibl. 250; at Corinth but only in foundations, Ward-Perkins (1981) 258, and at Ephesus for "petit appareil," 273, or in a Cappadocian city, Elaeussa, for reticulate work in a baths, Dodge (1987) 107 and Dodge (1990) 112; a general treatment of concrete use in Waelkens (1987), e.g. 95–100 at Pergamon ("petit appareil") and Ephesus (Roman-constructed Tropaion, temple by Antony?, temple of Caesar and Roma). *Opus caementicium* is also found, of various degrees of recognizable Roman-ness, and the alternation of bands of *reticulatum* and *quadratum*. Connection of Italian-type work with customers of western origin is noted by Waelkens (101).

79. Thompson (1987) 7.

80. Brandon (1996) 28, 40; Roller (1998) 135, 138.

81. Walls, in Leveau (1984) 18, 32, and Roller (1998) 143; water-works at Caesarea, ibid. 42, 46f., 136, 142; theater, 42 and 152, marble, Jos., BJ 1.408, amphitheater, Roller

140f. (and above, n. 52) and a "Capitolium," 138f.; an Augusteum on a 15' podium at Samaria, Barag (1993) 7f.; vaulting, 98f., reticulate stone-work, 99, and vaulting, 98f. and Ward-Perkins (1981) 310f., with concrete structure in theater.

82. Jos., AJ 16.5.1 (136–39), in 12 B.C.

83. Baths at Masada, ibid. 313; paving of Antioch's "show" street, Roller (1998) 216f.; amphitheater entertainment, e.g. Jos., AJ 15.267ff.; 16.136, Caesarea.

84. Jos., BJ 1.21.7 (414); the gym, e.g. at Damascus, "un édifice symbolique d'un polis grecque," Will (1994) 34f.

85. AJ 15.8.1 (267–71), in reference to the amphitheater, theater, games, and musical compositions in Jerusalem, exceeding all πολιτεία or σεμνοπρέπεια through his φιλοτιμία τοῦ διάσημον αὐτῷ γενέσθαι τὴν ἐπίδειξιν; compare 15.9.5 (326f.), he rules partly through inspiring fear, partly through his μεγαλόψυχος . . . πρὸς τὴν βασιλείαν εὐπρεπῶς; 328, reference to his φιλοτιμία and θεραπεία, flattering attention toward Augustus and the Romans; 138, Augustus praises his μεγαλοψαχία; and again, 16.5.3 (149), his display at Olympia of φιλοτιμία; finally, the one central motive in his personality, totally possessing him, φιλότιμος ὤν, "since he was so given to great displays" (153).

86. Caesar's great generosity striking in Suet., Caes. 28, Caesar Italiae Galliarumque et Hispanarum, Asiae quoque et Graeciae potentissimas urbes praecipuis operibus exornans; but notice his freedman, above, n. 52; the title "benefactor," above, n. 18; on Gabinius, cf. Barag (1993) 4 and Roller (1998) 98ff.; Athens, Thompson (1987) 5f.; on the Greek tradition, good Augustan illustrations in e.g. Gauthier (1985) 13f., and the whole history of the ethos, ibid. passim.

87. Bejor (1979) 130f. and Kienast (1982) 361f. gather the Italian evidence (much); on Balbus, Bejor (1979) 129 and the crucial texts, Suet., Caes. 81.3 and Aug. 29.8.

88. Most evidence for these values can be found in the Empire (in most part valid retrospectively), cf. MacMullen (1988) 81f., 101f., 108, and idem (1990) 196; but there has been much discussion of the Republican evidence. I would single out for recommendation (as does Deniaux [1993] 7f.) the older treatments by Gelzer (1912; 1969) and the infallible Brunt (1988), chap. 7, re-writing his article of 1964; otherwise, Deniaux herself.

89. IGLS 718=FIRA, ed. 2, 1.308f.=Johnson et al. (1961) 110f.

90. Plassart (1926) 441, the demos of Thebes pays honor to M. Licinius Crassus, τὸν ἑαυτοῦ πάτρωνα; IG ed. min. 4, 1.592, Epidaurus erects a statue to C. Iulius Lachares, "patron and benefactor;" Agrippa declared (in Latin) patronus of a voting tribe at Corinth, West (1931) 15.

91. Imperial cult rites are sometimes specified and, then, explicitly Greek, e.g. at Gythion, above, n. 18, or at Mytilene, OGIS 456; on the Delian Competeliasts' rites, Mellor (1975) 65f., Hellenistic in style, I suppose. See note 87.

92. Above, n. 64, and Suic (1976) 145, Iader; at Aenon, Kienast (1982) 349 n. 157; the Capitoline triad in Athens, Walbank (1997) 112 Fig. 6.

93. Millar (1993) 280f.

94. Bulard (1908) 18, 21–40, 88; Bezerra de Meneses and Sarian (1973) 79f., 99f., 104.

95. Above, at n. 41; Fränkel (1895) 264.

96. "That monstrous festival, the so-called Rosalia after holy Easter, an evil custom in the rural districts," says a twelfth century source, Tomaschek (1868) 370, but it contin-

ued as feasts of SS. Nicholas and John, Fränkel (1895) 266, and "of the Trinity" throughout the Balkans and Roumania, Mihaescu (1993) 300, so to the present day in the Eastern Church, Delehaye et al. (1920) 193 and RE s.v. "Rosalia" 1115. Occurrences in Macedonia reported by Perdrizet (1900) 299ff., doubted as Italian (not rather native) by Robert (1937) 244 n. 3, but later accepted, cf. J. and L. Robert, REG 83 (1970) 512; 85 (1972) 408; 86 (1973) 392; in Asia, doubted as the origin of rites of rose-burning, by Picard (1922) 199, but in other respects the Rosalia are clearly attested, Fränkel (1895) 262, Leclercq in Dictionnaire d'arch. chrétienne et de liturgie s.v. "Rosalies" (1950), SEG 1.330 (Thrace, a. 138), Hermann and Polatkan (1969) 8ff., 144 (early date); Sahin (1979–82) 1.71a, 87a; 2.49a, 199a; Schwertheim (1985) 83 (graveside banquet scene); and Becker-Bertau (1986) 104.

97. Christol and Drew-Bear (1999) MS. 23ff. Professor Drew-Bear kindly tells me that similar burials can be found in rural regions of Phrygia and Galatia. Cormack (1997) 139–48 offers a good survey of burial practices in Asia Minor without, however, supplying anything relative to Augustus' time nor, in fact, much for later periods that looks Roman.

98. Hoët-van Cauwenberghe (1999) MS. 1ff., 10f.

99. Above, n. 16; Box (1932) 180; Rizakis (1996) 15ff., with my thanks to Prof. Drew-Bear for steering me toward the publication.

CHAPTER II: AFRICA

1. Marius' colonists inland I pass over in my account, but cf. e.g. Pflaum (1973) 57 or Freis (1980) 360f. As to Sittius, after his death in 42 the Four Cirta Colonies were absorbed into "Old" Africa, cf. below, n. 18. Regarding "Sarnia," from the river of that name in the Campanian region, and the other three "nicknames," see Romanelli (1959) 135f. There is doubt as to some "Caesarian" colonies, whether of Caesar or Augustus: see Broughton (1929) 54f.; Vittinghoff (1951) 82–84 n. 5, 111, 147; Chevallier (1958) 88; Romanelli (1959) 138, 140, 185 (castella); Brunt (1971) 236, 593f.; Pflaum (1973) 58f.; Lassère (1982) 410f., 413; and Gascou (1982) 141; on Carthage only, Le Glay (1985) 238.

2. Brunt (1971) 261 suggesting 2–3000, accepted by Yavetz (1983) 145 (the 3,000 to Carthage in 29 B.C. are anomalous; and Romanelli preferred a much smaller coregroup of colonists, 300–500); Vittinghoff (1951) 23 and Lopez Paz (1994) 173f. on distributions by military rank.

3. Romanelli (1959) 196, Pflaum (1973) 58, Lassère (1982) 413, and Broughton (1929) 55 n. 64.

4. Février (1982) 336, listing possibly six settlements ex nihilo; cf. Kolendo and Kotula (1977) 178; on ILS 9400 and Augustan villages like Suturnurca or Medeli southwest of Carthage, see Vittinghoff (1951) 114, Romanelli (1959) 197, idem (1974) 186, and the map attaching to Pflaum (1970) 80, 82; on the pattern of Augustan policy, Desanges (1980) 82.

5. My settler-total excludes the civilians from Rome (below, chap. 5 n. 22). For the whole of the African provinces, Deman (1975) 58 n. 181 quotes an estimate of 1,300,000 (Lezine's) as being a third of the total population, another (G.-C. Picard's) as bringing the total to just over four millions. These figures seem to refer to the height of the empire, for whatever value they may have even at that date.

6. Hinrichs (1989) 122f.
7. Chevallier (1958) 97, cf. legionary road-building Oea-Sabratha later in the reign, Di Vita (1982) 576, and around Maktar and Sousse also, M'Charek (1987–89) 153, 160ff.; wall-building, *Aen.* 1.263f., 365, 423; at Cyrene, Leveau (1987) 152; at Curubis, Utica, and Uzitta, cf. Jouffroy (1986) 176f., 198; also in Mauretania Caesariensis, Leveau (1984) 26.
8. Favory (1983) 132 and Trousset (1995) 76, 78 (olive trees); one program of centuriation centered in the camp of Leg. III at Ammaedara, ibid. 73; the legion and surveying, and eventual effects of "sédentarisation," in Le Bohec (1989) 538f.
9. Chevallier (1958) 88 n. 3; compare that of Pola, still smaller. The *centuria*=ca. 50ha.
10. Trousset (1995) 72ff., five different centuriations in Tunisia, but in regard to the two at Carthage, current opinion, not Trousset, favors a date of 146 or immediately after for the land-survey.
11. Pre-Roman gridding, in Chevallier (1958) 64, speaking of several regions in Algeria, and Mattingly (1997) 120, perhaps not speaking of grids but only *termini*, ditches, &c.
12. Kolendo (1985) 57f. on M. Caelius Rufus, C. Rabirius Postumus, M. Vipsanius Agrippa, and (61) the ancestors behind Nero's confiscations, along with still others.
13. Broughton (1929) 38, 61, and Jacques (1993) 63ff., on Caelii and L. Aelius Lamia (cos. A.D. 3 or praet. 42 B.C.?); ibid. on L. Domitius Ahenobarbus (procos. Afr. 12 B.C.), and M. Lurius Varus of Actian fame—these three being only among several possibilities.
14. Clavel-Lévêque and Smajda (1980) 34, the term *villa* in known use from late Augustan years on.
15. An estimate of the likely size of a veteran's plot at 15 *iugera*, in Garnsey (1978) 230.
16. Lassère (1979) 83ff. (vague about dates but generally descriptive of post-Augustan times); Mattingly (1995) 70f., 140f., with a warning on page 160: "It is assumed here that the colonial age [i.e. 19th and 20th century] dichotomy between African nomads and 'Roman' sedentary farmers is now discredited."
17. Broughton (1929) 53, 64, but the evidence is exiguous.
18. Jouffroy (1986) 198, Curubis' II*vir* in 46 B.C.; Gascou (1981) 324.
19. T. Herennius, *eques Romanus* at Leptis, in Cic., II *Verr.* 5.155, perhaps with known descendants, cf. Birley (1998) 3; chartering at Musti, by Caesar, but only with Latin rights; Utica and Hippo Regius by Augustus: Broughton (1929) 51, Vittinghoff (1951) 84, and Gascou (1982) 141; Portus Magnus, Freis (1980) 370; and not Semta, Pflaum (1970) 82; on *conventus*, Broughton (1929) 39f., 43f.; and especially Lassère (1982) 405f.: Hadrumetum, Thapsus, Utica.
20. Broughton (1929) 70, 211f., 217; Romanelli (1959) 193; Le Glay (1985) 238f.
21. Desanges (1980) 82; on *curiae*, Kotula (1968) 31ff., 48, and passim; Di Vita (1982) 539f.; on their size etc., Duncan-Jones (1982) 277–82; Curubis etc., Broughton (1929) 55 and Di Vita (1982) 538, adding other Punic anomalies attested at least in a later (2nd century) period, 543ff.; other centers in "Old" Africa with *sufetes*, Pflaum (1970) 85, Kotula (1973) 75f., and G.-C. Picard (1974) 131, Thugga, also with *portae*; the tri-lingual inscription of ca. 50 B.C. dated by *sufetes* in Uthina, Oudhna (1998) 38f.; and Volubilis' son and heroic commander of armed levies against the rebel Aedemon, M. Valerius Severus son of Bostar, *sufes*, aedile, *duumvir*, etc., who won Roman

citizenship for the city from Claudius in A.D. 44, Chatelain (1942) 17 no. 56 and 35 no. 116.

22. Oea and Sabratha, cf. Burnett et al. (1992) 1.206; Le Glay (1968) 215 and Musso (1995) 335, Leptis' *sufetes* even into 3rd cent.; Benabou (1981) 254; Di Vita-Evrard (1981) 199, dating the status only to Vespasian; and Sznycer (1975) 66.

23. Reynolds and Ward-Perkins (1952) 97, no. 319, of 8 B.C., the *sufes* being also the *flamen* in charge of ritual, and the underlying Punic text of the inscription here noted; also Février (1982) 349f. on the text, and Ward-Perkins (1970) 15 and De Ruyt (1983) 104 on the *macellum*; on the theater, Gros (1996) 292f. with Fig. 346. and Brouquier-Reddé (1992) 166 on Ceres Augusta. Carthage perhaps also had an Augustan theater, Ros (1996) 483.

24. Jouffroy (1986) 180, 191, IRT 324; the paved forum of the governor, IRT 520; Forum Vetus, Ward-Perkins (1982) 30; on the beginning of marble at the end of the 1st cent. B.C., Musso (1995) 337.

25. Temples, in Smajda (1978) 176ff.; Ward-Perkins (1981) 373 (stairs compared to temple of Venus Genetrix) and idem (1982) 30, 43; Floriani Squarciapino (1966) 82, stairs compared to temple of *divus Caesar*. The temple's style and stairs may be found in a number of later African temples; date of completion, A.D. 14–19; its earlier service to the local (?) Milk'Ashtart, in Brouquier-Reddé (1992) 88. On Capitolia, Jouffroy (1986) 183ff., Carthage, and Kienast (1982) 353, Sabratha.

26. The *curia* apparently late Augustan, on the site of a Hellenistic-style *synedrion*, cf. Floriani Squarciapino (1966) 85.

27. Ward-Perkins (1982) 15 (and the same influences visible in 1st century B.C. Utica's column capitals).

28. Ibid. 32; Smajda (1978) 183; an older grid, ibid. 173 and Di Vita (1982) 553ff., who would throw the grid-system back to the first half of the 1st cent., around the "Old" forum, cf. Musso (1995) 335.

29. IRT 520, cf. Floriani Squarciapino (1966) 81 and *Buried City* (1964) 85, *pace* Di Vita (1982) 555f., who would apply the donative inscription of Cn. Papirius Carbo, governor, to the small temple.

30. A good plan of the city in MacDonald (1986) 40; proportions of space-use in MacMullen (1974) 62f. and G.-C. Picard (1975) 110, instancing Cuicul, Thuburbo Maius, among sites made Roman in Augustus' times. For Carthage's amphitheater, see (*pace* Bomgardner [1989] 97f., proposing a Trajanic date) Jouffroy (1986) 195 and Ros (1996) 462 n. 35, 483; on Utica's amphitheater, Caes., BC 2.25; on Curubis' wall of 45 B.C., Jouffroy 198.

31. Di Vita-Evrard (1981) 198; Burnett et al. (1992) 27, 185, and 187–204 on the cities of Proconsularis; Alexandropoulos (1987) 65ff., 72f.; imitation of Roman standards carries into bronze coinage, cf. 68 n. 18; for deities on coins, 72ff.

32. Brouquier-Reddé (1992) 44; Di Vita (1982) 552.

33. On the general subject of *interpretatio* I limit myself to representative good pages by Le Glay (1975) and a glimpse into a debate sharpened by Benabou, cf. Benabou (1976) 373, with, e.g., Mattingly (1995) 38f., 166. On Liber Pater at Leptis Minus as Italic, not Punic (=Shadrap), Seston (1967) 73ff., endorsed by Lassère (1982) 406.

34. Brouquier-Reddé (1992) 88ff.

35. Ibid. 201, on IRT 301 of A.D. 6; Di Vita (1982) 558 on *numen* cult; located in a *sacellum* in the *chalcidicum*, Floriani Squarciapino (1966) 54.

36. At Sousse, Cintas (1947) 48, a mid-1st cent. change in sacrifices; at Carthage, where the credibility of Tert., *Apol.* 9.2ff. is central, cf. ibid. 75ff., 78; Freis (1980) 367; Brown (1991) 23, 25; and Lancel (1992) 248.

37. Le Glay (1968) 237f., on Thugga under Tiberius, the first known Saturn-temple.

38. CIL 10.6104, the freedman M. Caelius Phileros.

39. Gsell (1972) 8.206ff.; Alföldi (1979) 69f.; and Leveau (1984) 13.

40. Vittinghoff (1951) 116; Brunt (1971) 596; Pflaum (1973) 59; Leveau (1981) 319; idem (1984) 16; Mackie (1983) 332, 340, 347f.; Oudhna (1998) 42, 216; and Freis (1980) 361f. on numbers of settlers, a thousand or less.

41. Fittschen (1979a) 227; Alföldi (1979) 70; the *mima* and Iulia Mimesis, and Leontius, in Gsell (1972) 8.236.

42. Gsell (1972) 8.245f.; on marble and copying of Rome, etc., Pensabene (1982) 120, 125, 132f. 136f.; Leveau (1983) 349f.; idem (1984) 16, colossal statue; Frézouls (1982) 391, chapels.

43. Leveau (1983) 350 and idem (1984) 37ff. (amphitheater), 51 and 61, hydraulic works; also idem and Paillet (1983) 231.

44. Février (1982) 334, pre-Roman at Utica; Di Vita (1982) 555, Leptis; Leveau (1984) 76f.

45. Ibid. 20, 26, 32; idem (1987) 153 Fig. 1, showing a couple of dozen pre-Augustan African centers with some defensive periphery; another 18 of Augustan date, including 11 in Juba's kingdom, and Caesarea's of 4,460m.

46. Euzennat and Hallier (1986) 73, 89f.

47. Leveau (1983) 353, architects?; Gsell (1972) 8.219 n. 1; Leveau (1981) 314f., 316.

48. Crawford (1985) 246f., 249; Burnett et al. (1992) 1, 1.27; Kienast (1982) 410.

49. Gsell (1972) 8.219, 222; Alföldi (1979) 70; Fittschen (1979a) 230.

50. Jouffroy (1986) 183ff., Banasa, Lixus, Sala.

51. *Buried City* (1966) Pl. 95 and caption at rear of volume; date, fixed by the paving inscription (above, n. 24); cf. at Gigthis, a *tabula lusoria* of a type common at Rusicade, Timgad, and Trier, in Constans (1914) 284 (notice, all Roman colonies).

52. Amadassi Guzzo (1988) 27 points out errors in the name of that other Leptis notable referred to above, Tapapius Rufus the donor of the theater, his name neither correctly nor traditionally Punic, nor Roman; Mattingly (1995) 58, citing A. R. Birley's study on the taking of Roman names randomly.

53. Apul., *Apol.* 118 [98.8] , in Constans (1916) 19; Amadassi Guzzo (1988) 23; Volterra (1952) 175f., a forum text of A.D. 53, with confusions in its Latin translation, 182ff.; and Mattingly (1995) 160f.

54. Mattingly (1995) on neo-Punic texts in 1st-century Leptis, often with Latin added; on coins, Polomé (1983) 526 and Burnett et al. (1992) 1.206, 208; Amadassi Guzzo (1988) 24f., with other contaminations of Latin texts and formulae by Punic conventions.

55. Brunt (1971) 250f. offers a little (but adequate) evidence on the raising of natives to citizenship in Utica or Simitthus; and Freis (1980) 368 reaches the same conclusion: "in the deduction of African colonies, the very great probability is that the native elite were given Roman citizenship." He instances a *duumvir* of 20 B.C., C. Iulius Malchio, at Curubis, a citizen with a Punic *cognomen* of sorts.

56. Poinssot (1959) 93ff., 103 on grammar and spelling mistakes, and names mostly Punic, all of Punic descent.

57. The focus in "Old" Africa and Numidia must be on the persistence of Punic and of Libyan=Berber. On names, Benabou (1976) 370, 374 has interesting points to make; Benzina Ben Abdallah (1990) 510, 514 offers new evidence; and Millar (1968) was full and careful, though now needing a little correction from Camps (1990–92) 39ff.

58. Gsell (1972) 8.232f.; Hesnard and Lenoir (1985) 49f.; on later (Flavian) production of fine pottery elsewhere in Africa, see Le Glay (1968) 231ff.; on importation, Kenrick (1996) 38ff.

59. The shield with "ob cives servatos," Galinsky (1996) 90.

60. Ibid. 150; Spaeth (1994) 95f.; cf. above, chap. 1 at n. 48, the relief with Romulus and Remus.

61. D. E. E. Kleiner (1985) 134, following P. Zanker.

62. Smajda (1978) 178, sculpture "directly related to the art of the Augustan court, demonstrating a loyalty to the dominant sculptural ideals"; and Bejor (1987) 104f., 109 (a similar early statue group in Hippo Regius).

63. Gsell (1972) 8.225f., comparing cuirassed statues of *divus Iulius* or Augustus in various sites of Rome; Leveau (1984) 16; and Fittschen (1979a) 232.

64. Fittschen (1979) 209f.; on coins, 491 Pl. 58 with text, p. 490, on the locks of hair, as his son Ptolemy copies the hair-style of Tiberius, p. 212 (date, late Augustan).

65. Gsell (1972) 8.246, 248ff.; Fittschen (1979a) 231, 234, 236, 238f.

66. Gsell (1972) 8.248, the Mahdia wreck off the southern Tunisian coast; but his dating is now to be corrected, to perhaps the 80s B.C., cf. Hallenkemper Salies (1994) 1.15, 21f., with corroborative evidence elsewhere in the same volume.

67. Leveau (1984) 202.

68. Le Glay (1968) 241ff., mostly on post-Augustan art; G.-C. Picard (1982) 181f.; and Mattingly (1995) 162.

CHAPTER III: SPAIN

1. Garcia y Bellido (1966) gives a careful summary of the evidence.

2. Even in the Ebro valley there were walled centers, cf. Dupré (1985) 285 or Gorges (1979) 24; on the northwest, Keay (1995) 320 and Richardson (1995) 346ff. and (1996) 157f.; Fear (1996) 24, on Augustus' resettlements of populations, Florus 2.33.52; add Strabo 3.2.15 and 3.3.5; Florus again, with Dio 54.11.5, regarding Agrippa's similar policy (19 B.C.), in Hanson (1988) 56; specific locations of resettlement, Diego Santos (1975) 545; Burillo Mozota (1991) 37–42 on Ebro valley towns as real centers of administration; Rodriguez Colmenero (1996) 157f., 182 on *castella*; Garcia y Bellido (1972) 481 on *vici*; and Braudel (1972) 1.34 and passim, on the dominant role of geographical features in acculturation, in the northwest and elsewhere.

3. Alföldy (1995) 122, the original Valentia destroyed, then re-established by Augustus; Lepida=Celsa virtually *ab ovo* in 44 B.C., Beltrán Lloris (1991) 135, or *contra*, it was a settlement on top of a native predecessor, Dupré (1985) 287; ibid., Caesaraugusta founded from scratch; and some unnamed entirely new centers, Keay (1995) 303; also, towns grown out of camps, ibid. and Garcia Marcos and Vidal Encine (1995) 373f., Kienast (1982) 405 n. 184, and Bendala Galán (1990) 36 (Asturica, Bracara, and Lucus Augusti); further, Curchin (1991) 74, Pisoraca grown from *canabae* of Leg. IV

Macedonica; and Emporiae's upper settlement, of ca. 100 B.C., built on and following the plan of the *praetorium* and *principia* of an earlier Roman camp, cf. Mar and Ruiz de Arbulo (1993) 47, 189, 218.

4. The list of sites chosen for the map passes over many disputed points, simply for convenience' sake. A foundation of the Triumviral period (Celsa) is attributed to "Augustus" (Octavian) only for that reason. Ercavica and Iulia Traducta, though Augustan *municipia*, are omitted because their location is unknown, Pompaelo as too questionable; likewise Onoba and Iptuci in Baetica, *pace* Martin-Bueno (1987) 109; and Iluro in the northeast, *pace* Olesti i Vila (1994) 302. For the most part I follow Galsterer (1971), e.g. in generally judging as Caesarian those foundations titled Julian, against other scholars' doubts, or regarding Pompaelo, *pace* Gorges (1979) 26; but in a few cases I depart from his dating, e.g. that of Italica, considered more likely to be by Augustus than by Caesar in the view of Rodriguez Hidalgo and Keay (1995) 399, or Segobriga, which I am persuaded not by Galsterer but by Roddaz (1996) 22 to place under Augustus; or regarding Dianium and Lucentum, likewise omitted by Galsterer, which I include following Alföldy (1995) 122. Galsterer omits *conventus*-centers entirely. But these and other points I think do not disturb the general picture.

5. Blazquez (1988) 214; Brunt (1971) 229, offering a guess at the number of Italians in Spain in the 40s B.C., i.e. before colonizing; compatible suggestions indicated by Roddaz (1996) 18; a Spain total offered by Le Roux (1995) 92; on *conventus* at Metellinum, Caecilius Vicus, Hispalis, and Corduba, see Wilson (1966) 15f. and Richardson (1996) 119; on legions rewarded after 25 B.C. and again in the early 'teens B.C., see Roddaz (1996) 407, 416, Burillo Mozota (1991) 43, and Ariño Gil (1990) 89.

6. Fear (1996) 74f. collects instances.

7. Strabo 3.5.3, Gades' 500 *equites*; Vittinghoff (1951) 72 collects reff. to *conventus* and *equites* in Spanish towns by the early 40s B.C.; on Balbus Maior, cf. RE s.v. "Cornelius" no. 69 cols. 1269f.

8. On Tarraco's title, Dupré i Raventós (1995) 361; Augustan creation of *conventus iuridici*, Dopico Cainzos (1986) 265; *pagi*, Curchin (1985) 342f. and (1991) 125, Baetica; also, exceptionally, around Emerita.

9. Rodriguez Colmenero (1996) 157f., 170 n. 253, 182; Richardson (1996) 157f., the Zoelae near Asturica under Tiberius; Lopez Paz (1994) 14f., on tribal *termini* in Lusitania.

10. Hinrichs (1989) 120 f. quotes CIL 10.680 on an Augustan *praefectus fabrum missus pro censore ad Lusitanos*, and Frontinus, on methods used there and in the Emerita region, in connection with taxation; on centuriated area on a tablet, including the Anas and Lacimurga, cf. Lopez Paz (1994) 28.

11. Details still to be read, Guy (1983) 317 (as in Africa, above, chap. 2 at n. 8); Fear (1996) 267 on oddities of terminology; Lopez Paz (1994) 184 on centuriation used in legal transfer; also, 104, on the double size of the module used at Emerita in 25 B.C., 40 × 20 *actus*; oddities at Caesaraugusta (a module of 15 × 15 *actus*), Ariño Gil (1990) 80 regarding the right bank of the Ebro, or at Italica, too (10 × 6 *actus*), Corzo Sanchez (1982) 305, compared to the normal at, e.g. Corduba, idem (1993) 73, with the boundaries to be read on the map at p. 65; but other colony areas were of the traditional Italian size, cf. Cosa compared with Carteia, etc., in Pfanner (1990) 63f.

12. Olesti i Vila (1994) 299f., 302, the Barcino area; Miret et al. (1991) 50ff. on Catalon-

ian, especially coastal, sites; Italian wine imported in 2nd half of 2nd century to Numantia, the northeast, Ebro, and Baetis, cf. Richardson (1996) 93; export by the earlier 1st century, ibid. 163 and Keay (1990) 129f., 135ff.; Curchin (1991) 127; esp. Gorges (1979) 23f., 267, 350, and idem (1994) 268f.; amphora-production for shipments from 2nd quarter of the 1st century, Revilla Calvo (1995) 314, 324 (Roman names on artifacts in villas); Cornelius Lentulus' vessels, ibid. 333 and Gianfrotta (1982) 475ff.

13. Blech (1993) 72; Keay (1990) 140; Gorges (1994) 270.
14. Etienne and Fontaine (1979) 140, Conimbriga, and Gorges (1979) 26ff., 32, and idem (1994) 270, 279, on mid- to late-Augustan Baetican villas with Arretine and Italic wares; Keay (1992) 304 on Corduba, Hispalis, Urso.
15. Gorges (1979) 32 (quoted); 96 (Emerita).
16. Emerita's size, d'Ors (1974) 262f.; Gorges (1979) 96, idem (1994) 279, and Lopez Paz (1994) 104; large areas left as *subseciva*, unoccupied, in Emerita as elsewhere, Hinrichs (1989) 121; allotments in colonies generally of 50, sometimes only of 25 *iugera*, suggesting a model for Spain, with 100 *iugera* almost sufficing for a curial census, cf. Keppie (1983) 99, 106.
17. Gorges (1979) 122f. and Pl. XXVIII.
18. MacMullen (1968) 339; elaboration by Hopkins (1978) 41, 58, and passim and idem, JRS 70 (1980) 101f., while disclaiming the need to consider taxes paid in kind; adopted by Keay (1990) 120, 128, 141f., and idem (1995) 294; but cf. Plut., *Caes.* 55, [Caes.], *Bell. Afr.* 97.3, 3 million pounds of olive oil exacted in kind from Leptis annually; and Duncan-Jones (1990) 188ff., 192, showing Spain's taxes collected in cash (70s B.C.) or in kind, somewhat later, and Africa's wealth in oil and grain tapped in kind, of which the oil could evidently be turned into cash without difficulty by the governing authorities; for Augustus' census in Spain (as elsewhere), cf. Van Nostrand (1937) 145 and d'Ors (1974) 256.
19. Knapp (1987) 19f.; Burnett et al. (1992) 1.26, Iberian silver rare in early 30s B.C., thereafter only by Carisius in Emerita in the 20s; otherwise, only bronze but from dozens of mints and in vast amounts, 1.66 and Richardson (1996) 145.
20. Beltrán Lloris (1990) 180, milestones at Lérida ca. 80km northwest of Tarraco; Richardson (1996) 91; the map, Abb. 57, with discussion in Nünnerich-Asmus (1993) 123ff., regarding pre-Roman roads, and 132ff. with Abb. 61 on the Augustan program.
21. Palarés (1970) 79; Chevallier (1976) 156 Fig. 32, 157ff.; Pallí Aguilera (1985) 92f., 97f., 109f., 118, and 207 Fig. 9, on the northeast branches and extensions; Richardson (1996) 160f.; Keay (1990) 137; Nünnerich-Asmus (1993) 132 Abb. 61, 133ff.; Sillieres (1994) 305ff. on Ianus Augustus; Bendala Galán (1990) 38 n. 65, no fewer than 15 Augustan milestones in southern stretches of the road.
22. Chevallier (1976) 157; Rodriguez Colmenero (1996a) 289.
23. Curchin (1991) 97.
24. *Hispania Antiqua* (1993) 320, Martorell bridge; Nünnerich-Asmus (1993) 140ff. on Emerita etc.; Trillmich (1990) 304 on the construction, Agrippan; on Ilici, Gorges (1983) 202; Ariño Gil (1990) 80, the alignment of Caesaraugusta's city-grid with the external one; and at Italica, lines of centuriation of the territory give orientation to the chief buildings of the "new" city in the mid-first century, cf. Corzo Sanchez

(1982) 311; for Portus Gaditanus built in the 40s B.C., its *insulae* oriented according to centuriation to the south, which in turn is oriented according to the Via Augusta, see Rambaud (1997) 76 Fig. 1, 79 Fig. 3, and 86. For instances in Gaul and Greece of a road ruling the cadastration-orientation, see Lopez Paz (1994) 52.

25. For example, in the southwest, Correia (1995) 250; Dupré (1985) 285, in the Ebro valley; Hauschild (1993) 218.

26. Gabba (1972) 90–92, 95–100, 108, walls built by magistrates around Verona, Brescia (91 n. 64), Sarsina, and Asisium; by a *patronus municipi* at Aeclanum, Caudium, and Tegianum; and otherwise attested, at many other sites. Notice the *duumvir* at Barcino responsible for the walls, towers, and gates, Curchin (1990) 182; 193, three *duumvirs'* walls at Carthago Nova.

27. Roldán Gómer (1992) 48, on Carteia; on Tarraco, Pfanner (1990) 63; Italian masons' marks on Tarraco's walls, Balil (1983) 231f., 235; *Hispania Antiqua* (1993) 260 (M. Blech), the Ibero-Roman site La Caridad ca. 200km west of Tarraco; Keay (1995) 298 on Valentia of 138 B.C.; Guitart Durán (1993) 57 on Baetulo; Keay (1995) 296 on Emporiae of ca. 100 B.C.; ibid. 317 on Segobriga; Hauschild (1993) 221; on Corduba, Ventura et al. (1993) 94f.; on Emerita, Pfanner (1990) 85 and Trillmich (1986) 302; lighter walls of Augustan times, Hauschild l.c.; Celsa unwalled, Beltrán Lloris (1991) 135; and the native-built town gate, cf. Stylow (1995) 220 supposing it was in anticipation of the hazards of civil war. For other building projects by magistrates, see above, n. 26, and below, nn. 32, 36, 42, 68.

28. Palol (1991) 235, Clunia's 130ha compared to Emerita, Augustobriga, and Caesaraugusta of roughly 50ha; of the old Italian style like Ostia or Cosa, less than 40ha, Lucus Augusti, Tarraco, Pyrgi, Barcino, etc., or (in Gaul) Arles, Pfanner (1990) 63f., 86f.; Caesaraugusta slow to fill up, ibid. 88; at the other extreme of size, the Augustan Caesarea in Palestine, 150ha, Leveau (1984) 31.

29. Grid, in Valentia, Keay (1995) 298; Emporiae, ibid. 296; at La Caridad, *Hispania Antiqua* (1993) 260; Corduba, Marquez (1998) 115, likewise Clunia, Augustan plan enclosing 130ha, Palol (1991) 234f.; Asturica, cf. Garcia Marcos and Vidal Encina (1995) 377; some comparable models of Italian city gridding in Galsterer (1992) 415f.

30. At Emporiae, four *insulae* form the forum, Ricardo Mar and Ruiz de Arbulo (1990) 145.

31. At Emporiae, Lv. 34.9.1, 195 B.C., and Santos Retolaza (1991) 20; Corduba, Stylow (1990) 266f., idem (1993) 77ff., and Fear (1996) 96f.; Celsa, Bendala Galán (1990) 33, and Tarraco and Italica, ibid. 35f., with towns titled "Gemella" like Acci and Tucci, not so named for a putative two-legion settlement.

32. Alarcão and Etienne (1977) 280; Ward-Perkins (1981) 216 with Fig. 132, p. 217; a general Vitruvian practice in Spanish fora, ibid. and Roddaz (1996) 22, pointing to imperial cult shrines on fora of Tarraco, Emporiae, Saguntum, and Baelo; Cortes (1987) 10f. on this latter feature at Tarraco, the dating of the city center's chief works perhaps post-Augustan, Dupré i Raventós (1990) 319; on lateral basilicas in Italy, like Conimbriga's, Jimenez Salvador (1986) 176, Emporiae, and Balty (1991) 365–76; on an *aedes Augusti* in the basilica on Emporiae's forum, cf. Keay (1995) 310; on a grand instance of terracing by a magistrate, at Saguntum, Richardson (1996) 143f.; other instances, Pfanner (1990) 76–81.

33. Balty (1991) 333, Barcino of about the turn of the era; for Conimbriga, Alarcão and Etienne (1977) 37, though Balty p. 3 argues from the presence of the *curia* that the town must have received *municipium* status. For a possible second example in the forum corner, ibid. 116f., Saguntum; in the northeast corner of the forum of the later Munigua, where, however, the temple projects into the forum space, cf. Balty (1991) 84f.; in a different position in the Caesarian plan of Tarraco, ibid. 337f.; and an Italian variant (Iuvanum) for a model, 342f.; p. 281f., Caesarian basilicas used for senate meetings; at Clunia, Palol (1987) 154, the general plan of the center being late Augustan, p. 153.

34. Competition for favor between the two focuses of cult in Augustan times, Jimenez Salvador (1986) 176; a *capitolium* assumed in Vitruvius, Gabba (1972) 107; a triad of temples at Baelo and Brescia, Gros (1996) 154; at Saguntum a three-celled 2nd-century temple, Aranegui (1987) 156, 161f., comparing the temples at Cosa and Luni, and Keay (1995) 298; at Italica, Bendala Galán (1982) 31, 69, though Richardson (1995) 346 denies the identification and the existence of any *capitolia* in any province before Augustus (!); other *capitolia* identified at Tarraco, of 71 B.C., cf. Dupré i Raventós (1995) 358; at Carteia and Emporiae, both Republican, cf. Rodríguez Hidalgo and Keay (1995) 398 and Keay (1990) 130f. with Fig. 10.6 and (1995) 296; the Carteian site not likely a *capitolium*, Roldán Gómer (1992) 94; also possible examples at Emerita and Bilbilis, cf. Cagiano de Azevedo (1941) 37ff. and Barton (1982) 267f.; but Keay (1990) 312 sees imperial cult here, and notes in "plan and decoration . . . close affinities with the temple of Venus Genetrix at Rome."

35. Pfanner (1990) 71f. on the Baelo example, late Republican or Augustan, *pace* De Ruyt (1983) 46 who prefers a date post A.D. 50, and, with over-delicate arguments for a date still later, Didierjean (1986) 257f. ("fragilité" of *macella*-dating generally); an inscription from Villajoyosa, a *macellum vetustate conlabsum*, already in ruins by the second century (originally Augustan?), De Ruyt (1983) 219; many examples in Italy, Jouffroy (1986) 44, 86f. (specifically Augustan).

36. Arches with colonnades paid for in Italica by a magistrate, Curchin (1990) 151; an aqueduct at Tarraco with 300 statues (Plin., NH 36.121), Alföldy (1979) 178; Aqua Augusta at Emerita, Pfanner (1990) 90; at Corduba built by Augustus, Stylow (1990) 270, Trillmich (1990) 304, and Ventura et al. (1993) 95, 98, capacity of 25–40,000m³ per diem; at Conimbriga, Kienast (1982) 405 n. 185 and Alarcão and Etienne (1977) 51, the length 2760m as the crow flies, longer in its actual course, and (58) parts built of *opus caementicium* and brick, along with ordinary cut stone.

37. Jouffroy (1986) 51f. lists Italian Republican *thermae*, cf. Yegül (1992) 54f.; 170 baths in Rome in 33 B.C., ibid. 30, 44, 55f.

38. *Lex Irnitana* in Gonzalez (1986) 182, trans. M. H. Crawford, and some lost mention in the Urso charter is supposed by Fear (1996) 10f.; baths in Valencia already in 138 B.C., Keay (1995) 298; in Baetulo, Guitart i Durán and Padros i Marti (1990) 170f. and Guitart Durán (1993) 58, 79, the date Augustan; at Conimbriga, Alarcão and Etienne (1977) 41, frescoes, 47f., compare the sculptures in Agrippan baths, Manderscheid (1981) Abb. 4 facing p. 10.

39. A race-track at Tarraco, Cortes (1987) 10f.; Augustan amphitheaters at Emerita and Segobriga, Keay (1995) 313, 317; the date of the Emerita building is 16/15, p. 313, or

8/7 B.C., Trillmich (1990) 305; at Carmo (ca. 10 miles northwest of Hispalis), half-wooden, Fear (1996) 198; another wooden structure at Emporiae, Keay (1990) 138; at Tarraco, Fishwick (1982) 232; and at Italica, Niemeyer (1993) 187.

40. Cic., Ad fam. 10.32.2, with ref. to fourteen rows of reserved seating, therefore in a large structure of some sort. He was quaestor in the then-Ulterior Spanish province, RE s.v. "Cornelius" no. 70, col. 1269.

41. Strabo 3.5.3 and Fear (1996) 40, 202.

42. Pfanner (1990) 72, with other theaters of the same period at Ronda la Vieja, Barcino, Bilbilis, Tarraco, Malaga, Metellinum, Italica, Saguntum, Carteia, and Clunia, with Emerita's next to the amphitheater, pp. 76, 79f.; 99; a gift of Agrippa, below, n. 60; and it is modelled on Pompey's theater in Rome, cf. Hispania Antiqua (1993) 239; but Italica's should perhaps be dated early under Tiberius, Rodríguez Hidalgo and Keay (1995) 402; dating of Tarraco's and Emerita's, Gros (1990) 386f.; Caesaraugusta's, Beltrán Lloris (1990) 199; and Carthago Nova's given by a local magnate in 5 B.C./ A.D. 1, cf. Abascal (1995) 141. On the deduction of a late Augustan theater at Corduba from column capitals, etc., see Marquez (1998) 126, 132.

43. Gros (1990) 386.

44. I thank my friend A. Stylow for his estimate that he "must have seen dozens, if not hundreds, of tabulae lusoriae in Spain," and M. Beltrán Lloris for very kindly writing to me in explanation of a particular example in a private house, datable to about A.D. 50, in Celsa, along with ref. to his (with others') study, Colonia Victrix Iulia Lepida-Celsa . . . (1984) 146 with n. 529, pointing to inscribed boards in other provinces and Rome. From his work, (1991) 148 Fig. 63, I reproduce the Celsa example as my Fig. 8, in the exedra of an Augustan home (the mosaic of the 50s A.D.). Add, in amphitheaters at Italica and Emerita, other examples, cf. Rothaus (1992) 365, 367; on the forum paving of Leptis Magna, cf. Buried City (1964) 85 and Pl. 95; and at Gigthis in Africa, an "essentially Roman" board with other examples all in Roman colonies (Trier, Timgad, Rusicade), cf. Constans (1914) 284 and (1916) 20. An article by Austin (1940) gathers reff. from literature but is of little use.

45. Representative passages in Zanker (1990) 18ff.; Pfanner (1990) 69, 82–85, 94 (Emerita's temple); León (1990), passim; Dupré i Raventós (1990) 319 and (1995) 365; or Roddaz (1996) 21f.

46. At Emporiae, Ricardo Mar and Ruiz de Arbulo (1990) 151 and Zanker (1990) 17; at Baelo, Pfanner (1990) 90f., with analogies in Italy.

47. Waelkens (1990) 61 n. 83 on Mamurra, Plin., N. H. 36.48; Hesberg (1992) 130 and passim on the attitude toward marble in Italian contexts, especially in Augustus' time; and his boast, Suet., Aug. 28.3.

48. Ramallo (1993) 226; Pfanner (1990) 100, 102f., Zanker (1990) 21, and Keay (1995) 308, local marble substitutes at Barcino, Ebora, Emerita, etc.; esp. at Emerita, in theater, amphitheater, etc., on a grand scale, both real and imitation marble-izing, cf. Pfanner (1990) 94 and Trillmich (1990) 310; in the basilica at Tarraco, Keay l. c.

49. Alarcão and Etienne (1977) 280f., 285; Cortes (1987) 10f. on modular (intercolumniar) planning of the Tarraco forum, temple, and circus, possibly Augustan.

50. Above, n. 29; Vicente Redón et al. (1991) 84; and the new meaning of modulus in Latin ("module" for a modern architect meaning not a notional measurement but a standard size for some element), cf. Coulton (1989) 85.

51. Dardaine (1983) 21 Fig. 3, the depth to interior rear being 7x, where x is the wall to either side of the cella entrance; at Carteia, Mar and Ruiz de Arbulo (1993) 220, 226, the temple cella's depth is 4x (x=intercolumniation), etc.
52. Aranegui (1987) 157ff., the foot used being the Italic of .2975m, so the overall width is 40'.
53. Palol (1991a) 329f., 331 Fig. 2 (Tiberian).
54. Correia (1995) 250, Lusitania; Vicente Redón et al. (1991) 95, 96 (some La Caridad houses); Dupré (1985) 286f., Ebro valley; and Zanker (1990) 17.
55. Examples, e.g., primitive and partial opus caementicium at Carteia, Roldán Gómer (1992) 46, late 3rd cent. B.C.; at Italica toward the turn of the 2nd cent. B.C., mortar bonding in walls, cf. Rodríguez Hidalgo (1995) 398; toward the same date, the same at Tarraco, Keay (1990) 127; at Rona la Vieja 50km west of Malaga, the late Republican theater showing opus caementicium, cf. Hispania antiqua (1993) 357; an Augustan example at Conimbriga, above, n. 36; of Julio-Claudian date in the basilica at Asturica, Garcia Marcos and Vidal Encinas (1995) 382; late Augustan/early Tiberian walls with plastering at Santiponce, Keay (1992) 293, or at Carteia's theater, Roldán Gómer p. 104; and opus reticulatum at Torre Ciega, Ramallo Asensio (1989) 120 and Ramallo (1993) 231. For a very close parallel, see Prieur (1986) 82f. at Aquileia.
56. León (1990) 368; Zanker (1990) 17; and cf. Strabo 3.4.2 on Malaga, "Punic-looking."
57. Santos Retolaza (1991) 20, Italian hands in Emporiae; Italian architects confidently assumed at work in Emerita and Bilbilis by Kienast (1982) 352; Ramallo (1993) 226, late Augustan column capitals at Emporiae by Italian hands "sin duda"; Zanker (1990) 21, with a question mark; earlier, Italian mason mark on Tarraco's opus quadratum, Balil (1983) 232ff., the explanation ignored by Richardson (1995) 347 and 353 n. 3, though accepted by Dupré i Raventós (1995) 356; and at Corduba, close copying of Rome's major Augustan monuments in the surviving architectural fragments of several structures thought to be the work of Italian masons, Marquez (1998) 119f.
58. Alarcão and Etienne (1979) 259.
59. Above, n. 36, re Emerita and Corduba; Kienast (1982) 352; Bonneville (1986) 190.
60. Ibid. 339 on Agrippa's wealth; CIL 2.474=ILS 130 of 16/15 B.C., cf. Hispania Antiqua (1993) 239, on the theater (called an amphitheater and the donor called Augustus by Keay [1995] 313); for the bas-relief, Trillmich (1986) 302.
61. Fear (1996) 109, municipi patronus (but "parens," p. 39); at Emporiae, Mar and Ruiz de Arbulo (1993) 279; for his aqueduct-decoration at Tarraco, above, n. 36.
62. Bonneville (1986) 184ff., 194; ibid. 187, on A. Terentius Varro Murena; and passim, other patroni of the highest fame, including princes; Kienast (1982) 352f. on building by (probably) imperial kinsmen at Caesaraugusta, Carthago Nova, Gades, Italica, Salaria, and Ulia for the reasons mentioned; Curchin (1991) 90, governors named patrons by Carthago Nova, Uxama, Emporiae, etc.; and the governor of Nearer Spain, T. Statilius Taurus, in CIL 2.3556=ILS 893, datable 25/15 B.C., Abad and Abascal (1991) 82.
63. RE s.v. "Cornelius" no. 69, cols. 1262f. (praefectus fabrum in 61 and 58 B.C., the second time in Gaul); 1268, familiarissimus Caesaris, Suet., Caes. 81. A similar success story on a smaller scale may lie behind the duumvir of Corduba honored for what, we cannot say—twice prefect of (prince) C. Caesar, CIL 2.1534.
64. Homo barbarus, Bell. Hisp. 35; another instance in Fear (1996) 36; but the Pacciaecus-

family is not a third native example, cf. Sebastián Hernández Fernández (1998) 164ff., 168, the family Italian settled in Spain.

65. Riccobono et al. (1968–72) 1.169, cap. 5, trans. Johnson et al. (1961) 64.

66. Veyne (1976) 487, in my translation based on Veyne (1990) 259, slightly condensed. He describes his work ([1976] 21) as a description of Hellenistic evergetism and of that of Rome, which followed and imitated it; derives it from the ambition for "honneur" (432, "exprimer leur splendeur," and passim), at home in Rome much before Augustus, cf. e.g. the Republican inscription comparable to the Res Gestae (487).

67. Ad Att. 1.13.6 of 61 B.C., Carcopino (1957) 1.74f. = (1951) 1.43, indicating the cost, three and a half million sesterces.

68. Of Augustus' building, an example in CIL 11.6218–9=ILS 104 of A.D. 9/10, gift to Fanum Fortunae of a city wall; examples of grand gifts to Aeclanum, etc., in the 80s to 60s, in Gabba (1972) 89f., 95, 98f., though his interpretation seems to me anachronistic; and parallels and more material above, chap. 1 at nn. 84f.

69. Riccobono et al. (1968–72) 1.184; Ventura et al (1993) 96f., gift of ornamental fountains by L. Cornelius, Corduban duumvir; Devijver and Wonterghem (1985) 147, gift of a campus by local magnate; Hispania epigraphica 2 (1990) 115, gift of road-building; Dupré i Raventos (1995) 359, arch at Tarraco, with interpretation by Alföldy (1977) 295; Pfanner (1990) 67 on a mine-owner of Carthago Nova and his generosity; Saguntum's whole forum the gift of a certain Cn. Baebius Geminus, Richardson (1996) 144; and above at nn. 27 and 42.

70. RE s.v. "Cornelius" no. 70; Strabo 3.5.3; Cic., Ad fam. 10.32.2f.; Fear (1996) 232; Rambaud (1997) 80 and passim.

71. Bellemore (1984) xxii and Nikolaos, Vita Caes. 12.26f. on this moment of προστασία (I use the editor's trans., changing δωρεάς, "gifts," to "boons").

72. Dyson (1980–81) 272f. on Fabii governors of Hither Spain and the striking numbers of Fabii in Saguntine epigraphy; a Fabius active in the northwest and perhaps patron of Bracaraugusta, Rodriguez Colmenero (1996) 177; Knapp (1978) 188 n. 6, 189; Castillo (1991) 238; on Agrippa patron of Carthago Nova and Emerita, Keay (1995) 310, 313; Juba patron of Spanish cities, Coltelloni-Tranoy (1993–95) 65 n. 50, with just the same client relations in Africa itself; and above, nn. 60f.

73. Garcia y Bellido (1966a) 149ff., from central Hispania Citerior=Tarraconensis of A.D. 14 (omnis for omnes, suorumqui for suorumque, civi for civis); idem (1972) 469f., with the earliest peninsular example of 1 B.C.; Rodriguez Colmenero (1996) 170 n. 253, 177; Nicols (1980) 550f., the phrase in fidem clientelamque normal (19 of 23) in early Spanish contracts; 561 no. 17, an example of 12 B.C. from Pompaelo, and five other Augustan ones, all from peregrine communities; Nesselhauf (1960) 142ff. on the assimilation of hopitium and patronatus toward a more Roman result; Dopico Cainzos (1986) 268f. and Castillo (1991) 238, re C. Asinius Gallus in A.D. 1, the community elsewhere called a castellum, and comparison with other new late-Augustan tesserae hospitales; generally, Pereira Menaut (1995) 294f. and Curchin (1991) 181; post-Augustan, Le Roux (1994) 343ff.

74. Curchin (1991) 87; Keay (1995) 293; and esp. Roddaz (1986) 319f.

75. Res gestae 25, iuraverunt in eadem verba provinciae Galliae, Hispaniae . . . in 32 B.C., cf. Etienne (1958) 357, with ref. also to Dio 50.6; Roddaz (1986) 320; Gonzalez (1988) 114 and passim.

76. Above, n. 62; Cic., Pro Balbo 50f., "Fabii" by act of Metellus or Pompey; and Knapp (1978) 188 n. 6, they "took their names before enfranchisement. The tendency was probably widespread. . . . Provincials not legally entitled to use Roman names seem to have adopted Roman nomina," cf. Curchin (1990) 94, accepting the evidence. But Knapp seems to have pushed beyond the limits of plausibility, as he forms his inferences into an argument.

77. Among many studies, cf. Etienne et al. (1976) 98ff. and Curchin (1990) 89–102; Fear (1996) 156, 159, on registration in the tribus Galeria (definitive for Caesarian and Augustan enrollments) and the total of Iulii (404) as compared to Valerii (365), Fabii (197), or Sempronii (143); Castillo Garcia (1975) 643, on Iulii; and Polomé (1983) 523 on the rush to Roman names in parts of Spain under Augustus.

78. Above, chap. 1 at n. 26, with Fear (1996) 96.

79. A good introduction to controversies in Humbert (1981) 207ff., 216ff.; Gonzalez (1986) 148, 203; Fear (1996) 39, 109, 115, on change in status in e.g. Carteia and Gades (given citizenship in 49 B.C. by Caesar, municipium status some years later); 117, Vittinghoff (1951) 79ff., and Galsterer (1988) 64, on general municipalization by Augustus, whether or not all with full-citizen rights (as is still disputed); Le Roux (1996) 246, Latin rights need not mean municipal forms of government.

80. Tab. Heracl. = Lex Iulia municipalis of ?44 B.C., cap. 28=146 Crawford (1996) 1.368; Lex Irnitana cap. 86=Gonzalez (1986) 196.

81. Curchin (1990) 22 (oversized curia in Irni); 37, anomalous magistracies in Celsa and Ulia; in un-Romanized centers, odd magistracies, G. Alföldy, CAH, ed. 2 (1996) 462; Nesselhauf (1960) 145; Hispania antiqua (1993) 266f.

82. The Saguntine text, CIL 2.3836=2.14, pp. 327f.=ILS 66, late Augustan according to Alföldy (1979) 266 and (1995) 126; Tiberian, Beltrán Lloris (1980) 47; the Italica text, CIL 2.1119, in Rodríguez Hidalgo and Keay (1995) 399; the Iliturgi text, Alföldy (1995) 47. For a similar recall of the Roman past in the imitation of Roman coins of ca. 100 B.C. celebrating Marius' Cimbric victories, on coins to celebrate Augustus' Cantabrian victories, see Trillmich (1990) 301.

83. On Salii, Beltrán Lloris (1980) 392f. and Alföldy (1986) 262, 281f.; on the sulcus-ceremony, Mierse (1990) 310, Fear (1996) 71, and Burnett et al. (1986) 1.119; Hispalis, Burnett et al. (1992) 1, 1.79; Rodríguez Hidalgo and Keay (1995) 399; Italica's relief, Bendala Galán (1982) 70; Ilerda, Burnett et al. 109; and a similar popularity enjoyed in African and eastern colonies by the figure of Marsyas at his revels, taken to show that Romans had no masters, cf. Veyne (1961) 87, 92f. On Italica's coins with GEN. POP. ROM., and PERMISSU AUG. (surely implying a cult), see Burnett et al. (1992) 1, 1.78.

84. [Caes.], Bell. Hisp. 42, cf. 35, homo barbarus is a native; Cic., Pro Balbo 42f., cf. Ad Q. frat. 1.1.27 (quoted in chap. 1, above), Roman administrators are set over immanes ac barbarae nationes. Fear (1996) 3, 46 makes good use of the first three of these texts.

85. Above, chap. 1 at n. 29; specifically on Spain, Gardner (1993) 188.

86. Cap. 81, nundinae in foro; MacMullen (1970) 333f., 338ff. The surviving tablets are Flavian, below, n. 90; but the post-Caesarian additions are agreed to be few and, where suspected, Augustan, not later.

87. Cap. 105, indignus . . . libertinus; equites, above, n. 40; capp. 125ff., proedria for decurions and special city guests, with permission to continue pre-charter=local customs

in *Lex Irnitana* 81, Gonzalez (1986) 195, and, for Italian models, Kolendo (1981) 303, 306.

88. Cap. 95; *Tab. Herac.* 2=4 Crawford (1996) 363, persons in *tutela*; provision to get a tutor, *Lex Irnitana* 29.

89. Caps. 22, 86 (*patria potestas*); 28, 72, 97 (manumission); and K (harvests)—trans. in Gonzalez (1986) 183, 187, 193, 199, and discussion of some of these, p. 148, with discussion of the discussion in Gardner (1993) 189 and Fear (1996) 134ff., 147.

90. *Lex col. gen. Iul. Urson.* 66, *ita uti . . . in quaque colonia*, and 70, 128, cults; taboos, 73, 95; Frederiksen (1965) 191, on pre-Caesarian law in the Urso charter with (195) some features added to its Flavian edition from Augustan laws; Augustan model, Gonzalez (1986) 150 and Crawford (1995) 426–29, arguing persuasively for this as constituting the great bulk of Flavian charters. Though Crawford (1996) 1.359 rejects ideas of any "unitary *lex municipalis*," one literally prescriptive and of a single authorization, he points (398) to dozens of points of overlap, verbatim or essential, between the Urso and Irni charters, and, in the two (chaps. 81/125; 82/104; 83/98; I/92; etc.), other close similarities in proedria, road-building, corvées, embassy management, etc., can be noticed.

91. *Lex Irnitana* caps. 31, 90, 92; Johnston (1987) 69 n. 40.

92. Fishwick (1982) 222, 231f.; Etienne (1958) 177f., 197, 205 and 293 (an Augustan inscription, *CIL* 2.6097, a *flamen* of ?Roma and Augustus); 363ff. on the Tarraco beginnings; 380ff. on diffusion in Spain, even to Urgavo in A.D. 11/12.

93. An *aedes Augusti* at Tarraco, Dupré i Raventós (1995) 359; Pfanner (1990) 97, Clunia, and (95) shrines not temples on the forum not only at Tarraco, but at Conimbriga and many other cities; above, nn. 32, 34, on Augustus-temples elsewhere.

94. Detecting the theater-connections of imperial cult, Kienast (1982) 170; parallels at Leptis, above, chap. 2 at n. 43; Ramallo (1993) 226, altar to prince Gaius in 5–1 B.C. at Carthago Nova; Gros (1990) 383 on the post-Augustan reff. in the *Tab. Siarensis* to *eum locum in quo statuae divo Augusto domuique Augustae dedicatae essent ab NN*, and imperial statues in niches of the stage back-drop at Emerita, 384; there but elsewhere too, in Niemeyer (1968) 33, 82; for Republican displays of statues in Italian theaters, Bejor (1979) 136 and Pfanner (1990) 100; for those in Greece, Egypt, and Mauretania, above, chap. 1 n. 72, and chap. 2 at n. 42; Tarraco-portico, *Hispania Antiqua* (1993) 274 and Gros 384, the two princes Gaius and Lucius portrayed there, Clavel (1970) 489f.

95. Trillmich (1990) 306; Keay (1995) 310, 312, 317; Alföldy (1979) 265, 268f., and (1995) 126; Barruol and Marichal (1987) 54, a mixed group at Ruscino, imperial and local magistrates; Alföldy (1995) 128, great Roman senators' statues in Ilici; Garcia y Bellido (1949) 1.39f., ?Livia at Azaila; 40ff., ?Octavia at Tarraco; the colossal "Augustus" in the temple on the Conimbriga forum, Alarcão and Etienne (1977) 31; and Etienne (1958) 390, Augustus-heads (some, posthumous) in small northwestern towns.

96. Private individuals in stone, normally magistrates, e.g. at Ruscino, Barruol and Marichal (1987) 54, or Emerita, Barcino, etc., Trillmich (1993) 54f., showing influence of an Agrippa-visage, 55 Abb. 10, and noting rapid response to Rome's fashions; passim, on imitation of Rome among women's and men's portraits in Spain; below, chap. 4 at n. 120 on control of public sculpture; in sign of this, Alföldy (1979) 189 notices the uniformity of bases in northeast Spain.

97. Zanker (1990) 15; Pfanner (1990) 69.
98. Curchin (1991) 183f., 185 Fig. 9.1; Rouillard (1997) 20; León (1990) 368ff., on architectural decoration as well as statuary; rare suggestions of native traditions in late- or post-Augustan work, Zanker (1990) 19 and Fear (1996) 245, 264; and warrior statues 25–50 km. from Asturica and Bracaraugusta, in Tranoy (1988) 219–26.
99. Trillmich (1986) 298; Fishwick (1982) 223, 226; on the *clipeus*, above, chap. 2 at n. 59.
100. Ramallo (1993) 226.
101. Above, at nn. 37f.; frescoes in private houses at Celsa (Pompeian IInd style), Beltrán Lloris (1991) 141f., 148; idem (1997) 14, 24, 26; near Hispalis, Keay (1992) 293.
102. Keay (1992) 293; Kreilinger (1993) 205; Guitart et al. (1991) 38, more elaborate mosaics at Baetulo, Carthago Nova, Emporiae.
103. Abad Casal and Aranegui Gasco (1993) 86, supplying my Fig. 10; Blech (1993) 95.
104. *Hispania Antiqua* (1993) 261 (ca. 175 km west of Dertosa); Blech (1993) 94 with Abb. 42, comparing another inscribed mosaic near Pompaelo in the upper Ebro also naming a Likine=Licinius, but from Bilbilis, and a certain Abulo (Celtiberian name), Abulo being taken as the house owner and Likine=Licinius as the mosaicist of both sites; accepted by De Hoz (1995) 73f.; but at La Caridad, I find this implausible, and prefer the view that Likine=Licinius was the house owner, given the prominent position of the name at the entrance of the *tablinum*, cf. Vicente Redón et al. (1991) 84, 92, 120ff.; also the fact that the excavators call it "the House of Likine."
105. Ibid. 95f., 104ff., 107, 123.
106. *Hispania Antiqua* (1993) 261; Beltrán Lloris (1991) 131–50, 155, comparing (150) other (not many) houses at other northeastern coastal sites; Roman-style floors appear at Tarraco and Corduba around the same time as Likine, Keay (1995) 295f.; for Emporiae houses, see Mar and Ruiz de Arbulo (1993) 239, 242, design of the turn of the 1st century B.C.
107. Gorges (1986) 222.
108. For example, Gorges (1994) 270, much Campanian ware in Republican *villa* sites in Ebro valley, Arretine in Baetica of Augustan times; similarly at Conimbriga, Etienne and Fontaine (1979) 140 and Alarcão and Etienne (1979) 262 (*terra sigillata* in Augustan times); Blech (1993) 72 and Keay (1992) 293f. on northeastern sites from 3rd quarter of 1st century on; but (ibid. 303) later in Baetica, cf. Gorges (1979) 29 and Bourgeois and Mayet (1991) 27, 40, 56ff.
109. In 1st-century Carteia and Italica, Iberian pottery predominates, Fear (1996) 36f., and, 91, "the pottery [at Ilici in Augustan times] is overwhelmingly Iberian in both decoration and design"; cf. Curchin (1991) 186.
110. Strabo 3.3.7, ζῦθος; the same drink in pre-Roman Illyricum/Pannonia, Tchernia (1986) 171.
111. Blech (1993) 72.
112. Strabo 3.2.15; *Hispania Antiqua* (1993) 265f.
113. Texts in Garcia y Bellido (1967) 11f. = idem (1972) 470f.: Plut. *Sert.* 22.2f.; Cic., *Pro Archia* 26, *pingue quiddam sonantes atque peregrinum; De div.* 2.131, 44 B.C.
114. Gomez Pallarès (1992) 154ff.; and Garcia y Bellido (1972) 478 lists indigenous success-stories suggestive of thorough Roman acculturation (besides the Balbi, Seneca Rhetor, Julius Hyginus, Acilius Lucanus, Moderatus Columella, and others).
115. Stylow (1995) 221, speaking of Baetica; Alföldy (1995) 123f., 128, speaking of the

central-east coast from late Republican times on, other areas a little later but still Augustan; idem (1991) 292 on the epigraphic curve datable to the same decades in Italy; De Hoz (1995) 66, Ebro valley epigraphy begins in Augustan times.

116. Above, at n. 73; Garcia y Bellido (1967) 10 = idem (1972) 470, on patronage-contracts and legal documents; Hübner (1893) 162, Augustan bilingual from Saguntum; Palol (1987) 153, ditto from Clunia; Mayer and Velaza (1993) 669; *Hispania Antiqua* (1993) 266f.; Garcia y Bellido (1967) 16 n. 29.

117. Garcia y Bellido (1972) 471, Polomé (1983) 524, and Crawford (1985) 213ff., latest Iberian-legend coins; Garcia y Bellido (1972) 472, 487 (both earlier and later testimonies to Iberian in inscriptions in pockets of population).

118. Garcia y Bellido (1967) 10.

119. Garcia y Bellido (1972) 482 lists auxiliary units with Spanish names/origins.

120. (At random:) Urso, caps. 1f., 28; Irni, caps. C, 85, 95; an early (97 B.C.) example of Iberian-speakers engaged in legal consultation requiring Latin, at Contrebia, Dupré (1985) 286.

121. Antonio Tovar was the chief investigator of the subject: (1973) 48–62 passim; Mariner Bigorra (1983) 822ff., in Spain as in other Latinate areas of the empire, as emphasized by Herman (1990) 12, 63, and 86, "identité monumentale" in provincial Latin; again, idem (1991) 34f.; Dardel (1992) 83; "old-fashioned" Latin, Garcia y Bellido (1972) 472; Fischer (1995) 479; and Stefenelli (1995) 35.

122. Pfanner (1990) 69; some random examples of indigenous traditions in funerary evidence: in art, Curchin (1991) 183ff. and Fig. 9.1; tomb-design, Fear (1996) 234, 241ff.; symbolism, Blazquez (1976) 67; or bilingualism, Mayer and Velaza (1993) 669.

CHAPTER IV: GAUL

1. Koch (1993) 46; Tranoy (1988) 225f.

2. Tierney (1959–69) 247ff., 264; date, Nash (1976) 111 (whose assumption, 124, that Poseidonios indicates conditions a generation earlier than when he wrote seems to me unlikely); ibid. 117 n. 19 and idem (1981) 13 on the place of gold in Celtic life (Strabo, Vergil, Caesar, etc.); above, chap. 3 n. 110 on pre-Roman beer drinking.

3. E.g., at Nîmes, Darde and Lassalle (1993) 15; Nîmes-area imported Italian pottery in warrior graves, Crawford (1985) 170; at Toulouse, Fouet (1969) 74ff., 87f., mid-Augustan wine amphorae (some uncorked), Italian pottery and local imitations; at Béziers, Ital. ware in burials, and at nearby Montfo, a wine-merchant's shop with stock of unsold amphorae, Clavel (1970) 97, 160; in the Moselle region, Demarolle (1994) 23, 27, esp. elevated sites=*oppida;* Nash (1976a) 114f.; Thill (1966) 484, 491 and Metzler (1984) 92, in mid-Augustan warrior graves 50 mis. SW of Trier (Goeblingen-Nospelt in Luxembourg), swords, an "ACO" goblet, a bronze wine service with Latin inscription of maker's name; 50km south-southeast of Caesarodunum, a warrior burial of ca. 10 B.C., having arms (most unusually: swords and spears), "ACO" cup, *terra sigillata,* amphorae, cf. Ferdière and Villard (1993) 16f., 27–44, 92 (date: 20–0 B.C.); similar burials in the region, 281ff.; burials with arms explained, ibid. 281, as auxiliary veterans; the long series of Trier-region rich warrior chamber tombs, with arms and increasingly Romanized luxury articles of every sort, from ca. 20 B.C., Reinert (1993) 179ff.; the well-known shipwreck of 90s B.C. off Albingau-

nun=Albenga with Italian wine and ceramic cargo, Lamboglia (1952) 153, 167–82; and ceramic imports in warrior graves. Viticulture was not unknown in Provincia, Py (1993) 215 (near Glanum), but importation from Italy became gigantic over later 2nd and to late 1st century, cf. e.g. at Toulouse, Tchernia (1986) 79f., 126, 164f.

4. Feugère (1993) 126f., with similar but delayed artifactual evidence in Britain, Philpott (1993) 167, and the prior underlying patterns in earlier Italian burials, Fasold (1993) 384. For Gallic wine production, cf. Tchernia (1986) 147, 150 (even some export to north Africa); for ceramic manufacture in Lyon from 15 B.C. on, including "ACO" cups of Italian style and local imitation of *terra sigillata* with imported stamps and moulds, cf. Lasfargues et al. (1976) 79 and Wells (1977) 135; for similar and slightly later (but still B.C.) production of *terra sigillata* at Mediolanum, Audin (1985) 73, the city and area having been the chief consumer of the product (including Perennius-ware) in western Gaul from 30 B.C. on, cf. Tilhard (1992) 231, 236f.; and at La Graufesenque in the Toulouse area toward the end of Augustus' reign, Vernhet (1979) 13, 18 and Demarolle (1994) 21. Warrior elite graves of the same sort and period may be compared in, e.g., Thrace (60s/50s), Künzl (1969) 336, or SE Britain (40s), Haselgrove (1984) 22.

5. On Béziers currencies, Clavel (1970) 192, 196ff.; Belgic coins, Scheers (1981) 18ff.; central Gaul, Wightman (1976) 409, 411, idem (1985) 19; 21, Rhone-Saône area; and Nash (1981) 16; concentration in oppida, Nash (1976a) 118; Crawford (1985) 171.

6. *Civitas*-mints from 80s, Nash (1976a) 125; issues in the 50s B.C., Scheers (1969) 22, 177 and (1972) 2ff., 6 (no native gold after 50); Nash (1981) 10f.; Crawford (1985) 214ff., and Burnett et al. (1992) 8, prevalence of *denarii* from Caesar on for a generation only; and Allen (1980) 24, 94, 99.

7. Nîmes-mint bronze to the end of Augustus' principate, Burnett et al. (1992) 20 (an earlier terminus in Clavel [1970] 197f.).

8. Allen (1980) 101, Hirtius in the 40s; Munatius Plancus, too, Crawford (1985) 217; and Octavian, from Nîmes, and in 30/29, Carinas, Allen p. 102 and Burnett et al. (1992) 152, 147; Minerva-head of late 40s/early 30s, wolf, etc., Scheers (1969) 30, 67; Crawford l. c.

9. Allen (1980) 121, coins of Munatius Plancus; Togirix in the 50s, Wightman (1976) 412 and (1985) 43, with Dumnorix also, or "Rex Adietuanus" with wolf, a supporter of Caesar from the Sotiates.

10. Allen (1980) 102, "Roman aquiescence"; "no attempt to impose the appearance and metrology of Roman coins on the provinces . . . , no general or coherent policy towards the coinage, other than to allow it, as far as possible, to take its natural course," Burnett et al. (1992) 53. Cf. above, chap. 1 n. 21.

11. M. Lejeune in *L'onomastique latine* . . . 1975 (Paris 1977) 324; cf. CIL 3.5232=ILS 1977, C. Iulius Vepo, *donatus civitate Romana viritim et immunitate ab divo Augusto*, to show the path to promotion.

12. Severed heads on coins e.g. of Armorica, Allen (1980) 39, 135f.; of central Gaul (p. 59: 1st half of 1st century B.C.); found at Alesia (p. 92 and Pl. 22 no. 317: 50s B.C.) with two names on them, and the quoted comment on Celtic art; over-all, Green (1996) 57.

13. Fasold (1993) 382, in Raetia no weapons after mid-1st century; in southern third of

Gaul, they cease under Augustus, Feugère (1993) 152; a late example, but its rarity
emphasized, Ferdière and Villard (1993) 30, supposing the warrior Bituriges of this
date had served under Caesar in the 40s B.C.

14. Private displays, Py (1993) 244ff.; on Ribemont-sur-Ancre, destroyed "soon after the
    conquest," King (1990) 232; on this and Gournay and the latter's date, Brunaux
    (1986) 17f., 21f.

15. Grenier (1958–60) 4,2.483–88, 2nd- and 1st-century sites in Aix area and St.-Rémy,
    with Poseidonios in later sources; Drioux (1934) 186f., adding other ancient texts;
    Maurin (1978) 250ff.; Brunaux (1996) 178, 193, 196, adding Pomponius Mela, and
    (p. 77, 87ff., 119ff.) skulls at sites mostly of Rouen-Soissons area.

16. Lucan 3.399ff.; Suet., Claud. 25.13; King l. c.

17. Brunaux (1986) 134f., on the misinterpretation; 126f., denying to Caesar any "sorte
    de programme de romanisation anticipé en matière religieuse," the Romans being
    "plus laxiste" in general; cf. Beaujeu (1976) 434, "On n'a jamais vu les Romains s'em-
    ployer, comme l'ont fait certains peuples colonisateurs des temps modernes, à extir-
    per les croyances et les dieux des peuples soumis et à les convertir à leur propre reli-
    gion. . . . (439) Le rôle de l'état romain, nous l'avons noté, était aussi exempt de
    prosélytisme que d'intolérance."

18. Suet., Claud. 25.13; Brunaux (1996) 127, 170, and passim; Druidism "political," CAH
    10 (1952) 209, 492, 499; Momigliano (1986) 108f.

19. Among many studies, see e.g., regarding cult pits, Galliou (1984) 192; displaced by
    above-ground altars, and more elaborate built structures, Brunaux (1996) 73f., 88;
    animal sacrifices, e.g. Lepetz (1993) 39f.; ceramic finds narrowed post-Augustus to
    offerings rather than vessels also used in rituals, Tuffreau-Libre (1994) 134; and
    prayers and thanks recorded in addresses to deities in Greco-Roman manner, De
    Sury (1994) 169–73.

20. King (1990) 225ff.; Bourgeois (1994) 73ff., changes to stone, of Augustan date at a
    hilltop site between Rouen and Paris; Brunaux (1996) 62f., 73f.; Bayard and Cadoux
    (1982) 85, a late Augustan commencement to built phases of a shrine at Ribemont-
    sur-Ancre.

21. Diod. 22.9; Grenier (1958–60) 4,2.479f., 685ff., on Mavilly, and the quotation,
    p. 694, comparing similar sculpture of early Tiberian date from Paris, where the fig-
    ures are identified with their names in Latin, a mixture of Roman and native, cf. also
    Hatt (1965) 95ff., 109; further on Mavilly, Thevenot (1955) 19ff., with general discus-
    sion of Mars in Gaul, passim; King (1990) 222, 230; Brunaux (1996) 51; idem (1986)
    77; and Lavagne (1979) 162ff., 175f., on the degree of Romanization of Mars' and
    Mercury's worshippers.

22. Drioux (1934) 11ff. and Fellmann (1975) 201.

23. Thevenot (1968) 133; Lavagne (1979) 159, 179ff.; Finocchi (1994) 95f.; and Brasseur
    (1996) 79ff.

24. Hill (1953) 206, 214, 222, where P.-M. Duval's 2nd-century dating is quoted with a
    question-mark; derivation of the pose and full discussion, Boucher (1976) 68f.,
    165f., 168, and Figs. 86f., 103, and 301, where dating may be arrived at through some
    fixed chronological points in Pompeian small bronzes and by comparison with, and
    superiority to, the Lyon Jupiter of the mid-1st century; and the quotation, 169; similar

poses etc., cf. Boucher and Tassinari (1976) 68ff.; recognition of the Baltimore work as Sucellus, Lavagne (1979) 181 n. 102.

25. Lv. *per.* 139; Grenier (1958–60) 4.507 and n. 3; Hatt (1970) 244; Fishwick (1978) 1204 and (1982) 226 n. 32.

26. On the number of tribes, Galsterer-Kröll (1996) 119. On roads, esp. Strabo 4.6.11; König (1970) 35–60, passim; Chevallier (1976) 160ff., on the *via Augusta* etc.; Kienast (1982) 412f.; Drinkwater (1983) 111, 121, 124f.; Wightman (1985) 49, 80, the first bridge to Trier dated 18/17 B.C.; Heinen (1984) 36f., 40, disputing the date of Agrippa's commencement of building; Roddaz (1984) 389, 393; Audin (1985) 63; Maurin (1991) 46f.; and Demarolle (1994) 18. Nash (1976) 95ff., 113, emphasizes the relatively better organized=urbanized condition of pre-27 B.C., even pre-conquest central and eastern Gaul; also Brunaux (1996) 58.

27. Abandonment of older centers: Grenier (1958–60) 3,1.234; Kienast (1982) 403, Vesunna displaced for Aventicum, etc.; Bedon (1985) 86; Ramage (1997) 122; new towns, Bedon and Ramage, locc. citt.; Vittinghoff (1951) 102; Grenier 245 n. 2; *Princeton Encyclopedia* (1976) 118; Kienast 404 and nn. 176ff.; Mertens (1985) 262 and (1994) 259, Bavai, Tongres, Tournai; Frézouls (1991) 110, Troyes; Maurin (1991) 49, Périgueux; Rebourg (1991) 101, Bibracte replaced by Augustodunum; Häussler (1993) 50; degree of novelty of *civitates* (53 unknown to Caes. and Poseidonios), Goudineau et al. (1980) 93; new centers tied to roads, 99.

28. Ward-Perkins (1970) 4; Goudineau et al. (1980) 90; Hinrichs (1989) 120, tax list center; Grenier (1958–60) 4, 1.122, aqueducts; C. Goudineau in *CAH* 10, ed. 2 (1996) 470, 493 (ascribing the amphitheater to the gift of the Mediolanum elite in A.D. 19); Desbat and Mandy (1991) 79; Burdy and Pelletier (1994) 7ff.; and Ramage (1997) 141, the amphitheater begun.

29. Beyond the often difficult mentions in Plin., *N. H.* (esp. 3.36f.), and omitting most scholarly sources used, I mention only the basic survey, now very old, Kornemann (1900); Grenier (1937) 488ff.; Vittinghoff (1951) 147 and passim; Kienast (1982); and Pelletier (1991) 29. On Lug. Convenarum, May (1996) 15; Nîmes, Darde and Lasalle (1993) 17; Vienne, Goudineau in *CAH* 10, ed. 2 (1996) 470; Nyon, Drack and Fellmann (1988) 20; and Avennio and other southern sites, Christol and Heijmans (1992) 38ff.

30. A selection of names taken to honor Caesar or Augustus in Grenier (1958–60) 3, 1.245 n. 2; Wightman (1985) 59, Latin-right *civitates*; C. Goudineau in *CAH* 10, ed. 2 (1996) 473ff.; and Johnson et al. (1961) 152, request from a town to take the emperor's (Vespasians's) name.

31. Goudineau cit. 475; idem (1975) 28ff.; idem et al. (1980) 326; above, chap. 1 n. 25, 2 n. 21, 3 n. 79; Kornemann (1900) 585; Maurin (1978) 148ff., 154ff.; Drinkwater (1983) 107.

32. Grenier (1958–60) 3, 1.86ff.; Audin (1985) 62f., 77; Galliou (1983) 62, gridding of A.D. 10–20 at Condate=Rennes; Mertens (1985) 262; Maurin (1991) 54f., Burdigala and Vesunna; Desbat and Mandy (1991) 94, 97, Lyon; Drack and Fellmann (1988) 125f., pre-Roman Swiss sites.

33. The late chronology of Gallia Comata's Roman urban development, rarely detectible archeologically before the end of the first century, was pointed out with surprise by Ward-Perkins (1970) 1 and again by C. Goudineau in *CAH* 10, ed. 2 (1996) 492f. Grid-

ding, generally, Drinkwater (1983) 143; at Augusta Raurica, Ward-Perkins p. 4; Autun, Grenier (1958–60) 3, 1.235f. with Fig. 63; at Mediolanum, construction only from 20s B.C., *Mediolanum* (1988) 303, with gridding, the highway being the *decumanus maximus*, Maurin (1978) 63, but without gridding, idem (1991) 54; at Tongres and other Belgic centers, Mertens (1994) 259; at Aventicum, Paunier (1994) 54; at Trier and Amiens, Wightman (1985) 77.

34. At Vienne, Leveau (1987) 152 and Gros (1987) 160, but doubts by P. André et al. (1991) 63; at Autun, Goudineau in *CAH* 10, ed. 2 (1996) 493 and Ramage (1997) 123.

35. Drinkwater (1983) 125; at Augusta Raurica, due north and south, Le Gall (1975) 318; presumed from position of new cities, Roddaz (1984) 393; but pre-Roman land-measurement even with its own measurement unit, the *candetum*, Favory (1983) 78; 89 n. 7, use of a *pes Drusianus* ($1^1/2$ Rom. ft) in Tongres area.

36. "Apparently" Augustan building at Limoges and Augustomagus, Ramage (1997) 123; *Princeton Encyclopedia* (1976) 126; aqueducts, Rebourg (1991) 105 and P. André et al. (1991) 67.

37. *Tegulae* and *imbrices*, *Mediolanum* (1988) 27, 303, residential of ca. 20 B.C.; cement, Bedon (1985) 92; late Augustan "petit appareil" at Alesia, Mangin (1986) 58; Maurin (1991) 54, 57, Mediolanum mosaics and, at Vienne, column capitals like those of the Roman Mars-Ultor temple, cf. also Audin (1985) 71.

38. Guillaumet and Rebourg (1987) 45, the late Augustan circuit being almost 6km.

39. Fora in Grenier (1958–60) 3, 1.364ff., 368ff., 383f.; Drack and Fellmann (1988) 106f., 109.

40. Balty (1991) 335f., later made Colonia Flavia Forum Segusiavorum; Vallette and Guichard (1991) 130.

41. Wightman (1975) 625 and Goudineau et al. (1980) 226 on Bibracte; Pelletier (1985) 176ff. on Lyon.

42. Le Glay (1991) 120.

43. MacMullen (1968) 337f. with some statistics on payrolls; Goudineau et al. (1980) 374, 376, 380, dismissive of the Hopkins thesis on the role of commerce (and see above, chap. 3 n. 18).

44. On Nyon, Vittinghoff (1951) 69 and Drack and Fellmann (1988) 20; Valentia not a military colony, Vittinghoff p. 7; Cenabum established with a mix of immigrants and indigenes, Strabo 4.2.3.

45. On Baeterrae villas, see Clavel (1970) 299, 307, and below, at nn. 54, 97; on the displacement of villages by villas in the area of Artois and Picardy, Agache (1975) 659f., 702, and passim, without, however, data easily distinguished as Augustan. Notice Strabo 4.1.11, the Allobrogian elite relocate from countryside to city; Goudineau (1991) 12, Latinitas "inevitably produced a draw toward the urban center, and in this sense, urbanization in Gaul was indeed Augustan, fundamentally;" J.-M. André (1991) 27, to the same effect, *re* Autun and generally; Wightman (1975) 624.

46. Maurin (1978) 148f., 181ff., with other less clear family stories of Saintes; Wightman (1975) 622, with more in Belgica, eadem (1985) 71; and above, at n. 11.

47. Soricelli (1995) 75, 101f.; Clavel (1970) 156, 197f.

48. Justin 43.5 tells of Trogus Pompeius' family rewarded for service to Pompey and Caesar; on the Valerii, Goudineau (1989) 61f. notices the texts, BG 1.47, 53, and 7.65, but

conflates the Helvetii and Helvii, and stretches the evidence in taking the young man to Rome. Holmes (1911) 52, 652, suggests Troucillus (BG 1.19.3)=Procillus, as is accepted "in general," cf. Soricelli (1995) 72 n. 41, who disagrees; but I side with the majority, and also suggest Caburus (1.47)=Caburus (7.65). In the Flaccus in question I would see the consul of 93, cf. Broughton (1951–52) 2.58. The Helvii lived in the Ardèche.

49. Examples above at n. 47, cf. *Archéologie à Nîmes* (1990) 203, showing the drift of *cognomen*-change from Celtic of the grandfather to Roman of the elder grandson, but not the younger; generally on Province name-shifts, Chastagnol (1990) 577ff. and Christol (1992) 29ff., 34, 59.

50. Gros (1986) 66ff.; G.-C. Picard (1963) 122; idem (1992) 121ff.; F. S. Kleiner (1977) 664f.

51. Burnand (1975) 36, 51, 230, 233, cf. Brunt (1971) 205 on the question, which Domitius gave the name to its later bearers in the Province (probably later Republican ones).

52. Fiches and Soyer (1983) 271ff. on the vast Nîmes area, where "the spread of habitation and cadastration seem to be connected phenomena, profoundly changing the countryside and exploitation of it"; Clavel-Lévêque and Favory (1992) 103; and Perez (1995) 16, cadastration promotes sedentarization.

53. Soricelli (1995) 117ff.; Brun (1993) 309f., 314; Kneissl (1988) 242.

54. Clavel (1970) 299, 302, 307; idem (1971) 15; Pelletier (1991) 33 on Clavel's evidence; and Clavel-Lévêque and Favory (1992) 102. Notice the small numbers of Caesarian veterans in Narbo, much outnumbered by native citizens, Gayraud (1981) 176.

55. Clavel (1970) 580; Pelletier (1991) 30f., with the statement, "the great period for giving out of citizenship arose after the conquest and the turn of the era"; Ramage (1997) 121. The 14 Latin-right towns that I count are, in my Fig. 11, nos. 1–3, 5, 20, 25, 27–28, 32–33, 35, 39, 43, and 46, including four (32–33, 35, 39) not in Pelletier's list of Latin colonies, (1991) 29, and excluding his Ruscino, Antibes, Saint-Paul—Trois-Chateaux, and Lodève (on which, of date A.D. 20? 60?, see Perez [1995] 155).

56. Grenier (1958–60) 3, 1.118; Deman (1975) 32; Darde and Lasalle (1993) 16; Chouquer (1983) 292ff.; and Perez (1995) 16, on "the degree to which, by Orange cadastration, . . . traditional structures, *solidarités*, were destroyed and traditional dependencies were erased to make way for new connections of clientage which can be divined through toponymy."

57. Pre-Roman cadastres, Favory (1983) 78, 98, 106 n. 161, and Clavel-Lévêque (1983) 217; Roman centuriation, ibid. 240, 257f.; Clavel (1970) 207 and map 7, 209; idem (1971) 12; Lopez Paz (1994) 354f., 366f., 380ff.; *termini* between Arausio and Aquae Sextiae, 13; Via Domitia rules, 52, and Clavel-Lévêque and Favory (1992) 104. For a broad update, Soricelli (1995) 92–107; and for a still-useful map, see CIL 12, ed. O. Hirschfeld (1888), Tab. I and II.

58. Grenier (1958–60) 3, 1.112, grid and 100-foot module in siting of major buildings at Fréjus; Ward-Perkins (1970) 4, Nîmes; Clavel (1971) 13, Béziers; and, on Orange, Assénat (1994–95) 44ff.; on bisecting of city centers by cadaster lines, Perez (1995) passim, e.g. 109 and 120 (Narbo, twice), 131ff., 148 (Baeterrae), 143 (Nîmes), and a gen-

eral statement emphasizing the role of Augustus, 245 n. 319; but of Hellenistic tradition, orthogonal elements (not so disciplined as the Roman would be) at Nages, Entremont, and Lattes, cf. Py (1993) 201, 204f., 208, 210.

59. Walls, at Nîmes, Varène (1987) 17, 19f., and Darde and Lassalle (1993) 49, 56.

60. Orange, Magdinier and Thollard (1987) 88f.; Arles and Fréjus, Goudineau et al. (1980) 260, noting, idem in *CAH*, ed. 2 (1996) 482, their small circuit (50ha) compared to Nîmes and Orange (200ha); also Aix's walls, Gros (1987) 160.

61. Bedon (1984) 27ff., 35f.; Ward-Perkins (1992) 15.

62. Nîmes' shrine to the eponymous god, Grenier (1958–60) 4, 2.495; Circius-shrine, Sen., *Quaest. nat.* 5.17f., *divus certe Augustus templum illi* [=Circio], *cum in Gallia moraretur et vovit et fecit*, cf. the imperial prince Gaius' gift of a *xystum*, an ornamental garden, to Nîmes, Grenier (1958–60) 3, 1.15; attestation of Augustus, Agrippa, or the princes as patrons of cities, at Baeterrae, Clavel (1971) 12; Nîmes' coin legends, Le Glay (1991) 124; Nîmes-gifts, Ward-Perkins (1970) 4.

63. Detection of a "Bauboom," e.g. Rolland (1958) 10 or Kienast (1982) 351f.

64. Augustan/Agrippan attribution, cf. Ward-Perkins (1981) 223 and Kienast (1982) 350 n. 159, citing H. Kähler, and Roddaz (1984) 400; ca. mid-1st cent., *Archéologie à Nîmes* (1990) 140 and Darde and Lassalle (1993) 26, 87.

65. Pelletier (1991) 33, Narbo; Maurin (1978) 98, 100, Saintes; Grenier (1958–60) 3, 4.49f., the Fréjus aqueduct with a relief of a builder, a soldier, in a veteran-settlement town; baths but no aqueduct, Goudineau et al. (1980) 285, late Augustan, at Vaison and Glanum—the latter, the earliest known in Gaul, ca. 40 B.C., cf. Ward-Perkins (1970) 3; and Mediolanum baths, Guyon et al. (1991) 99, late Augustan.

66. Theaters near cult centers are well known, cf. e.g. Grenier (1958–60) 3, 2.854–59; 4, 2.725; Provost (1994) 210ff.; Gallic design, Gros (1996) 296, e.g. at Naintré, Augustan; without evident cult connection, at Lugdunum Convenarum, Guyon et al. (1991) 108, late Augustan; at Nîmes, with an amphitheater too, Ramage (1997) 141, with a theater also at Arausio; at Arelate, Forum Iulii, and Apta, Kienast (1982) 350 n. 162 and Goudineau et al. (1980) 294; at Vaison, Pelletier (1991) 33; and many of Augustan date in the Three Gauls, e.g. Burdy and Pelletier (1994) 21, Augustan, seating 5,000.

67. Gros (1991) 384ff., with the same under Tiberius at Arles.

68. Special tracks &c in south Gaul, Courtois (1998) 98, 100; on funding, Pelletier (1991) 33 is quite right to assume theaters were all built by evergetes. On *proedria*, indicated at an early date in Narbo for *flamines, inter decuriones senatoresque subsellio primo spectandi ludos publicos*, cf. *FIRA*, ed. 2, 1.199 line 5.

69. Arles' altar, Gros (1987a) 347 and (1991) 137; others, those seven in Spain at Emerita, the northwest, etc., deriving in some sense from the one in Mytilene, Etienne (1958) 378, 380–88, and in the east at Miletus, Balty (1991) 284 and at Milyas in 5/4 B.C., Mitchell (1993) 1.103.

70. Nîmes' altar, Christol and Goudineau (1987–88) 102ff. and Ramage (1997) 153, disagreeing with P. Gros, who sees a joint cult of Roma and Augustus here.

71. C. Goudineau, *CAH*, 10 ed. 2 (1996) 486; cf. the two temples at Magdalensburg of ca. 15 B.C., Alföldy (1974) 70; and May (1996) 37f. on the late Augustan imperial cult temple on the Mediolanum forum. Note the adherence to the festal calendar of Rome in the Narbo-altar decree, Fishwick (1991–93) 2.482. For Capitolia, cf. Barton (1982) 268 listing Arausio, Baeterrae, and perhaps Vienna, also Lugdunum; also Badie et al.

(1994) 119 willing to accept only this last as certain; but the Narbo capitol is ruled out by Gayraud (1981) 259.

72. Johnson et al. (1961) 131 n. 1a on the *flamen-Dialis* parallels; Fishwick (1991–93) 2.379, 478f.; Riccobono et al. (1968–72) 1.199ff.; J.-M. André (1991) 24f. Compare below, n. 75.

73. Clavel (1970) 456f.; Goudineau l. c.; Gros (1991) 137; the decree's later appearances, MacMullen (1981) 13f.; its text discussed, Kneissl (1980) 294f., . . . *ceterae leges huic arae titulisque eadem sunto, quae sunt Dianae in Aventino* . . . ; 301 on festivals; and Johnson et al. (1961) 130 on the flamen-rules.

74. Hill (1953) 222; Finocchi (1994) 96; 110 known deities in Province, Lavagne (1979) 193; add, the "Temple of Diana" (identification uncertain, but certainly not a Greco-Roman huntress!) at Nîmes, Darde and Lassalle (1993) 68f. Which gods temples served, e.g. at Lugdunum Convenarum or Glanum ("Twin Temples"), can rarely be told.

75. Known from literary mention and unlikely to be afterthoughts in the monumental-ization of the center, Capitolia at Narbo and Tolosa, Grenier (1958–60) 3, 1.270, though evidence on Narbo's does tilt toward a 2nd-century date, Fishwick (1991–93) 1.252f.; otherwise identified at Arelate, Grenier 182, and Arausio, 269, with still more in Badie et al. (1994) 115, the Baeterrae temple on a podium but not a Capi-tolium.

76. Date of Glanum forum, Gros and Varène (1984) 29ff., from the 20s B.C. with changes over the latter years of Augustus; Roth-Congès (1987) 191; and Février et al. (1989) 306.

77. The Augusta Bagiennorum forum plan adapted from Assandria and Vacchetta (1925) Pl. 1 and Ward-Perkins (1970); Feurs' forum in Balty (1991) 335 and Fig. 169, pointing (342ff.) to similarities of *curia*-location with the central Italian town of Iuvanum; Val-lette and Guichard (1991) 113 and Fig. 2, adducing (152f.) many Gallic parallels to the tripartite plan. Several plans can be seen in Grenier (1958–60) 3, 1.291 (Arles, the basilica on a long side as at Conimbriga), Lugdunum Convenarum, 331, or Augst, 370; discussion and plans in Ward-Perkins (1970) 6ff. and (1977) 200f.; some com-parative remarks and other tripartite fora in Gros (1996) 220f.; Italian models, 210ff., or Balty (1991) 360ff.

78. Forums, e.g. Ward-Perkins (1970) 1; Roddaz (1984) 399; Ramage (1997) 141; and on square-C cryptoporticoes, at Feurs, below, n. 83; at Narbo as a *horreum* of late 40s roughly 51m × 38m, Solier (1973) 315, 324, and Gayraud (1981) 254f; at Arles (not a *horreum*), roughly 89m × 59m with double aisles nearly 4m wide, some walls of "pe-tit appareil," some of rubble in layers, Amy (1973) 276f., 282f., and Rouquette and Sintès (1989) 41ff.; use of "petit appareil" and *opus reticulatum*, Solier (1973) 317 and Amy (1973) 277.

79. At Glanum and Ruscino, Goudineau et al. (1980) 274; Alesia, cf. Grenier (1958–60) 3, 1.344f.; at Alba and perhaps Nîmes, Balty (1991) 101f., 108f.

80. Grenier (1958–60) 3, 1. 138 and Pelletier (1991) 33; Lugdunum Convenarum, cf. Guyon et al. (1991) 92, dating is late Augustan or early Tiberian; mosaics, 102, 106; Badie et al. (1994) 119, a date ca. A.D. 15; but cf. May (1996) 43f., saying the building went up "after A.D. 20," but on foundations of ca. 20 B.C. (?).

81. Above, nn. 39, 60; Grenier (1958–60) 3, 1.32 on Pont du Gard and La Turbie;

Goudineau (1979) Pl. 80, intercolumniation as module for peristyle-design in a Vaison dwelling.

82. House of Likine, La Caridad, above, chap. 3 nn. 104f.; Vaison, in Goudineau (1979) 99, date ca. 40 B.C. (93, 115, 190). Cf. the interaxial measurement of the corner columns of the Ostian model temple, exactly one Roman foot (below, n. 90, and Pensabene [1997] 129).

83. Glanum, cf. Roth-Congès (1987) 196 with n. 16; Feurs forum, Vallette and Guichard (1991) 113, 141, 143, 150, dated to 2nd half of 1st century B.C.

84. Jeppesen (1989) 31, on Vitr. 8.3.24f. (cf. 1 pr. 2); Schrijvers (1989) 16; and the not very great possibility that he served as *praefectus fabrum*, *Der kleine Pauly* 5 (1975) s.v. "Vitruvius" 1309f. or *Ox. Class. Dict.*, ed. 3 (1996) s.v. "Mamurra."

85. Glanum baths by the 40s B.C., Grenier (1958–60) 4, 1.248 and Goudineau (1979) 103f., 108, 123; at Vaison and Arles, 254ff., 263; frescoes from 1st quarter of 1st century B.C., Février et al. (1989) 318 and Barbet (1990) 105, 132–34, offering spectacular color "restitutions"; in significant quantity in Provincia (not Tres Galliae) from 40s B.C., Barbet (1982–83) 54, 66ff.; late Augustan in Raetia, Drack (1983) 9; tile roofs, *Mediolanum* (1988) 27 (with date, ca. 20 B.C., p. 303), Goudineau (1979) 102f., and *Archéologie à Nîmes* (1990) 49; mosaics at Nîmes in 1st half of 1st century, Darde and Lassalle (1993) 25, or at Béziers, Clavel (1970) 158; "petit appareil," Ward-Perkins (1970) 4 or Goudineau (1979) 191f., 196f., citing many sites and kinds of buildings; but pervasive persistence also of traditional construction materials and methods, Goudineau et al. 240; Clavel l. c., central impluvium, hypocausts, painted walls; plans, Chevallier (1975) 758–63; and frescoes in eight sites not colonial (Glanum, Ensérune, etc.), Soricelli (1995) 118.

86. Goudineau et al. (1980) 181.

87. Chap. 3, above, at nn. 55 (the Didius mausoleum) and 122; the same scholar there quoted, speaking of Narbo and Arelate, Pfanner (1990) 69, cf. C. Goudineau, *CAH*, ed. 2 (1996) 486, quoted, instancing Augusta Tricastinorum; a full survey of eastern Province in Roth-Congès (1993) 389f., 30 examples from 2nd quarter of 1st century B.C., most around the turn of the era and (393f.) showing military careers of native elite.

88. The early Augustan Sestino mausoleum, Verzar (1974), the fold-out Zeichnung I, i, facing p. 444, adducing parallels from all over the peninsula (391ff., 410ff.) and (412 n. 1) St.-Rémy, with eastern in-put perceptible, 422; also, Tamassia (1984) 90f., on Mantova and still other late Republican or early Augustan Italian sites, F. S. Kleiner (1977) 676–79, and Prieur (1986) 80–85, surveying the whole Mediterranean for comparison with Glanum.

89. I make the Actium connection from the conjectures of Gros (1981) 165f.; for the Italian connection (but much earlier), as he points out, Pairault (1972) 44f., 123f., 126–33 with Pls. 48a, 49, 51–53, 55f., 64,, 72f., 75f.; for a suggestion that the services were to Caesar, the Monument of 30–20 B.C., cf. Gros (1986) 68, with which G.-C. Picard (1964) 20 seems to agree.

90. Other Mars-Ultor copying, above, n. 37 (Vienne) and chap. 3 nn. 47, 100; copying of other Rome buildings, F. S. Kleiner (1977) 666. Heilmeyer (1970) 108, 111f., 115f., Ward-Perkins (1981) 227, and Gros (1987a) 343 suggest a real Roman immigrant stone-cutter, cf. tomb-decoration, Goudineau in *CAH* 10, ed. 2 (1996) 486, or wall-

painting, Barbet (1982–83)165, and, for Spain, Ramallo (1993) 226; but local copying is the answer, says Goudineau (1979) 242 n. 231, italicizing "à partir de cartons diffusées par l'Urbs [=Rome] . . . On observe, à tous les niveaux, une volonté constante, sinon toujours bien servie par les artisans locaux, d'imiter jusque dans le moindre détail les créations contemporaines de la capitale." For the late Republican Ostian model and the Vitruvius text, see Pensabene (1997) 129ff., the Ostian miniature temple following the rules of modules with a scale of 1:32 (the actual temple on the Piazza delle Corporazioni?), and Haselberger (1997) 80f., 93, comparing the idea of resort to a few precious imported models of building parts, Trillmich (1993) 52, with copies of varying skill (plain in Pl. 56a–b).

91. F. S. Kleiner (1977) 668ff., 672, Iulii-Monument sculptors working also at Lyon and Avennio; Rolland (1977) 32, Glanum Arch artists working also at Carpentras; Arles stone-cutters at work also in Cabelio and Arausio, Janon (1986) 43.

92. F. S. Kleiner (1977) 680f.; on the Maison Carrée column capitals, Heilmeyer (1970) 108f. and Gros (1983) 442f.

93. Above, chap. 2 at n. 60 and chap. 3 at n. 99.

94. Gros (1987a) 346f. The date for the shield, 26 B.C., which other scholars are agreed on, Gros (1991) 137 would now move down by a decade, with reasons I can't evaluate; and Christol (1995) 51 sticks to the earlier.

95. Ward-Perkins (1981) 227 and Sauron (1983) 62f.; at Arles, Ramage (1997) 144.

96. Above, n. 61; Gros (1987a) 343; Pensabene (1972) 323, (1989) 45, and (1982) 119 n. 14, the St. Tropez wreck; and Ward-Perkins (1981) 227, quoted.

97. Barbet (1982–83) 130, "on suppose la simultanéité de l'adoption des modes décoratives entre Italie et la Gaule à l'époque d'Auguste," with parallels in promptness at Lyon, 164.

98. On the passivity of the emperor, not initiating change, cf. Millar (1977), essentially accepted even by those who would disagree, e.g. Ste. Croix (1981) 375, or who are confronted by those who agree, cf. reff. in MacMullen (1984) 162 n. 3.

99. Vine scrolls of the Ara Pacis are offered "explicitement" to diffuse a style, the acanthus is elevated to an Apollinian image, cf. Sauron (1988) 9f., 36f.; and (I quote only from the major scholars championing this interpretation of the style) its "meaning is clear: it evokes through its unfolding . . . the virtues of the Golden Age renewed through the Princeps; its vision is that of a natural abundance, exuberant but disciplined and warranted by the Augustan peace," Gros (1996) 159 on the Maison Carrée frieze; Zanker (1991) 203 and (1988) 266, "the new political imagery"; "official ideology" expressed in art consistent with "the central plan of moral restoration," M. Torelli in CAH 10, ed. 2 (1996) 932, with "programmatic foundations in the ideology of the state . . . for the propagation of the religious, political and symbolic elements of this revival" (933), with a "type of message . . . loftier and richer in ethical or political content" (940).

100. Quoted from Zanker (1988) 282, 284.

101. Blanckenhagen and Alexander (1962) 35, 58 with n. 109, and 60f.; Torelli p. 948, agreeing with the derivation of the style from Julia's and Agrippa's Rome house, contrasted (949) with something less Augustan in Augustus' own house in the preceding decade.

102. Perennius' the mother-atelier for terra sigillata, Paturzo (1996) 68; Zanker (1988) 266.

103. Balil (1959) 312f., Figs. 2f.; 311, quoted ("common themes"); 312, quoted ("noble"); Greifenhagen (1963) 75, 77ff. and Abb. 73, with the quotation from p. 80. A good color plate in Johns (1982) 129, with comment on the work's "reticence," etc., p. 125. For an entirely different kind of erotic scene, obviously popular because common, see e.g. Oswald (1937) Pls. 90f.

104. Quoted, M. Torelli in CAH 10, ed. 2 (1996) 951, describing the gilt-silver cup from Hoby (Denmark); K. F. Johansen (1930) 273ff. and Paturzo (1996) chap. 5 passim, esp. 83, and discussion of the Hoby cup, 84 and its ceramic match.

105. The silver Warren/Thomas cup now at Oxford, Vermeule (1963) 38 and Pl. 14, 2, 4, and 6 = Johns (1982) 103 Fig. 84 and 113 Fig. 25.

106. For Vitruvius' "encyclopédisme de façade," cf. Frézouls (1989) 39; for his silence about patrons while speaking of painting, cf. Leach (1982) 140, with Vitruv. 7.5.3ff. on dealing with frescoists, and 7.4.4, the architect controls the over-all decor and, 7.9.2, if the customer intervenes, he's a fool; and the outburst in 7.5.4, esp. ad fin., castigating haec falsa [= bad art] videntes homines [=patrons] non reprehendunt sed delectantur.

107. E.g. Att. 1.3 and 14; Fam. 7.23; above, chap. 3 n. 67; and Plin., N. H. 35.116, an Augustan frescoist much admired and "his fees small," cf. 35.50—though better yet are painters on tabulae which the owner can take with him if he moves. Of imperial commissions, I agree with the conjecture of Zanker (1988) 108, that "the princeps himself set the guidelines by determining the location and the level of expenditure for raw materials and building costs" (but, I would add, anything beyond that was the artist's affair). For luxury silver and bronze vessels, figurines, and furniture en route to the Province, see Parker (1992) 183, 377.

108. Plin., N. H. 35.120, an Augustan artist gravis ac severus . . . , paucis horis pingebat, id quoque cum gravitate, quod semper togatus quamquam in machinis.

109. Gruen (1992) 132ff., 140; Schrijvers (1989) 14; Gros (1983) 437, architects virtually invisible, lowly technicians, and (444) the customer surely ignorant of their technique and vocabulary (yes, I agree).

110. Gilbert (1998) 399, 404, 412 (quoted), 446.

111. For example, a guild determines on a commission, to be executed in a style similar to something already on display by a well-known artist, in Vasari (1965) 106f.; and other artists are consulted on whom to hire for the job, ibid. 108; and on agents, cf. Gilbert (1998) passim, e.g. 401, 408, 417.

112. Ibid. 422 on Justice, and idem (1980) 197.

113. The phrase, Gilbert (1998) 398, with Gilbert's sardonic comments on the present-day "career advantage in research postulating widespread symbolic supervision" by patron, where in fact such theories are "relatively immune to disproof" (p. 445).

114. Rolland (1977) 42 compares the Glanum arch with Avennio's, Arelate's, Narbo's; Ramage (1997) 125 lists ten or twelve in the Province, Carpentras, Baeterrae, etc.; G.-C. Picard (1992) 127 and Perez (1995) 247 date the Arausio arch to a late-Augustan commencement, with its final dedication under Tiberius.

115. Gros (1996) 59 finds an "astonishing" detail of control in the Tabula Siarensis of 19 B.C. (cf. Potter and Damon [1999] 26 lines 75, 83, and Tac., Ann. 2.83), but it doesn't reach to art and symbolism. Alföldy (1979) 180 adds Tac., Ann. 1.74.

116. The northeast pair are taken to be both males by Rolland (1977) 35 and Clavel-

Lévêque and Lévêque (1982) 690; but the violation of symmetry seems to me most unlikely, other details seem to me decisive (height of supposed second male, costume), and a uniform pairing of male-female is seen by Espérandieu, *Recueil* 1.90, G.-C. Picard (1957) 197, Gros (1981) 161 n. 18, and Ramage (1997) 127.

117. Rolland 35 (Pergamene echoes); 46, a post-Caesarian war recalled (so also, Ramage 130); G.-C. Picard (1957) 197, it is Caesar's conquest recalled.

118. Clavel-Lévêque and Lévêque (1982) 680f.; Duval (1965) 124f.; and Ramage (1997) 125.

119. Clavel-Lévêque and Lévêque (1982) 680, compare the program empire-wide, D. E. E. Kleiner (1985) 116 or at Glanum, Gros (1981a) 126f., 143; and surviving busts of the imperial family sometimes in clusters, at e.g. Béziers, Clavel (1971) 12f. or Arles, Ramage (1997) 154, or Ruscino, Barruol and Marichal (1987) 54. Notice the colossal Carrara-marble head of Augustus for delivery somewhere in the Province, but shipwrecked, Parker (1992) 366. For the Marius-head at Narbo, see Balty (1981) 97.

120. Above, n. 68.

121. Above, nn. 86 (private houses) and 92; traces of "originality," "vitality," or "tradition," beyond mere incompetence, noticed by Janon (1986) 90 (Narbo), Gros (1996) 155 (Glanum), 157 (Nîmes), and characteristic of the region, cf. Heilmeyer (1970) 113f.

122. Torque noticed by G.-C. Picard (1963) 124 and Rolland (1958) 104, who finds it unmatched in Gaul; on the akroterion's general style, ibid and C. Picard (1963a) 132ff.

123. King (1990) 228.

124. On epigraphy in Italy, cf. Alföldy (1991) 292; on Augustus' role in spreading epigraphy, 298, 322; in Narbonensis, Christol (1995) 52.

125. Strabo 4.1.12, in Herman (1983) 1046 and (1990) 54, 148; Varro in Jerome's chronicle, cf. Polomé (1983) 527 n. 51; and Iren., *C. haer.* 1 pr. 3. I do not cite Tac., *Ann.* 3.43, mentioning "a school of liberal studies at Autun for the offspring of Gaul's highest nobility," since this is in a context of the A.D. 20s (though Maurin [1991] 59 thinks the school "sans doute" contemporary with the city's founding).

126. Very much bilingualism, cf. Herman (1990) 153f.; one single Latin found empire-wide, 12, 24, 36, 47, 63; Dardel (1992) 83; Stefenelli (1995) 35; and Fischer (1995) 479.

127. Flobert (1992) 106, 111ff.; a similar rabbit of Claudian date in Oswald (1937) 133 and Pl. LXXXI 2106, etc.; and C. Goudineau, in *CAH* 10, ed. 2 (1996) 485, instances from an early date, not exactly indicated, a Vaison graffito on a sherd, "Don't steal me," which addresses a world assumed by the inscriber to be Latin-speaking.

128. Balsan (1970) 179 Fig. 1.6, among a selection of sherds of the turn of the era on to Tiberian.

129. Tuffreau-Libre (1996) 58; Passelac (1996) 11, 13–17.

130. Flobert (1992) 259.

131. Ettlinger (1987) 5f., Narbo production for western armies, Lyon (p. 8) for the north; Wells (1977) 135f.; Flobert (1992) 104; repaired pots, Mayet (1984) 1.239.

132. Supposing a push from Italy, C. Goudineau, in *CAH* 10, ed. 2 (1996) 479, and Wells (1977) 135, though conceding some small-scale local initiatives; but Passelac (1996) 11 shows the potential success of purely local enterprise on a small scale; and the remarkable publication of Mayet (1984) shows how, from Claudian times, the same en-

terprise in northern and southern Spain at two sites could, by Flavian times, give rise to another really big business in ceramic manufacture (I pp. 16f., 54, 91, 94f., 210ff., and passim).

133. MacMullen (1968) 339; Baatz (1977) 148ff., 153f.; Tuffreau-Libre (1996) 59; and, on Pollentia in Mallorca and Rhine army stations, Berlin (1993) 38ff.

134. The texts that count, at least for the Province, are Cic., Font. 33, equating the barbari and bracati still to be found in Gaul in ca. 70 B.C., but then Pomponius Mela 2.74 in the A.D. 40s, fuit aliquando Bracata nunc Narbonensis, with Plin., N. H. 3.31, Narbonensis . . . bracata antea dicta; Wild (1985) 377, 384, 410; women's wear doesn't change, p. 413 and MacMullen (1990) 63.

135. Wightman (1985) 126.

CHAPTER V: REPLICATION

1. Lugli (1957) 371, 375, 450; Carettoni et al. (1960) 1.81, 95; Sear (1982) 74; MacMullen (1993) 61f.

2. Explained by Lugli 387f. (use of cassoni lignei), 416; by Goudineau (1979) 190f., 195, "opus caementicium required both less time and less specialization," to which, add as a variant or development opus reticulatum, representing, "one may say, industrialization . . . , techniques of mass production, and use of shuttering, coffrages de bois recuperables à l'infini"; also MacDonald (1982) 147, who offers further information in conversation (my cordial thanks to my omniscient friend). Grenier (1958–60) 3, 1.24 was right to emphasize the call for very large numbers of unskilled or semi-skilled labor that must explain the "building-boom" in Gaul under Augustus. Cf. the ca. 11,000,000 quite uniform blocks required for a single project, Autun's walls, Varène (1987) 45.

3. Roman production of "spawls" for concrete, of any size, cannot have been different from the method (quoted) in eighteenth-century Weymouth, England, Smeaton (1793) 65.

4. On opus incertum and reticulatum, Lugli 372, 422, 446, esp. 488; Goudineau 196, "petit appareil constitutes the equivalent of reticulatum. It represents a regional adaptation of the Italian technique and its attribution to Roman influence can give rise to no disagreement."

5. Above, on exported Roman wall techniques, chap. 1 nn. 78, 81; 3 n. 55; 4 n. 85; in the Province, Goudineau (1979) 191f.; and cryptoporticoes, chap. 4 n. 78 (to say nothing of those in Spain, e.g. Conimbriga).

6. Grenier (1958–60) 3, 1.15, a sphaeristerium in A.D. 4.

7. Chaps. 1 at n. 67; 2 at n. 7; 3 at nn. 3, 10, 22f.; and 4 at n. 65.

8. Barcelona, cf. Pfanner (1990) 70f., 87 (date in 30s B.C.?), compared with Ostia or other Italian colony plans; Balty (1991) 361 versus Euzennat and Hallier (1986) 90, 96f., nn. 110, 112, both citing MacMullen (1959) 221f. and nn; and above, chap. 1 n. 67 and 3 n. 3. Cf. Kienast (1982) 364, supposing "that the greater part of Augustan construction . . . was carried through by soldiers."

9. Above, chap. 2 n. 8, 3 n. 18, and 4 nn. 52, 84.

10. Lopez Paz (1994) 333; Blume et al. (1967) 1.172 lines 2f. and 194 lines 9f.; on the surveyor Balbus, 239 lines 15ff., with controversy in Dilke (1971) 38, Moatti (1993) 93,

and Perez (1995) 45, from all which, I see the man in question as, at the least, handling sources of Augustus' time, and perhaps himself of that time. On the fragments of the Arausio plan, first extensively studied by A. Piganiol, see e.g. Hinrichs (1989) 123 n. 28, 125, Assénat (1994–95) 53f., and Moatti (1993) chaps. 2, 3, 5, and passim, to show that durability on which Lopaz Paz insists (and to refute the suggestion of N. Purcell in a review, JRS 80 [1990] 180, that the map amounted only to "the rhetoric of display of wealth" without relevance to "the ability to retrieve meaningful information from the record.")

11. Chap. 3 at nn. 51ff., 4 at nn. 59, 81ff.

12. The best explanation of technique that I know is Paturzo (1996) 128f., 132ff., 141; or see A. Stenico, s. v. "Aretini, vasi" in the Enciclopedia delle arte antica classica e orientale 1 (1958) cols. 609f.; in English, Baur (1941) 245f. (with thanks for reff. to my friend C. Lucas).

13. Whittaker (1985) 50.

14. Grenier (1958–60) 4, 2.796; Menzel (1985) 160, where the identical nature is clear in the photographs, Pl. 13; compare the identical (or virtually identical) Jupiter bronzes in discussions of Sucellus-figurines, above, chap. 4 n. 24.

15. Antony's portrait, e.g. Braemer (1948–49) 112f. or Holtzman and Salviat (1984) 265f., 271f., Thasos, Narbo, etc.; Caesar's portrait, above, chap. 1 n. 18, Lämmer (1975) 102, and Keay (1995) 310; colossal statues for Augustus, in the east, above, chap. 1 n. 18; in Africa, chap. 2 n. 42, Gsell (1972) 8.225, Smajda (1978) 180 (with smallest size for princes, p. 181), Bejor (1987)104f., Leveau (1984) 16, and Fittschen (1979a) 232; and in Spain, chap. 3 n. 95 and Garcia y Bellido (1949) 1.22f. For group displays, cf. above, chap. 1 nn. 18, 72; 2 nn. 42, 62f.; and 3 nn. 94f. Totals in Walker and Burnett (1981) 25 with map, 48, and Pfanner (1989) 178, proposing a total of 25–50,000.

16. Trillmich (1993) 57; Fittschen (1979) 218.

17. Pfanner (1989) 188 or Boschung and Pfanner (1990) 138 Fig. 12a-b-c; but I prefer to cite the 1989 article, which the 1990 severely abbreviates.

18. Pfanner (1989) 194, the method sketched; its accuracy, 205–12 with Abb. 22–30; a half-dozen examples of Augustan times of "puntelli," 237f., 240, 245, 247, 250; further thorough, excellent discussion, passim; and the quotation, 226, with emphasis on the accompanying "Gleichförmigkeit und ihre normative Monotonie," or standardization. Cf. G.-C. Picard (1982) 180 on "the uniformity of imperial Roman art . . . , the chief types of official sculpture turn out almost identical in the different parts of the empire" (as is self-evident in any large selection of photographs). On plaster casts, presumed as vehicles of copying, see Fittschen (1979) 212 or Zanker (1983) 8 or (1991) 215.

19. Chap. 4 at nn. 115ff.; Pfanner cit., 226, "überall sehr ähnliche Bauten mit ähnlichem Bauschmuck . . . mit Recht als Ausdruck einer 'Reichskunst' an[zu]sehen;" Alföldy (1979) 189 on "the remarkable strictness of unity in the character of monumental statue bases"; and Landwehr (1990) 148, remarking on "une véritable industrie. L'art de la copie connut un premier sommet sous le règne d'Auguste." For a good illustration of the supply of the market, cf. Gsell (1972) 248ff.

20. Caes., BC 1.35, neque sui iudicii neque suarum esse virium discernere, utra pars iustiorem habeat

causam; Pompey's *beneficia*, 2.18, matched by Caesar, 2.21, with Dio 41.24.1 and Galsterer (1988) 63f., regarding Gades, cf. chap. 3 at n. 59, on [Caes.], *Bell. Hisp.* 42, *beneficia* to Hispalis.

21. On the "Latinization" of Provincia attributed to Caesar, see Sherwin-White (1973) 232 or C. Goudineau in *CAH* 10, ed. 2 (1996) 473, without the process being really explained or the attribution well defended. There is a tendency to see Caesar as more generous with citizenship than Augustus, but cf. Vittinghoff (1951) 97f. and Sherwin-White (1973) 233. The latter (225) finds generosity during wartime, where I emphasize its role in post-war settlements. Of urban centers, several dozen were made *municipia* by Caesar or Augustus in the east, Africa, and Spain, and perhaps 14 Latin colonies in Gaul.

22. Mattern (1999) 84, 38 legions at Philippi; at Actium, 16 (Octavian's) and 23 (Antony's, undersized); more complicated calculations in Brunt (1971) 480–501; the land costs, ibid. 337 (*Res Gestae* 16.1). My total of Augustan colonies is arrived at from the lists attached to my four maps, excluding the titular colonies of Gaul, with results considerably larger than Brunt's (cf. his App. 15); for my totals of pre-Augustan colonies, see the maps, again; and for the civilians, Suet., *Iul.* 42.1, "80,000 citizens distributed among [Caesar's] overseas colonies, to relieve the crowding of the overstrained city."

23. MacMullen (1990) 226; above, n. 5 with reff.

24. MacMullen (1990) 64.

25. The foremost is the elder Balbus, chap. 3 and n. 70; for other examples, sure or likely, of non-Roman individuals taking an active part in the civil wars and being rewarded afterwards, see above, chap. 1 nn. 18, 29, 31, 72, 89; chap. 3 nn. 7. 63f.; and chap. 4 nn. 11, 13, 46, 48, 87, 89.

26. Apparently not in a hostile sense, in [Caes.], *Bell. Hisp.* 35; clearly hostile, against an artifactually or institutionally or morally backward society, ibid. 35; Caes., *B. G.* 2.15, 5.34, 36; Cic., *Pro Balbo* 19.43; *Ad. Q. frat.* 1.1.27, quoted in the first chapter, above; Strabo 4.1.12; 4.4.4ff.; Pomp. Mela, *Chorography* 3.2.18f., from Poseidonios, in Brunaux (1996) 196.

27. Virg., *Aen.* 1.263, on Aeneas' destiny to give laws, etc., is aimed only at Italy and is either irrelevant or significant in what it does not say. Plin., *N. H.* 3.39, quoted, on *Italia* and *Roma, numine deum electa quae caelum ipsum clarus faceret, sparsa congregaret*, etc.; and Tac., *Agr.* 21, where I borrow parts of the translation of Birley (1999) 17, with (p. 80) an alternative English for *domus* which I adopt, and the comment, "This chapter is unique in the literary sources for Roman history as a record of officially sponsored 'Romanization.'" But I prefer my own ([1990] 64) translation of the two Latin words that Birley gives as "they began to compete with one another for his approval."

28. Ibid., and Fear (1996) 17ff. and Haley (1997) 496, and "the new orthodoxy" in between, noted by Hanson (1997) 67, which "sees the process [of Romanization] as an incidental, even accidental one." To this, Hanson doesn't subscribe, nor Ramage (1997) 150, "Romanization was surely one of the long-term goals . . . ," nor Whittaker (1997) 144, e.g., "It was cultural regeneration that was the intention of Augustus"(!), to be sought empire-wide through "the ideology of cities coupled to the moral order of society as a whole."

29. Lassèrre (1983) 889–93.

30. Frézouls (1991a) 100–111.
31. Engelmann and Knibbe (1989) 102—and add in explanation Suet., *Caes.* 42.
32. Vittinghoff (1951) 9 describes the Roman "imperial conception" in a long emphatic statement, too long to quote; similarly, Syme in 1983, quoted with agreement by Koch (1993) 24, on Rome's "kulturpolitischer Indifferenz," with all of which I agree; Beaujeu and Brunaux to the same effect, abov, chap. 4 n. 17; also Thébert (1978) 72, leaving more room for the *Agricola*-passage and (77), with Frézouls (1991) 112f., seeing the Roman elite in friendly, tolerant yoke with provincial elites, regardless of way of life.
33. Fuhrmann (1949) 65; *per contra*, the most effective advocate for an ideological content in Augustan art, Zanker (1988), with equal thoroughness, includes in his presentation generally rare objects, many post-Augustan for lack of contemporary works, and selected out of a mass that generally ignores the motifs he emphasizes, esp. pottery—in sum, an evidentiary base less sure than it seems. See further the arguments in chap. 4 at nn. 97ff., above.
34. Pflaum (1973) 67, going on to say, quite rightly, "Still, this behavior was a function of Rome's power;" and still, "the Romans never wanted to Romanize."

BIBLIOGRAPHY

NOTE: explanation of a few standard abbreviations such as ANRW, JRS, REA, may be found in *Année philologique*.

Abad and Abascal (1991)—Abad, L., and J. M. Abascal, *Textos para la historia de Alicante*, Alicante 1991.

Abad Casal and Aranegui Gasco (1993)—Abad Casal, L., and C. Aranegui Gasco, "Las ciudades romanas del los ámbitos levantino y barbarico," *La ciudad hispanorromana*, ed. C. Diez Rodrigo, Madrid 1993, 84–107.

Abascal (1995)—Abascal, J. M., "La temprana epigrafia latina de Carthago Nova," *Roma y el nascimiento de la cultura epigrafica en Occidente. Actas del Colloquio . . . 1992*, ed. F. Beltrán Lloris, Zaragoza 1995, 139–49.

Agache (1975)—Agache, R., "La campagne à l'époque romaine dans les grandes plaines du Nord de la France d'après les photographie aériennes," ANRW II, 4, Berlin 1975, 658–713.

Alarcão and Etienne (1977)—Alarcão, J., and R. Etienne, *Fouilles de Conimbriga*, I: *L'architecture*, Paris 1977.

Alarcão and Etienne (1979)—Alarcão, J., and R. Etienne, *Fouilles de Conimbriga*, VII: *Trouvailles diverses—conclusions générales*, Paris 1979.

Alexandropoulos (1987)—Alexandropoulos, J., "L'iconographie monétaire en Afrique proconsulaire sous Auguste et Tibère," *Karthago* 21 (1987) 65–80.

Alföldi (1979)—Alföldi, M. R., "Die Geschichte des numidischen Königreiches und seiner Nachfolder," *Die Numider. Reiter und Könige nördlich der Sahara*, eds. H. G. Horn and C. B. Rüger, Köln 1979, 43–74.

Alföldy (1974)—Alföldy, G., Noricum, trans. A. Birley, London 1974.

Alföldy (1977)—Alföldy, G., "L'onomastique de Tarragone," *L'onomastique latine*, Paris 1977, 293–95.

Alföldy (1979)—Alföldy, G., "Bildprogramme in den römischen Städten des Conventus Tarraconensis—Das Zeugnis der Statuenportamente," *Revista de la Universitad Complutense*, Ser. 2, 28, iv (1979) 177–275.

Alföldy (1986)—Alföldy, G., *Die römische Gesellschaft. Ausgewählte Beiträge*, Stuttgart 1986.

Alföldy (1991)—Alföldy, G., "Augustus und die Inschriften: Tradition und Innovation. Die Geburt der imperialen Epigraphik," *Gymnasium* 98 (1991) 289–324.

Alföldy (1995)—Alföldy, G., "Die Entstehung der epigraphischen Kultur der Römer an der Levanteküste," *Roma y el nacimiento de la cultura epigrafica en Occidente. Actas del Coloquio . . . 1992*, ed. F. Beltrán Lloris, Zaragoza 1995, 121–37.

Allen (1980)—Allen, D. F., *The Coins of the Ancient Celts*, Edinburgh 1980.

Alzinger (1972–75)—Alzinger, W., "Das Regierungsviertel," *Jahresheft oesterr. arch. Inst.* 50 (1972–75), Beibl. 230–99.

Amadassi Guzzo (1984)—Amadassi, M. G., "Les divinités dans les inscriptions de Tripolitaine: essai de mise au point," *Bull. arch. Comité trav. hist.*, Ser. 2, 17B (1984) 189–96.

Amadassi Guzzo (1988)—Amadassi Guzzo, M. G., "Cultura punica e cultura latina in Tripolitania. Osservazioni in base alle iscrizioni puniche e alle iscrizioni bilingui," *Bilinguismo e biculturalismo nel mondo antico. Atti del colloquio . . . 1987*, eds. E. Campanile et al., Pisa 1988, 23–33.

Amy (1973)—Amy, R., "Les cryptoportiques d'Arles," *Les cryptoportiques dans l'architecture romaine. Colloque internationale . . . 1972*, Rome 1973, 275–91.

J.-M. André (1991)—André, J.-M., "L'encadrement juridique des fondations augustéennes," *Les villes augustéennes de Gaule. Actes du colloque . . . 1985*, Autun 1991, 17–28.

P. André et al. (1991)—André, P. et al., "Données nouvelles sur la Vienne augustéenne," *Les villes augustéennes de Gaule. Actes du colloque . . . 1985*, Autun 1991, 61–77.

Aranegui (1987)—Aranegui, C., "Algunas construcciones preaugusteas de Sagunto," *Los Asentamientos ibericos ante la Romanización. Coloquio . . . 1986*, Madrid 1987, 155–62.

Archéologie à Nîmes (1990)—*Archéologie à Nîmes. Bilan de 40 années de recherches et découverts 1950–1990*, Nîmes 1990.

Ariño Gil (1990)—Ariño Gil, E., *Catastros Romanos en el Convento Juridico Caesaraugustano, La Region Aragonesa*, Zaragoza 1990.

Assandria and Vacchetta (1925)—Assandria, G., and G. Vachetta, "Augusta Bagiennorum. Planimetria generale degli scavi con cenni illustrativi," *Atti della Società piemontese di archeologia e belle arti* 10 (1925) 184–95.

Assénat (1994–95)—Assénat, M., "Le cadastre colonial d'Orange," *Rev. archéologique de Narbonnaise* 27–28 (1994–95) 43–55.

Attolini (1984)—Attolini, I., "La riscoperta della centuriazione: Falbe," *Misurare la terra: centuriazione e coloni nel mondo romano*, ed. R. Bussi, Modena 1984, 166–69.

Attolini (1984a)—Attolini, I., "La riscoperta della centuriazione: Kandler," *Misurare la terra: centurazione e coloni nel mondo romano*, ed. R. Bussi, Modena 1984, 170–71.

Audin (1985)—Audin, P., "L'équipement des villes entre Gironde et Loire d'Auguste à Claude," *Caesarodunum* 20 (1985) 61–82.

Austin (1940)—Austin, R. G., "Greek board games," *Antiquity* 13 (1940) 257–71.

Baatz (1977)—Baatz, D., "Reibschale und Romanisierung," *Rei cretariae Romanae fautorum acta* 17–18 (1977) 147–58.

Badie et al. (1994)—Badie, A., et al., *Saint-Bertrand-de-Comminges: 1. Le Temple du Forum et le monument à enceinte circulaire*, Bordeaux 1994.

Baldus (1987)—Baldus, H. R., "Syria," *The Coinage of the Roman World in the Late Republic. Proceedings of a Colloquium . . . 1985*, eds. A. M. Burnett and M. H. Crawford, Oxford 1987, 121–51.

Balil (1959)—Balil, A., "Vasos aretinos decorados conservados en el Museo Arqueologico de Barcelona y en el Museo Monografico de Ampurias," *Ampurias* 21 (1959) 310–23.

Balil (1983)—Balil, A., "Segni di scalpellino sulle mura romane di Tarragona," *Epigraphica* 45 (1983) 231–36.

Balsan (1970)—Balsan, L., "La louve de Romulus et Remus dans le céramique de la Graufesenque," *Riv. di Studi Liguri* 36 (1970) 176–82.

Balty (1991)—Balty, J. C., *Curia ordinis. Recherches d'architecture et d'urbanisme antiques sur les curies provinciales du monde romain*, Bruxelles 1991.

Bammer (1976–77)—Bammer, A., "Das Denkmal des C. Sextilius Pollio in Ephesos," *Jahresheft oesterr. arch. Institut* 51 (1976–77) Beibl. 78–91.

Barag (1993)—Barag, D., "King Herod's royal castle at Samaria-Sebaste," *Palestine Exploration Quarterly* 125 (1993) 3–18.

Barbet (1982–83)—Barbet, A., "La diffusion du IIIe style pompéien en Gaule," *Gallia* 40 (1982) 53–82; 41 (1983) 111–65.

Barbet (1990)—Barbet, A., "Les peintures de Glanum: une relecture," *Gallia* 47 (1990) 103–34.

Barruol and Marichal (1987)—Barruol, G., and R. Marichal, "Le forum de Ruscino," *Los foros romanos de la provincias occidentales*, Madrid 1987, 45–54.

Barton (1982)—Barton, I. M., "Capitoline temples in Italy and the provinces (esp. Africa)," *ANRW* II, 12, 1, Berlin 1982, 259–342.

Baur (1941)—Baur, P. V. C., "Megarian bowls in the Rebecca Darlington Stoddard Collection of Greek and Italian vases in Yale University," *Am. Jnl Archaeology* 45 (1941) 229–48.

Bayard and Cadoux (1982)—Bayard, D., and J.-L. Cadoux, "Les thermes du sanctuaire gallo-romain de Ribemont-sur-Ancre (Somme)," *Gallia* 40 (1982) 83–105.

Beaujeu (1976)—Beaujeu, J., "Cultes locaux et cultes d'empire dans les provinces d'Occident aux trois premiers siècles de notre ère," *Assimilation et résistance à la culture gréco-romaine dans le monde ancien. Travaux du VI Congrès international d'Etudes Classiques* . . . 1974, ed. D. M. Pippidi, Paris 1976, 433–43.

Becker-Bertau (1986)—Becker-Bertau, F., *Die Inschriften von Klaudiu Polis*, Bonn 1986.

Bedon (1984)—Bedon, R., *Les carrières et les carriers de la Gaule romaine*, Paris 1984.

Bedon (1985)—Bedon, R., "Les incidences de la réorganisation urbaine à l'époque d'Auguste sur la population des Trois Gaules," *Caesarodunum* 20 (1985) 83–102.

Bejor (1979)—Bejor, G., "L'edificio teatrale nell'urbanizzazione Augustea," *Athenaeum* 57 (1979) 125–38.

Bejor (1987)—Bejor, G., "Documentazione epigrafica di complessi statuari nell'Africa romana: alcuni esempi," *Africa Romana. Atti del IV Convegno* . . . 1986, Sassari 1987, 101–116.

Bellemore (1984)—Bellemore, J., ed., *Nicolaus of Damascus, Life of Augustus*, Bristol 1984.

Beltrán Lloris (1980)—Beltrán Lloris, F., *Epigrafia latina de Saguntum y su territorium (cronologia, territorium, notas prosopograficas, cuestiones municipales)*, Valencia 1980.

Beltrán Lloris (1990)—Beltrán Lloris, M., "El valle medio del Ebro y su monumentalización en época republicana y augustea," *Stadtbild und Ideologie. Die Monumentalisierung hispanischer Städte zwischen Republik und Kaiserzeit*, eds. W. Trillmich and P. Zanker, München 1990, 179–204.

Beltrán Lloris (1991)—Beltrán Lloris, M., "La colonia Celsa," *La Casa urbana hispanorromana. Ponencias y comunicaciones*, Zaragoza 1991, 131–64.

Beltrán Lloris (1997)—Beltrán Lloris, *Colonia Celsa*, Zaragoza 1997.

Benabou (1976)—Benabou, M., "Résistance et romanisation en Afrique du Nord sous le Haut-Empire," *Assimilation et résistance à la culture gréco-romaine dans le monde ancien. Travaux du VI Congrès international d'Etudes classiques* . . . 1974, ed. D. M. Pippidi, Paris 1976, 367–75.

Benabou (1981)—Benabou, M., "Anomalies municipales en Afrique romain?" *Ktema* 6 (1981) 253–60.

Bendala Galán (1982)—Bendala Galán, M., "Excavaciones en el Cerro de los Palacios," *Italica (Santiponce Sevilla). Actas* . . . 1980 [Excavaciones arqueológicas en España 121], Madrid 1982, 29–73.

Bendala Galán (1990)—Bendala Galán, M., "El plan urbanístico de Augusto en Hispania: precedentes y pautas macroterritoriales," *Stadtbild und Ideologie. Die Monumentalisierung hispanischer Städte zwischen Republik und Kaiserzeit*, eds. W. Trillmich and P. Zanker, München 1990, 25–42.

Benzina Ben Abdallah (1990)—Benzina Ben Abdalla, Z., "Une cité sufétale d'Afrique proconsulaire: Limisa," MEFRA 102 (1990) 509–515.

Berlin (1993)—Berlin, A. M., "Italian cooking vessels and cuisine from Tel Anafa," Israel Exploration Jnl 43 (1993) 35–44.

Bezerra de Meneses and Sarian (1973)—Bezerra de Menesses, U., and H. Sarian, "Nouvelles peintures liturgiques de Délos," Etudes Déliennes, Paris 1973, 77–109.

Birley (1998)—Birley, A. R., "Names at Leptis Magna," Libyan Studies 19 (1998) 1–19.

Birley (1999)—Birley, A. R., Tacitus, Agricola and Germany translated with an Introduction and Notes, Oxford 1999.

Biscardi (1993)—Biscardi, A., "Gai 3.134 e il diritto internazionale privato," Studi Senesi 105 (1993) 26–67.

Blanckenhagen and Alexander (1962)—Blanckenhagen, P. H. von, and C. Alexander, The Paintings from Boscotrecase, Heidelberg 1962.

Blazquez (1976)—Blazquez, J. M., "Rechazo y asimilación de la cultura romana en Hispania (siglos IV y V)," Assimilation et résistance à la culture gréco-romane dans le monde ancien. Travaux du VI Congrès international d'Etudes classiques . . . 1974, ed. D. M. Pippidi, Paris 1976, 63–94.

Blazquez (1988)—Blazquez, J. M., "Hispania en época julio-claudia," Estudios sobre la Tabula Siarensis, eds. J. Gonzalez and J. Arce, Madrid 1988, 201–32.

Blech (1993)—Blech, M., "Archäologische Quellen zu den Anfängen der Romanisierung," Hispania Antiqua. Denkmäler der Römerzeit, eds. W. Trillmich et al., Mainz 1993, 71–110.

Blume et al. (1967)—Blume, F., et al., eds., Die Schriften der römischen Feldmesser, ed. 2, 2 vols., Hildesheim 1967.

Bomgardner (1989)—Bomgardner, D. L., "The Carthage amphitheater: a reappraisal," Am. Jnl Archaeology 93 (1989) 85–103.

Bonneville (1986)—Bonneville, J.-N., "Les patrons du municipe d'Emporiae (Ampurias, Espagne)," Rev. des études anciennes 88 (1986) 181–200. Borbein (1975)—Borbein, A. H., "Die Ara Pacis Augustae. Geschichtliche Wirklichkeit und Programm," Jahrbuch deut. arch. Inst. 90 (1975) 242–66.

Boschung and Pfanner (1990)—Boschung, D., and M. Pfanner, "Les méthodes de travail des sculpteurs antiques et leur signification dans l'histoire de la culture," Pierre éternelle du Nil au Rhin. Carrières et préfabrication, ed. M. Waelkens, Bruxelles 1990, 127–42.

Boucher (1976)—Boucher, S., Recherches sur les bronzes figurés de Gaule pré-romaine et romaine, Rome 1976.

Boucher and Tassinari (1976)—Boucher, S., and S. Tassinari, Bronzes antiques du

Musée de la civilisation gallo-romaine à Lyon, 1: *Inscriptions, statuaire, vaisselle*, Paris-Lyon 1976.

Bourgeois (1994)—Bourgeois, L., "Le sanctuaire de Bennecourt (Yvelines): structures et rituels du IIe siècle av. J.-C. au IVe siècle de notre ère," *Le sanctuaires de tradition indigène en Gaule romaine. Actes du colloque . . . 1992*, ed. C. Goudineau et al., Paris 1994, 73–77.

Bourgeois and Mayet (1991)—Bourgeois, A., and F. Mayet, *Belo VI: Les sigillés*, Madrid 1991.

Bowersock (1965)—Bowersock, G. W., *Augustus and the Greek World*, Oxford 1965.

Box (1932)—Box, H., "Roman citizenship in Laconia, 1," *JRS* 22 (1932) 165–83.

Bradford (1957)—Bradford, J., *Ancient Landscapes. Studies in Field Archaeology*, London 1957.

Braemer (1948–49)—Braemer, F., "Un buste présumé de Jules César," *Bull. Soc. Nationale des Antiquaires de France* 1948–49, 112–16.

Brandon (1996)—Brandon, C., "Cement, concrete, and settling barges at Sebastos: comparisons with other Roman harbor examples and the descriptions of Vitruvius," *Caesarea Maritima. A Retrospective after Two Millennia*, eds. A. Raban and K. G. Holum, Leiden 25–40.

Brasseur (1996)—Brasseur, M., *Les Celtes. Les dieux oubliés*, Rennes 1996.

Braudel (1972)—Braudel, F., *The Mediterranean and the Mediterranean World in the Age of Philip II*, ed. 2, 2 vols., trans. S. Reynolds, New York 1972.

Broughton (1929)—Broughton, T. R. S., *The Romanization of Africa Proconsularis*, Baltimore 1929.

Broughton (1951–52)—Broughton, T. R. S., *The Magistrates of the Roman Republic*, 2 vols., New York 1951–52.

Brouquier-Reddé (1992)—Brouquier-Reddé, V., *Temples et cultes de la Tripolitaine*, Paris 1992.

Brown (1991)—Brown, S. S., *Late Carthaginian Child Sacrifice and Sacrificial Monuments in their Mediterranean Context*, Sheffield 1991.

Brun (1993)—Brun, J.-P., "L'oléiculture et la viticulture antiques en Gaule: instruments et installations de production," *La production du vin et de l'huile en Méditerranée. Actes du symposium . . . 1991*, Paris 1993, 307–41.

Brunaux (1986)—Brunaux, J.-L., *Les Gaulois. Sanctuaires et rites*, Paris 1986.

Brunaux (1996)—Brunaux, J.-L., *Les religions gauloises. Rituels celtiques de la Gaule*, Paris 1996.

Brunt (1971)—Brunt, P., *Italian Manpower 225 B.C.—A.D. 14*, Oxford 1971.

Brunt (1974)—Brunt, P. A., "C. Fabricius Tuscus and an Augustan dilectus," *Zeitschr. Papyrologie und Epigraphik* 13 (1974) 161–85.

Brunt (1988)—Brunt, P., *The Fall of the Roman Republic and Related Essays*, Oxford 1988.

Bulard (1908)—"Peintures murales et mosaïques de Délos," *Monuments Piot* 14 (1908) 8–213.

Burdy and Pelletier (1994)—Burdy, J., and A. Pelletier, *Guide du Lyon gallo-romain*, Lyon 1994.

The Buried City: Excavations at Leptis Magna, intro. R. Bianchi Bandinelli, text by E. Vergara Caffarelli and G. Caputo, trans. D. Ridgway, New York 1964.

Burillo Mozota (1991)—Burillo Mozota, F., "The evolution of Iberian and Roman towns in the middle Ebro valley," *Roman Landscapes. Archaeological Survey in the Mediterranean Region*, eds. G. Barker and J. Lloyd, London 1991, 37–46.

Burnand (1975)—Burnand, Y., *Domitii Aquenses, une famille de chevalliers romains de la région d'Aix-en-Province, mausolée et domaine*, Paris 1975.

Burnett et al. (1992)—Burnett, A., et al., *Roman Provincial Coinage*, I: *From the Death of Caesar to the Death of Vitellius* (44 B.C.—A.D. 69), Pt I: *Introduction and Catalogue*; II, *Indexes and Plates*, London 1992.

Cagiano de Azevedo (1941)—Cagiano de Azevedo, M., "I 'Capitolia' dell'impero romano," *Atti della Pont. Accad. Rom. di arch.*, Ser. 3, Memorie 5 (1941) 1–76.

Callu (1993)—Callu, J.-P., "Eres et monnayages à l'orée de l'Empire romain," *Ktema* 18 (1993) 113–29.

Calzolari (1993)—Calzolari, M., "Divisioni agrarie di età romana nella *Venetia* meridionale,' *La mostra archeologica didattica di Villadose*, ed. E. Maragno, Padova 1993, 151–68.

Camps (1990–92)—Camps, G., "'Punica lingua' et épigraphie libyque dans la Numidie d'Hippone," *Bull. arch. Comité trav. hist.*, Ser. 2, 23 (1990–92) 33–49.

Carcopino (1951)—Carcopino, J., *Cicero. The Secrets of his Correspondence*, 2 vols., trans. E. O. Lorrimer, New Haven 1951.

Carcopino (1957)—Carcopino, J., *Les secrets de la correspondance de Cicéron*, 2 vols., Paris 1957.

Carettoni et al. (1960)—Carettoni, G., et al., *La pianta marmorea di Roma antica. Forma urbis Romae*, 2 vols., Roma 1960.

Castillo Garcia (1975)—Castillo Garcia, C., "Städte und Personen der Baetica," *ANRW* II, 3, Berlin 1975, 601–54.

Castillo (1991)—Castillo, C., "El progreso de la epigrafia romana en Hispania (1983–1987)," *Emerita* 59 (1991) 225–73.

Centuriazione (1993)—*La centuriazione dell'agro di Adria. La mostra archeologica didattica di Villadose*, ed. E. Maragno, Padova 1993.

Chastagnol (1990)—Chastagnol, A., "L'onomastique du type pérégrin dans les cités de la Gaule narbonnaise," *MEFRA* 102 (1990) 573–93.

Chatelain (1942)—Chatelain, L., *Inscriptions latines du Maroc*, Paris 1942.

Chevallier (1958)—Chevallier, R., "Essai de chronologie des centuriations romaines de Tunisie," *MEFRA* 70 (1958) 61–128.

Chevallier (1975)—Chevallier, R., "Gallia Narbonensis. Bilan de 25 ans de recherches historiques et archéologiques," *ANRW* II, 3, Berlin 1975, 686–828.

Chevallier (1976)—Chevallier, R., *Roman Roads*, trans. N. H. Field, London 1976.

Chouquer (1983)—Chouquer, G., "Localisation et expression géographique des cadastres affichés à Orange," *Cadastres et espaces rurales: approches et réalités antiques. Table ronde . . . 1980*, ed. M. Clavel–Lévêque, Paris 1983, 275–95.

Christol (1992)—Christol, M., ed., *Inscriptions antiques de la cité de Nîmes*, Nîmes 1992.

Christol (1995)—Christol, M., "De l'Italie à la Gaule méridionale: transferts d'influences, d'après les inscriptions de la fin du 1er siècle avant J.-C. et du 1er siècle après J.-C.," *Roma y el nacimiento de la cultura epigráfica en Occidente. Actas del Coloquio . . . 1992*, ed. F. Beltrán Lloris, Zaragoza 1995, 49–56.

Christol and Drew-Bear (1995)—Christol, M., and T. Drew-Bear, "Une famille d'Italiens en Lydie," *Arkeoloji Dergisi* 3 (1995) 117–33.

Christol and Drew-Bear (1999)—Christol, M., and T. Drew-Bear, "Vétérans et soldats légionnaires à Antioche en Pisidie," *Actes di IXe Rencontre franco-italienne sur l'épigraphie du monde romain . . . 1995*, Rome 1999 [pagination not available].

Christol and Goudineau (1987–88)—Christol, M., and C. Goudineau, "Nîmes et les Volques Arécomiques au 1er siècle avant J.-C.," *Gallia* 45 (1987–88) 87–103.

Christol and Heijmans (1992)—Christol, M., and M. Heijmans, "Les colonies latines Narbonnaise: un nouveau document d'Arles mentionnant la *Colonia Iulia Augusta Avennio*," *Gallia* 49 (1992) 37–44.

Cintas (1947)—Cintas, P., "Le sanctuaire punique de Sousse," *Rev. afr.* 91 (1947) 1–80.

Clavel (1970)—Clavel, M., *Béziers et son territoire dans l'Antiquité*, Paris 1970.

Clavel (1971)—Clavel, M., "Béziers gallo-romain," *Béziers et le Biterrois (Fédération historique du Languedoc. . . XLIIIe Congrès . . . 1970)*, Montpelier 1971, 9–19.

Clavel-Lévêque (1983)—Clavel-Lévêque, M., "Cadastres, centuriations et problèmes d'occupation du sol dans le Biterrois," *Cadastres et espaces rurales: approches et réalités antiques. Table ronde . . . 1980*, ed. M. Clavel-Lévêque, Paris 1983, 207–58.

Clavel-Lévêque and Favory (1992)—Clavel-Lévêque, M., and F. Favory, "Les *gromatici veteres* et les réalités paysagères: présentation de quelques cas," *Die römische Feldmesserkunst. Interdisziplinäre Beiträge zu ihrer Bedeutung für die Zivilisationsgeschichte Roms*, eds. O. Behrends and L. Capograssi Colognesi, Göttingen 1992, 88–137.

Clavel-Lévêque and Lévêque (1982)—Clavel-Lévêque, M., and P. Lévêque, "Impérialisme et sémiologie: l'espace urbain à Glanum," MEFRA 94 (1982) 675–98.

Clavel-Lévêque and Smajda (1980)—Clavel-Lévêque, M., and E. Smajda, "Le passage à l'époque romaine," Dossiers d'archéologie 43 (1980) 34–40.

Collas-Heddeland (1999)—Collas-Heddeland, E., "Une famille bilingue d'Antioche," Actes di IXe Rencontre franco-italienne sur l'épigraphie du monde romain . . . 1995, Rome 1999, pagination not available].

Coltelloni-Tranoy (1993–95)—Coltelloni-Tranoy, M., "Les liens de clientèle en Afrique du Nord, du IIe siècle av. J.-C. jusqu'au début du Principat," Bull. arch. du comité des trav. hist., Ser. 2, 22 (1993–95) 59–82.

Constans (1914)—Constans, L.-A., "Inscriptions de Gigthis," MEFRA 34 (1914) 267–86.

Constans (1916)—Constans, L.-A., "Rapports sur une mission archéologique à Bou-Ghara (Gigthis) (1914 et 1915)," Nouvelles archives des missions scient. et litt.2 14 (1916) 1–115.

Corinth (1966)—Corinth. Results of Excavations VIII Part III: The inscriptions, ed. J. H. Kent, Princeton 1966.

Cormack (1997)—Cormack, S., "Funerary monuments and mortuary practice in Roman Asia Minor," The Early Roman Empire in the East, ed. S. E. Alcock, Oxford 1997, 137–56.

Correia (1995)—Correia, V. H., "The Iron Age in south and central Portugal and the emergence of urban centers," Social Complexity and the Development of Towns in Iberia from the Copper Age to the Second Century A.D., eds. B. Cunliffe and S. Keay, Oxford 1995, 237–62.

Cortes (1987)—Cortes, R., "Los foros de Tarraco," Los foros romanos de la provincias occidentales, Madrid 1997, 9–24.

Corzo (1993)—Corzo, R., "Topografia y territorio de la Códoba romana," Colonia Patricia Corduba. Una Reflexión arqueologica, ed. P. León, Córdoba 1993, 63–75.

Corzo Sánchez (1982)—Corzo Sánchez, R., "Organización del territorio y evolución urbana en Italica," Italica (Santiponce Sevilla). Actas . . . 1980 [Excavaciones arqueologicas en Espan 121], Madrid 1982, 299–319.

Coulton (1987)—Coulton, J. J., "Roman aqueducts in Asia Minor," Roman Architecture in the Greek World, eds. S. Macready and F. H. Thompson, London 1987, 72–84.

Coulton (1989)—Coulton, J. J., "Modules and measurements in ancient design and modern scholarship," Munus non ingratum. Proc. of the International Symposium on Vitruvius' De Architectura and the Hellenistic and Republican Architecture . . . 1987, eds. H. Geertman and J. J. de Jong, Leiden 1989, 85–89.

Courtois (1998)—Courtois, C., "Le bâtiment de scène des théâtres romains du Sud

de la Gaule, des provinces d'Espagne et d'Afrique du Nord. Etude comparée,"
Latomus 57 (1998) 96–104.

Crawford (1985)—Crawford., M., *Coinage and Money under the Roman Republic: Italy and the Mediterranean Economy*, London 1985.

Crawford (1988)—Crawford, M., "The laws of the Romans: knowledge and diffusion," *Estudios sobre la Tabula Siarensis*, eds. J. Gonzalez and J. Arce, Madrid 1988, 127–40.

Crawford (1995)—Crawford, M. H., "Roman towns and their charters: legislation and experience," *Social Complexity and the Development of Towns in Iberia from the Copper Age to the Second Century A. D.*, eds. B. Cunliffe and S. Keay, Oxford 1995, 421–30.

Crawford (1996)—Crawford, M. H., ed., *Roman Statutes*, 2 vols., London 1996.

Curchin (1985)—Curchin, L. A., "*Vici* and *pagi* in Roman Spain," REA 87 (1985) 327–43.

Curchin (1990)—Curchin, L. A., *The Local Magistrates of Roman Spain*, Toronto 1990.

Curchin (1991)—Curchin, L. A., *Roman Spain. Conquest and Assimilation*, London 1991.

Dardaine (1983)—Dardaine, S., "Historique des fouilles," Belo II, Paris 1983, 7–36.

Darde and Lassalle (1993)—Darde, D., and V. Lassalle, *Nîmes antique. Monuments et sites*, Paris 1993.

Dardel (1992)—Dardel, R. de, "Niveaux de langue intermédiaires entre le latin classique et le protoroman," *Latin vulgaire—latin tardif III. Actes du IIème colloque international . . . 1991*, eds. M. Iliescu and W. Marxgut, Tübingen 1992, 83–91.

De Hoz (1995)—De Hoz, J., "Escrituras en contacto: iberica y latina," *Roma y el nacimiento de la cultura epigrafica en Occidente. Actas del Coloquio . . . 1992*, ed. F. Beltrán Lloris, Zaragoza 1995, 57–84.

Delehaye et al. (1920)—Delehaye, H., et al., "Bulletin des publications hagiographiques," *Analecta Bollandiana* 38 (1920) 177–240.

Deman (1975)—Deman, A., "Matériaux et réflexions pour servir à une étude du développement et du sous-développement dans les provinces de l'Empire romain," ANRW II, 3, Berlin 1975, 3–97.

Demarolle (1994)—Demarolle, J.-M., "Les importations de céramiques en Gaule mosellane fournissent-elles des repères significatifs des début de la romanisation?" *Caesarodunum* 28 (1994) 1.17–31.

Deniaux (1993)—Deniaux, E., *Clientèles et pouvoir à l'époque de Cicéron*, Rome 1993.

Denti (1989)—Denti, M., "La scultura ellenistica delle regioni transpadane nel 1 secolo a. C.: problemi e prospettive di ricerca," *Dialoghi di archeologia 3* 7 (1989) 9–26.

Derow and Forrest (1982)—Derow, P. S., and W. G. Forrest, "An inscription from Chios," *Annual Brit. Sch. Rome* 77 (1982) 79–82.

De Ruyt (1983)—De Ruyt, C., *Macellum. Marché alimentaire des Romains*, Louvain-la-Neuve 1983.

Desanges (1980)—Desanges, J., "Permanence d'une structure indigène en marge de l'administration romaine: la Numidie traditionelle," *Ant. afr.* 15 (1980) 77–89.

Desbat and Mandy (1991)—Desbat, A., and B. Mandy, "Le développement de Lyon à l'époque augustéenne: l'apport des fouilles récentes," *Les villes augustéennes de Gaule. Actes du colloque . . . 1985*, Autun 1991, 79–97.

De Sury (1994)—De Sury, B., "L'ex voto d'après l'épigraphie. Contribution à l'étude des sanctuaires," *Les santuaires de tradition indigène en Gaule romaine. Actes du colloque . . . 1992*, eds. C. Goudineau et al., Paris 1994, 169–73.

Devijver and Van Wonterghem (1985)—Devijver, H., and F. Van Wonterghem, "Neue Belege zum 'campus' der römischen Städte in Italien und im Westen," *Zeitschr. Papyrologie und Epigraphik* 60 (1985) 147–58.

Didierjean (1986)—Didierjean, F, *Belo III: Le macellum*, Madrid 1986.

Diego Santos (1975)—Diego Santos, F., "Die Integration Nord–und Nordwestspaniens als römische Provinz in der Reichspolitik des Augustus. Von der konsularischen zur hispanischen 'Ara'," *ANRW* II, 3, Berlin 1975, 523–71.

Dilke (1971)—Dilke, O. A. W., *The Roman Land Surveyors. An Introduction to the Agrimensores*, Newton Abbot 1971.

Di Vita (1982)—Di Vita, A., "Gli *Emporia* di Tripolitania dall'età di Massinissa a Diocleziano: un profilo storico-istituzionale," *ANRW* II, 10, 2, Berlin 1982, 515–95.

Di Vita-Evrard (1981)—Di Vita-Evrard, G., "Municipium Flavium Lepcis Magna," *Bull. arch. du comité des trav. hist.*, Ser. 2, 17 (1981) 197–209.

Dodge (1987)—Dodge, H., "Brick construction in Roman Greece and Asia Minor," *Roman Architecture in the Greek World*, eds. S. Macready and F. H. Thompson, London 1987, 106–16.

Dodge (1990)—Dodge, H., "The architectural impact of Rome in the East," *Architectural Sculpture in the Roman Empire*, ed. M. Henig, Oxford 1990, 108–20.

Donderer (1996)—Donderer, M., *Die Architekten der späten römischen Republik und der Kaiserzeit. Epigraphische Zeugnisse*, Erlangen 1996.

Dopico Cainzos (1986)—Dopico Cainzos, M. D., "Los conventus iuridici. Origen, cronologia y naturaleza histórica," *Gerion* 4 (1986) 265–83.

Downey (1961)—Downey, G., *A History of Antioch in Syria from Seleucus to the Arab Conquest*, Princeton 1961.

Drack (1983)—Drack, W., "Les peintures romaines en Suisse trouvées depuis

1950," *La peinture murale romaine dans les provinces de l'Empire. Journées d'étude*... 1982, ed. A. Barbet, Oxford 1983, 9–25.

Drack and Fellmann (1988)—Drack, W., and R. Fellmann, *Die Römer in der Schweiz*, Stuttgart 1988.

Dreizehnter (1975)—Dreizehnter, A., "Pompeius als Städtegründer," *Chiron* 5 (1975) 213–45.

Drinkwater (1983)—Drinkwater, J. F., *Roman Gaul: The Three Provinces, 58* B.C.–A.D. 260, Ithaca 1983.

Drioux (1934)—Drioux, G. L., *Cultes indigènes des Lingons. Essai sur les traditions religieuses d'une cité gallo-romaine avant le triomphe du christianisme*, Paris 1934.

Duncan-Jones (1982)—Duncan-Jones, R., *The Economy of the Roman Empire. Quantitative Studies*, ed. 2, Cambridge (England) 1982.

Duncan-Jones (1990)—Duncan-Jones, R., *Structure and Scale in the Roman Economy*, Cambridge (England) 1990.

Dupré (1985)—Dupré, N., "Les villes ibéro-romaines de la vallée de l'Ebre du IIe s. avant J.-C. au milieu du Ier s. après J.-C.," *Caesarodunum* 20 (1985) 281–91.

Dupré i Raventos (1990)—Dupré i Raventos, X., "Un gran complejo provincial de epoca flavia en Tarragona: aspectos cronologicos," *Stadtbild und Ideologie. Die Monumentalisierung hispanischer Städte zwischen Republik und Kaiserzeit*, eds. W. Trillmich and P. Zanker, München 1990, 319–24.

Dupré i Raventos (1995)—Dupré i Raventos, X., "New evidence for the study of the urbanism of Tarraco," *Social Complexity and the Development of Towns in Iberia from the Copper Age to the Second Century* A.D., eds. B. Cunliffe and S. Keay, Oxford 1995, 355–69.

Dyson (1980–81)—Dyson, S. L., "The distribution of Roman Republican family names in the Iberian peninsula," *Anc. Society* 11–12 (1980–81) 257–99.

Ehrenberg and Jones (1955)—Ehrenberg, V., and A. H. M. Jones, eds., *Documents Illustrating the Reigns of Augustus and Tiberius*, ed. 2, Oxford 1955.

Engelmann and Knibbe (1989)—Engelmann, H., and D. Knibbe, "Das Zollgesetz der Provinz Asia," *Epigraphica Anatolica* 14 (1989) 1–209.

Engels (1990)—Engels, D., *Roman Corinth: An Alternative Model for the Classical City*, Chicago 1990.

Etienne (1958)—Etienne, R., *Le culte impérial dans la péninsule ibérique d'Auguste à Dioclétien*, Paris 1958.

Etienne et al. (1976)—Etienne, R., et al., "Les dimensions sociales de la romanisation dans la Péninsule ibérique des origines à la fin de l'Empire," *Assimilation et résistance à la culture gréco-romaine dans le monde ancien. Travaux du VI Congrès international d'Etudes Classiques*... 1974, ed. D. M. Pippidi, Paris 1976, 95–107.

Etienne and Fontaine (1979)—Etienne, R., and J. Fontaine, "Histoire et archéologie de la péninsule ibérique antique. Chronique II—1937–1977," REA 81 (1979) 105–205.

Ettlinger (1987)—Ettlinger, E., "How was Arretine ware sold?" Rei cretariae Romanae fautorum acta 25–26 (1987) 5–19.

Euzennat and Hallier (1986)—Euzennat., M., and G. Hallier, "Les forums de Tingitane. Observations sur l'influence de l'architecture militaire sur les constructions civiles de l'Occident romain," Ant. afr. 22 (1986) 73–103.

Farrington (1995)—Farrington, A., The Roman Baths of Lycia: An Architectural Study, Ankara 1995.

Fasold (1993)—Fasold, P., "Romanisierung und Grabbrauch: Uberlegungen zum frührömischen Totenkult in Rätien," Römerzeitliche Gräber als Quellen zu Religion, Bevölkerungsstruktur und Sozialgeschichte. Internationale Fachkonferenz . . . 1991, ed., M. Struck, Mainz 1993, 381–96.

Favory (1983)—Favory, F. "Propositions pour une modélisation des cadastres ruraux antiques," Cadastres et espaces rurales: approches et réalités antiques. Table ronde . . . 1980, ed. M. Clavel-Lévêque, Paris 1983, 51–135.

Fear (1996)—Fear, A. T., Rome and Baetica. Urbanization in Southern Spain c. 50 B.C.- A.D. 150, Oxford 1996.

Fellmann (1975)—Fellmann, R., "Quelques aspects de syncrétisme en territoire helvète," Les syncrétismes dans les religions de l'antiquité. Colloque . . . 1973, eds. F. Dunand and P. Lévêque, Leiden 1975, 200–203.

Ferdière and Villard (1993)—Ferdière, A., and A. Villard, La tombe augustéenne de Fléré-la-Rivière (Indre) et les sépultures aristocratiques de la cité des Biturigues, Saint-Marcel 1993.

Feugère (1993)—Feugère, M., "L'évolution du mobilier non céramique dans les sépultures antiques de Gaule méridionale (IIe siècle av. J.-C. –début du Ve siècle ap. J.-C.)," Römerzeitliche Gräber als Quellen zu Religion, Bevölkerungsstruktur und Sozialgeschichte. Internationale Fachkonferenz . . . 1991, ed. M. Struck, Mainz 1993, 119–65.

Février (1982)—Février, P.-A., "Urbanisation et urbanisme de l'Afrique romaine," ANRW II, 2, Berlin 1982, 321–97.

Février et al. (1989)—Février, P., et al., La Provence des origines à l'an mil: histoire et archéologie, Rennes 1989.

Fiches and Soyer (1983)—Fiches, J.-L., and J. Soyer, "Occupation du sol et cadastres antiques: l'exemple de la carte de Nîmes," Cadastres et espace rural. Approches et réalités antiques. Table ronde . . . 1980, ed. M. Clavel-Lévêque, Paris 1983, 258–74.

Finocchi (1994)—Finocchi, P., Dizionario delle divinità indigene della Gallia Narbonense, Roma 1994.

Fischer (1995)—Fischer, I., "Les normes du latin dans quelques inscriptions officielles de l'Empire," *Latin vulgaire—latin tardif. Actes du 4e colloque international . . . 1994*, ed. L. Callebat, Hildesheim 1995, 467–81.

Fishwick (1978)—Fishwick, D., "The development of provincial ruler worship in the western Roman empire," ANRW II, 16, Berlin 1978, 1201–53.

Fishwick (1982)—Fishwick, D., "The altar of Augustus and the municipal cult of Tarraco," *Madrider Mitt.* 23 (1982) 222–33.

Fishwick (1991–3)—Fishwick, D., *The Imperial Cult in the Latin West. Studies in the Ruler Cult of the Western Provinces of the Roman Empire*, 2 vols. [vol.1, ed. 2, 1993; vol. 2, 1992], Leiden.

Fittschen (1979)—Fittschen, K., "Bildnisse numidischer Könige," *Die Numider. Reiter und Konige nördlich der Sahara*, eds. H. G. Horn and C. B. Rüger, Köln 1979, 209–25.

Fittschen (1979a)—Fittschen, K., "Juba II. und seine Residenz Jol/Caesarea (Cherchel)," *Die Numider. Reiter und Konige nördlich der Sahara*, eds. H. G. Horn and C. B. Rüger, Köln 1979, 227–42.

Flobert (1992)—Flobert, P., "Les graffites de La Graufesenque: un témoignage sur le gallo-latin sous Néron," *Latin vulgaire—latin tardif III. Actes du IIème colloque international . . . 1991*, eds. M. Iliescu and W. Marxgut, Tübingen 1992, 103–14.

Floriani Squarciapino (1966)—Floriani Squarciapino, M., *Leptis Magna*, Basel 1966.

Fouet (1969)—Fouet, G., "Les nouvelles fouilles de la Caserne Niel à Toulouse," *Rev. archéologique de Narbonnaise* 2 (1969) 65–95.

Fränkel (1895)—Fränkel, M., *Die Inschriften von Pergamon*, Berlin 1895.

Freis (1980)—Freis, H., "Das römische Nordafrika—ein unterentwickeltes Land?" *Chiron* 10 (1980) 357–90.

Frederiksen (1965)—Frederiksen, M. W., "The Republican municipal laws: errors and drafts," *JRS* 55 (1965) 183–98.

Frézouls (1982)—Frézouls, E., "Aspects de l'histoire architecturale du théâtre romain," ANRW II, 12, 1, Berlin 1982, 343–441.

Frézouls (1989)—Frézouls, E., "Fondements scientifiques, armature conceptuelle et *praxis* dans le *De Architectura*," *Munus non ingratum. Proceedings of the Int. Symposium on Vitruvius' De Architectura and the Hellenistic and Republican Architecture . . . 1987*, eds. H. Geertman and J. J. de Jong, Leiden 1989, 39–48.

Frézouls (1991)—Frézouls, E., "Villes augustéennes de l'est et du nord-est de la France," *Les villes augustéennes de Gaule. Actes du colloque . . . 1985*, Autun 1991, 107–15.

Frézouls (1991a)—Frézouls, E., "La perception des rapports gouvernants/gouvernés à la fin de la République," *Cahiers des études anciennes* 26a (1991) 95–113.

Fuhrmann (1949)—Fuhrmann, H., "Zwei Reliefbilder aus der Geschichte Roms," *Mitt. des deutschen arch. Inst.* 2 (1949) 23–68.

Furnée-van Zwet (1956)—Furnée-van Zwet, L., "Fashion in women's hair–dress in the first century of the Roman Empire," Bull. van de Vereeniging tot Bevordering der Kennis van der Antieke Beschaving 31 (1956) 1–22.

Gabba (1972)—Gabba, E., "Urbanizzazione e rinnovamenti urbanistici nell'Italia centro-meridionale del I sec. a. C." Studi classici e orientali 21 (1972) 73–112.

Galinsky (1996)—Galinsky, K., Augustan Culture: An Interpretive Introduction, Princeton 1996.

Galliou (1984)—Galliou, P., L'Armorique romaine, Brasparo 1983.

Galsterer (1971)—Galsterer, H., Untersuchungen zum römischen Städtewesen auf der iberischen Halbinsel, Berlin 1971.

Galsterer (1986)—Galsterer, H., "Roman law in the provinces: some problems of transmission," L'impero romano e le strutture economiche e sociali delle province, ed. M. Crawford, Como 1986, 13–27.

Galsterer (1988)—Galsterer, H., "The Tabula Siarensis and Augustan municipalization in Baetica," Estudios sobre la Tabula Siarensis, eds. J. Gonzalez and J. Arce, Madrid 1988, 61–74.

Galsterer (1992)—Galsterer, H., "Die Kolonisation der hohen Republik und die römische Feldmesskunst," Die römische Feldmesskunst. Interdisziplinäre Beiträge zu ihrer Bedeutung für die Zivilisationsgeschichte Roms, eds. O. Behrends and L. Capogrossi Colognesi, Göttingen 1992, 412–28.

Galsterer-Kröll (1996)—Galsterer-Kröll, B., "Latinisches Recht und Municipalisierung in Gallien und Germanien," Teoria y practica del ordinamiento en Hispanias. Actas del Symposium . . . 1993, Bilbao 1996, 117–29.

Garcia y Bellido (1949)—Garcia y Bellido, A., Esculturas Romanas de España y Portugal, 2 vols., Madrid 1949.

Garcia y Bellido (1966)—Garcia y Bellido, A., "Los 'mercatores', 'negotiatores' y 'publicani' como vehiculos de romanización en la España romana preimperial," Hispania. Revista española de historia 26 (1966) 497–512.

Garcia y Bellido (1966a)—Garcia y Bellido, A., "Tessera hospitalis del año 14 de la Era hallada en Herrera de Pisuerga," Boletin de la Real Acad. de la Historia 159 (1966) 149–66.

Garcia y Bellido (1967)—Garcia y Bellido, A., "La latinización de Hispania," Archivo Español de Arqueologia 40 (1967) 3–29.

Garcia y Bellido (1972)—Garcia y Bellido, A., "Die Latinisierung Hispaniens," ANRW I, 1, Berlin 1972, 462–500.

Garcia Marcos and Vidal Encinas (1995)—Garcia Marcos, V., and J. M. Vidal Encinas, "Recent archeological research at Asturica Augusta," Social Complexity and the Development of Towns in Iberia from the Copper Age to the Second Century A.D., eds. B. Cunliffe and S. Keay, Oxford 1995, 371–94.

Gardner (1993)—Gardner, J. F., *Being a Roman Citizen*, London 1993.

Garnsey (1978)—Garnsey, P. D. A., "Rome's African empire under the principate," *Imperialism in the Ancient World*, ed. idem and C. R. Whittaker, Cambridge (England) 1978, 223–54.

Gascou (1981)—Gascou, J., "Les magistratures de la confédération cirtéenne," *Bull. arch. du comité des trav. hist.*, Ser. 2, 17 (1981) 323–35.

Gascou (1982)—Gascou, J., "La politique municipale de Rome en Afrique du Nord," ANRW II, 10, 2, Berlin 1982, 136–320.

Gauthier (1985)—Gauthier, P., *Les cités grecques et leurs bienfaiteurs*, Paris 1985.

Gayraud (1981)—Gayraud, M., *Narbonne antique des origines à la fin du IIIe siècle*, Paris 1981.

Gelzer (1912)—Gelzer, M., *Die Nobilität der römischen Republik*, Wiesbaden 1912.

Gelzer (1969)—Gelzer, M., *The Roman Nobility*, trans. R. Seager, Oxford 1969,.

Gianfrotta (1982)—Gianfrotta, P. A., "Lentulo Augure e le anfore laietane," *Epigrafia e ordine senatorio. Atti del colloquio internazionale . . .* 1981, Roma 1982, 2.475–79 [Tituli 4].

Gilbert (1998)—Gilbert, C. E., "What did the Renaissance patron buy?" *Renaissance Quarterly* 51 (1998) 392–450.

Gomez Pallarès (1995)—Gomez Pallarès, J., "Cultura literaria en el *Corpus* de los CLE Hispaniae hasta época Flavia," *Roma y el naciemiento de la cultura epigrafica en Occidente. Actas del Coloquio . . .* 1992, ed. F. Beltrán Lloris, Zaragoza 1995, 151–62.

Gonzalez (1986)—Gonzalez, J., "The Lex Irnitana: a new copy of the Flavian municipal law," JRS 76 (1986) 147–243.

Gonzalez (1988)—Gonzalez, J., "The first oath pro salute Augusti found in Baetica," *Zeitschr. Papyrologie und Epigraphik* 72 (1988) 113–27.

Gorges (1979)—Gorges, J.-G., *Les villas hispano-romaines. Inventaire et problématique archéologiques*, Paris 1979.

Gorges (1983)—Gorges, J.G., "Remarques sur la détection des cadastres antiques en péninsule ibérique: à propos d'Elche et de Mérida," *Cadastres et espace rural. Approches et réalités antiques. Table ronde . . .* 1980, ed. M. Clavel-Lévêque, Paris 1983, 199–206.

Gorges (1986)—Gorges, J.G., "Prospections archéologiques autour d'Emérita Augusta. Soixante-dix sites ruraux en quête de signification," REA 88 (1986) 215–36.

Gorges (1994)—Gorges, J.G., "Les villas hispano-romaines: un panorama des connaisance," *Caesarodunum* 28 (1994) 1.267–83.

Goudineau (1975)—Goudineau, C., "La romanisation des institutions en Transalpines," *Cahiers ligures de préhistoire et d'archéologie* 24 (1975) 26–34.

Goudineau (1979)—Goudineau, C., *Les fouilles de la maison au Dauphin. Recherches sur la romanisation de Vaison-la-Romaine*, Rome 1979.

Goudineau (1989)—Goudineau, C., "A propos de C. Valerius Procillus, un prince helvien qui parlait. . . gaulois," *Etudes celtiques* 26 (1989) 61–62.

Goudineau (1991)—Goudineau, C., "Introduction," *Les villes augustéennes de Gaule. Actes du colloque. . . 1985*, Autun 1991, 7–15.

Goudineau et al. (1980)—Goudineau, C. et al., "Le réseau urbain" and "Les antécédents: y a-t-il une ville protohistorique?" and "Les villes de la paix romaine," *Histoire de la France urbaine*, ed. G . Duby, Paris 1980, 42–137, 138–231, and 232–398.

Green (1996)—Green, M., "Art and religion: aspects of identity in pagan and Celtic Europe," *Studia Celtica* 30 (1996) 35 –58.

Greifenhagen (1963)—Greifenhagen, A., *Beiträge zur antiken Reliefkeramik*, Berlin 1963.

Grenier (1937)—Grenier, A., "La Gaule romaine," *Economic Survey of Ancient Rome*, ed. T. Frank, 3, Baltimore 1937, 379–664.

Grenier (1958–60)—Grenier, A., *Manuel d'archéologie gallo-romaine*, vols. 3–4, Paris 1958–60.

Grether (1946)—Grether, G., "Livia and the Roman imperial cult," *AJP* 67 (1946) 222–52.

Gros (1981)—Gros, P., "Note sur deux reliefs des 'Antiques' de Glanum: le problème de la romanisation," *Rev. arch. de Narbonnaise* 14 (1981) 159–72.

Gros (1983)—Gros, P., "Statut social et rôle culturel des architectes (période hellénistique et augustéenne)," *Architecture et société de l'archaïsme grec à la fin de la République romaine. Actes du colloque. . . 1980*, Paris 1983, 425–52.

Gros (1986)—Gros, P., "Le mausolée des Julii et le statut de Glanum," *Rev. archéologique* 1986, 65–80.

Gros (1987)—Gros, P., "Rapport de synthèse," *Les enceintes augustéennes dans l'Occident romain (France, Italie, Espagne, Afrique du Nord). Actes du colloque. . . 1985*, ed. M.-G. Colin, Nîmes 1987, 159–64.

Gros (1987a)—Gros, P., "Un programme augustéen. Le centre monumental de la colonie d'Arles," *Jahrbuch deut. arch. Inst.* 102 (1987) 339–63.

Gros (1990)—Gros, P., "Théâtre et culte impérial en Gaule narbonnaise et dans la péninsule ibérique," *Stadtbild und Ideologie. Die Monumentalisierung hispanischer Städte zwischen Republik und Kaiserzeit*, eds. W. Trillmich and P. Zanker, München 1990, 381–90.

Gros (1991)—Gros, P., "Nouveau paysage urbain et cultes dynastiques: remarques sur l'idéologie de la ville augustéenne à partir des centres monumentaux d'Athènes, Thasos, Arles et Nîmes," *Les villes augustéennes de Gaule. Actes du colloque* . . . 1985, Autun 1991, 127–40.

Gros (1996)—Gros, P. *L'architecture romaine du début du IIIe siècle av. J.-C. à la fin du Haut-Empire*, 1: *Les monuments publics*, Paris 1996.

Gros and Varène (1984)—Gros, P., and P. Varène, "Le forum et la basilique de Glanum: problèmes de chronologie et de restitution," *Gallia* 42 (1984) 21–52.

Gruen (1992)—Gruen, E., *Culture and National Identity in Republican Rome*, Ithaca 1992.

Gsell (1972)—Gsell, S., *Histoire de l'Afrique du Nord*, 8 vols., reprint Osnabrück 1972.

Guillaumet and Rebourg (1987)—Guillaumet, J.-P., and A. Rebourg, "L'enceinte d'Autun," *Les enceintes augustéennes dans l'Occident romain (France, Italie, Espagne, Afrique du Nord). Actes du colloque* . . . 1985, Nîmes 1987, 41–49.

Guitart Durán (1993)—Guitart Durán, J., "La ciudad romana en el ambito de Cataluña," *La ciudad hispanorrama*, ed. C. Diez Rodrigo, Madrid 1993, 54–83.

Guitart et al. (1991)—Guitart. J. et al., "La casa urbana en Baetulo," *La casa urbana hispanorromana. Ponenciás y comunicaciones*, Zaragoza 1991, 35–47.

Guitart i Durán and Padros i Marti (1990)—Guitart i Durán, J., and P. Padros i Marti, "Baetulo, cronologia y significación de sus monumentos," *Stadtbild und Ideologie. Die Monumentalisierung hispanischer Städte zwischen Republik und Kaiserzeit*, eds. W. Trillmich and P. Zanker, München 1990, 165–77.

Guy (1983)—Guy, M., "Existence de bornages divisionnaires dans une centuriation antique," *Cadastres et espaces rurales: approches et réalités antiques. Table ronde* . . . 1980, ed. M. Clavel-Lévêque, Paris 1983, 215–17.

Guyon et al. (1991)—Guyon, J., et al., "From *Lugdunum* to *Convenae*: recent work on Saint-Bertrand-de-Comminges (Haute-Garonne)," *Jnl Rom. Archeology* 4 (1991) 89–122.

Haley (1997)—Haley, E., "Town and country: the acculturation of S. Spain," *Jnl Rom. Archeology* 10 (1997) 495–503.

Hallenkemper Salies (1994)—Hallenkemper Salies, G., "Der antike Shiffsfund von Mahdia. Entdeckung und Forschung," *Das Wrack. Der antike Shiffsfund von Mahdia*, eds. eadem et al., Köln 1994, 1.5–29.

Hänlein-Schäfer (1985)—Hänlein-Schäfer, H., *Veneratio Augusti. Eine Studie zu den Templen des ersten römisches Kaisers*, Rome 1985.

Hanson (1988)—Hanson, W. S., "Administration, urbanisation and acculturation in the Roman west," *The Administration of the Roman Empire (241 B.C.-A.D. 193)*, ed. D. C. Braund, Exeter 1988, 53–68.

Hanson (1997)—Hanson, W. S., "Forces of change and methods of control," *Dialogues in Roman Imperialism. Power, Discourse, and Discrepant Experience in the Roman Empire*, ed. D. J. Mattingly, Portsmouth 1997, 67–80.

Haselberger (1997)—Haselberger, L., "Architectural likenesses: models and plans of architecture in classical antiquity," Jnl Roman Archeology 10 (1997) 77–94.

Haselgrove (1984)—Haselgrove, C., "'Romanisation' before the conquest: Gaulish precedents and British consequences," Military and Civilian in Roman Britain. Cultural Relationships in a Frontier Province, eds. T. F. C. Blagg and A. C. King, Oxford 1984, 5–63.

Hatt (1965)—Hatt, J.-J., "Essai sur l'évolution de la religion gauloise," REA 67 (1965) 80–125.

Hatt (1970)—Hatt, J.-J., Les Celtes et les Gallo-Romains, Genève 1970.

Hatzfeld (1919)—Hatzfeld, J., Les trafiquants italiens dans l'Orient hellénique, Paris 1919.

Hatzopoulos and Loukopoulou (1992)—Hatzopoulos, M. B., and L. D. Loukopoulou, Recherches sur les marches orientales des Temenidès (Anthemonte-Kalindoia), 1, Athens 1992.

Hauschild (1993)—Hauschild, T., "Traditionen römischer Stadtbefestigungen der Hispania," Hispania Antiqua. Denkmäler der Römerzeit, eds. W. Trillmich et al., Mainz 1993, 217–31.

Häussler (1993)—Häussler, R., "The Romanisation of the Civitas Vangionum," Bull. Inst. of Archaeology 30 (1993) 41–104.

Hayes (1973)—Hayes, J. W., "Roman pottery from the South Stoa at Corinth," Hesperia 42 (1973) 416–70.

Heilmeyer (1970)—Heilmeyer, W.-D., Korinthisches Normalkapitelle. Studien zur Geschichte der römischen Architekturdekoration, Heidelberg 1970.

Heinen (1984)—Heinen, H., "Augustus in Gallien und die Anfänge des römischen Trier," Trier—Augustusstadt der Treverer, Stadt und Land in vor–und frührömischer Zeit, Mainz 1984, 32–47.

Herman (1983)—Herman, J., "La langue latine dans la Gaule romaine," ANRW II, 29, Berlin 1983, 1045–60.

Herman (1990)—Herman, J., Du latin aux langues romanes. Etudes de linguistique historique, ed. S. Kiss, Tübingen 1990.

Herman (1991)—Herman, J., "Spoken and written Latin in the last centuries of the Roman Empire. A contribution to the linguistic history of the western provinces," Latin and the Romance Languages in the Early Middle Age, ed. R. Wright, London 1991, 29–43.

Herrmann and Polatkan (1969)—Herrmann, P., and K. Z. Polatkan, Das Testament des Epikrates und andere neue Inschriften aus dem Museum von Manisa (Sitz.ber. 265, Oesterr. Akad. Wiss., Phil.-hist. Kl.), Wien 1969.

Herz (1978)—Herz, P., "Kaiserfeste der Prinzipatszeit," ANRW II, 16, Berlin 1978, 1135–2000.

Hesberg (1992)—Hesberg, H. von, "Publica magnificentia. Eine antiklassizistichen Intention der frühen augusteischen Baukunst," *Jahrbuch deut. arch. Inst.* 107 (1992) 125–47.

Hesnard and Lenoir (1985)—Hesnard, A., and M. Lenoir, "Les négociants italiens en Maurétanie avant l'annexion (résumé)," *Bull. arch. du comité des trav. hist.*, Ser. 2, 19B (1985) 49–50.

Hicks (1889)—Hicks, E. L., "Inscriptions from Casarea, Lydae, Patara, Myra," *JHS* 10 (1889) 46–85.

Hill (1953)—Hill, D. K., "Le 'dieu au maillet' de Vienne à la Walters Art Gallery de Baltimore," *Gallia* 11 (1953) 205–22.

Hinrichs (1989)—Hinrichs, F. T., *Histoire des institutions gromatique. Recherches sur la répartition des terres, l'arpentage agraire, l'administration et le droit foncier dans l'Empire Romain*, trans. D. Minary, Paris 1989.

Hispania Antiqua (1993)—*Hispania Antiqua. Denkmäler der Römerzeit*, ed. W. Trillmich, Mainz 1993.

Hispania epigraphica (1989–)—*Hispania epigraphica*, ed. L. Mangas, Madrid 1989–.

Hobson (1993)—Hobson, D. W., "The impact of law on village life in Roman Egypt," *Law, Politics and Society in the Ancient Mediterranean World*, eds. B. Halpern and D. W. Hobson, Sheffield 1993, 193–219.

Hochuli-Gysel (1977)—Hochuli-Gysel, A., *Kleinasiatische glasierte Reliefkeramik (50 v. Chr. bis 50 n. Chr.) und ihre oberitalischen Nachahmungen*, Bern 1977.

Hoët-van Cauwenberghe (1996)—Hoët-van Cauwenberghe, C., "Onomastique et diffusion de la citoyenneté romaine en Arcadie," *Roman Onomastics in the Greek East. Social and Political Aspects. Proceedings of the International Colloquium . . . 1993*, Athens 1996, 207–14.

Hoët-van Cauwenberghe (1999)—Hoët-van Cauwenberghe, C., "Statius Anicius, Décurion d'Antioche," *Actes du IXème Rencontre franco–italienne sur l'épigraphie du monde romain . . . 1995*, Rome 1999 [pagination not available].

Hoff (1994)—Hoff, M. C., "The so-called Agoranomion and the imperial cult in Julio-Claudian Athens," *Archäologischer Anz. des deut. arch. Inst.* 1994, 93–117.

Holtzman and Salviat (1984)—Holtzman, B., and F. Salviat, "Les portraits sculptés de Marc-Antoine," *Bull. de Correspondance hellénique* 105 (1984) 265–88.

Holmes (1911)—Holmes, T. R., *Caesar's Conquest of Gaul*, ed. 2, Oxford 1911.

Hopkins (1978)—Hopkins, K., "Economic growth and towns in classical antiquity," *Towns in Societies. Essays in Economic History and Historical Sociology*, eds. P. Abrams and E. A. Wrigley, Cambridge (England) 1978, 35–78.

Horsfall (1996)—Horsfall, N., *La cultura della plebs romana*, Barcelona 1996.

Hübner (1893)—Hübner, E., *Monumenta linguae ibericae*, Berlin 1893.

Humbert (1881)—Humbert, M., "Le droit latin impérial: cités latines ou citoyen-neté latine?" *Ktema* 6 (1981) 207–26.

Hurst (1998)—Hurst, H., *The Sanctuary of Tanit at Carthage in the Roman Period: a Re-interpretation*, Ann Arbor 1998.

Inschriften von Ephesos (1981)—*Die Inschriften von Ephesos* VII, 1, eds. R. Meric et al., Bonn 1981.

Jacques (1993)—Jacques, F., "L'origine du domaine de la Villa Magna Variana id est *Mappalia Siga* (Henchir Mettich): une hypothèse," *Antiquités afr.* 29 (1993) 63–69.

Janon (1986)—Janon, M., *Le décor architectonique de Narbonee. Les rinceaux*, Paris 1986.

Jeppesen (1989)—Jeppesen, K., "Vitruvius in Africa," *Munus non ingratum. Proc. of the International Symposium on Vitruvius' De Architectura and the Hellenistic and Republican Architecture . . . 1987*, eds. H. Geertman and J. J. de Jong, Leiden 1989, 31–33.

Jimenez Salvador (1986)—Jimenez Salvador, J. L., "Los modelos constructivos en la arquitectura forense de la Península Ibérica," *Los foros romanos de la provincias occidentales*, Madrid 1987, 173–77.

F. S. Johansen (1967)—Johansen, F. S., "Antichi ritratti di Caio Giulio Cesare nella scultura," *Analecta Romana Instituti Danici* 4 (1967) 7–68.

K. F. Johansen (1930)—Johansen, K. F., "An antique replica of the Priam bowl from Hoby," *Acta archaeologica* 1 (1930) 273–77.

Johns (1982)—Johns, C., *Sex or Symbol: Erotic Images of Greece and Rome*, London 1982.

Johnson et al. (1961)—Johnson, A. C., et al., *Ancient Roman Statutes: A Translation, Commentary, Glossary, and Index*, Austin 1961.

Johnston (1987)—Johnston, D., "Three thoughts on Roman private law and the Lex Irnitana," *JRS* 77 (1987) 62–787.

Jones (1971)—Jones, A. H. M., *The Cities of the Eastern Roman Provinces*, ed. 2, rev. M. Avi-Yonah et al., Oxford 1971.

Jouffroy (1986)—Jouffroy, H., *La construction publique en Italie et dans l'Afrique romaine*, Strasbourg 1986.

Keay (1990)—Keay, S., "Processes in the development of the coastal communities of Hispania Citerior in the Republican period," *The Roman Empire in the West*, eds. T. Blagg and M. Millett, Oxford 1990, 120–50.

Keay (1992)—Keay, S., "The 'Romanization' of Turdetania," *Oxford Jnl of Archaeology* 11 (1992) 275–315.

Keay (1995)—Keay, S., "Innovation and adaptation: the contribution of Rome to urbanism in Iberia," *Social Complexity and the Development of Towns in Iberia: From the Copper Age to the Second Century AD*, eds. B. Cunliffe and S. Keay, Oxford 1995, 291–338.

Keil and Wilhelm (1931)—Keil, J., and A. Wilhelm, *Denkmäler aus dem rauhen Kilikien* (MAMA III), Manchester 1931.

Kenrick (1996)—Kenrick, P. M., "The importation of Italian sigillata to Algeria," *Antiquités afr.* 32 (1996) 37–44.

Keppie (1983)—Keppie, L., *Colonisation and Veteran Settlement in Italy 47–14 B.C.*, London 1983.

Kienast (1982)—Kienast, D., *Augustus, Prinzeps und Monarch*, Darmstadt 1982.

King (1990)—King, A., "The emergence of Roman-Celtic religion," *The Early Roman Empire in the West*, eds. T. Blagg and M. Millett, Oxford 1990, 220–41.

D. E. E. Kleiner (1985)—Kleiner, D. E. E., "Private portraiture in the age of Augustus," *The Age of Augustus. Interdisciplinary Conference . . . 1982*, ed. R. Winkes, Providence 1985, 107–35.

F. S. Kleiner (1977)—Kleiner, F. S., "Artists in the Roman world. An itinerant workshop in Augustan Gaul," MEFRA 89 (1977) 661–96.

Klingenberg (1993)—Klingenberg, G., "Ein Irrtum über eine locale *consuetudo*," *Ars boni et aequi. Festschrift für W. Waldstein . . .* , eds. M. J. Schermaier and Z. Végh, Stuttgart 1993, 167–75.

Knapp (1978)—Knapp, R. C., "The origins of provincial prosopography in the West," *Anc. Society* 9 (1978) 187–226.

Knapp (1987)—Knapp, R. C., "Spain," *The Coinage of the Roman World in the Late Republic. Proceedings of a Colloquium . . . 1985*, eds. A. M. Burnett and M. Crawford, Oxford 1987, 19–41.

Kneissl (1980)—Kneissl, P., "Entstehung und Bedeutung der Augustalität. Zur Inschrift der ara Narbonensis (CIL XII 4333)," *Chiron* 10 (1980) 291–326.

Kneissl (1988)—Kneissl, P., "Zur Wirtschaftsstruktur des römischen Reiches: das Beispiel Gallien," *Alte Geschichte und Wissenschaftsgeschichte. Festschrift für K. Christ*, ed. idem and V. Losemann, Darmstadt 1988, 234–55.

Koch (1993)—Koch, M., "Animus . . . meus . . . praesagit, nostram Hispaniam esse," *Hispania Antiqua. Denkmäler der Römerzeit*, eds. W. Trillmich et al., Mainz 1993, 1–40.

Kolendo (1981)—Kolendo, J., "La répartition des places aux spectacles et la stratification sociale daans l'Empire romain. A propos des inscriptions sur les gradins des amphithéâtres et théâtres," *Ktema* 6 (1981) 301–15.

Kolendo (1985)—Kolendo, J., "Les domaines des Caelii en Afrique au Ier siècle avant notre ère," *Bull. arch. du comité des trav. hist.*, Ser. 2, 19B (1985) 53–62.

Kolendo and Kotula (1977)—Kolendo, J., and T. Kotula, "Quelques problèmes du développment des ville en Afrique romaine," *Klio* 59 (1977) 175–84.

König (1970)—Kolendo, I., *Die Meilenstein der Gallia Narbonensis. Studien zum Strassenwesen der Provincia Narbonensis*, Bern 1970.

Kornemann (1900)—Kornemann, E., "Coloniae," RE 4, Stuttgart 1900, cols. 513–88.

Kotula (1968)—Kotula, T., *Les curies municipales en Afrique romaine*, Wroclaw 1968.

Kotula (1973)—Kotula, T., "Remarques sur les traditions puniques dans la constitution des villes de l'Afrique romaine," *Akten des VI. Internationalen Kongresses für griechische und lateinische Epigraphik . . . 1972*, München 1973, 73–83.

Kränzlein (1993)—Kränzlein, A., "*Ius municipum*. Zu Art. 93 Lex Irnitana," *Ars boni et aequi. Festschrift für W. Waldstein . . .*, eds. M. J. Schermaier and Z. Végh, Stuttgart 1993, 177–86.

Kreilinger (1993)—Kreilinger, U., "Zu römischen Mosaiken in Hispanien," *Hispania Antiqua. Denkmäler der Römerzeit*, eds. W. Trillmich et al., Mainz 1993, 205–15.

Kroll (1997)—Kroll, J. H., "Coinage as an index of Romanization," *The Romanization of Athens. Proceedings . . . 1996*, eds. M. C. Hoff and S. I. Rotroff, Oxford 1997, 135–50.

Künzl (1969)—Künzl, E., "Der augusteische Silbercalathus im Rheinischen Landesmuseum Bonn," *Bonner Jbb* 169 (1969) 321–92.

Lamboglia (1952)—Lamboglia, N., "La nave romana di Albenga," *Rivista di studi liguri* 18 (1952) 131–236.

Lämmer (1975)—Lämmer, M., "Die Kaiserspiele von Cesarea im Dienste der Politik des Königs Herodes," *Kölner Beitr. zur Sportswiss.* 3, 1974 (1975) 95–164.

Lancel (1992)—Lancel, S., *Carthage*, Paris 1992.

Landwehr (1990)—Landwehr, C., "Bronze grec original, moulage en plâtre et copie romaine en marbre," *Pierre éternelle du Nil au Rhin. Carrières et préfabrication*, ed. M. Waelkens, Bruxelles 1990, 143–61.

Lasfargues et al. (1976)—Lasfargues, J. and A., and H. Vertet, "L'atelier de potiers augustéen de la Muette à Lyon: la fouille de sauvetage de 1966," *Notes d'épigraphie et d'archéologie Lyonnaises*, Lyon 1976, 61–80.

Lassère (1979)—Lassère, J., "Rome et 'le sous-développement' de l'Afrique," *REA* 81 (1979) 67–104.

Lassère (1982)—Lassère, J.-M., "L'organisation des contacts de population dans l'Afrique romaine, sous le République et Haut-Empire," *ANRW* II, 10, 2, Berlin 1982, 397–426.

Lasserre (1983)—Lasserre, F., "Strabon devant l'Empire romain," *ANRW* II, 30, Berlin 1983, 867–96.

Lavagne (1979)—Lavagne, H., "Les dieux de la Gaule Narbonnaise: 'romanité' et romanisation," *Jnl des Savants* 1979, 155–83.

Leach (1982)—Leach, E. W., "Patrons, painters, and patterns: the anonymity of Romano-Campanian painting and the transition from the Second to the Third

Style," *Literary and Artistic Patronage in Ancient Rome*, ed. B. K. Gold, Austin 1982, 135–73.

Le Bohec (1989)—Le Bohec, Y., *La troisième Légion Auguste*, Paris 1989.

Le Gall (1975)—Le Gall, J., "Les Romains et l'orientation solaire," MEFRA. 87 (1975) 287–319.

Le Glay (1968)—Le Glay, M., "Les flaviens et l'Afrique," MEFRA 80 (1968) 201–46.

Le Glay (1975)—Le Glay, M., "Les syncrétismes dans l'Afrique ancienne," *Les syncrétismes dans les religions de l'antiquité. Colloque . . . 1973*, eds. F. Dunand and P. Lévêque, Leiden 1975, 123–51.

Le Glay (1985)—Le Glay, M., "Les premiers temps de Carthage romaine: pour une révision des dates," Bull. arch. du comité des trav. hist., Ser. 2, 19B (1985) 235–48.

Le Glay (1991)—Le Glay, M., "Le culte d'Auguste dans les villes augustéennes . . . et les autres," *Les villes augustéennes de Gaule. Actes du colloque . . . 1985*, Autun 1991, 117–26.

León (1990)—León, P., "Ornamentación esculturica y monumentalización en las ciudades de la Betica," *Stadtbild und Ideologie. Die Monumentalisierung hispanischer Städte zwischen Republik und Kaiserzeit*, eds. W. Trillmich and P. Zanker, München 1990, 367–79.

Lepetz (1993)—Lepetz, S., "Les restes animaux dans les sépultures gallo-romains," *Monde des morts, monde des vivants en Gaule rurale. Actes du colloque . . . 1992*, ed. A. Ferdière, Tours 1993, 37–44.

Le Roux (1994)—Le Roux, P., "La tessère de Montealegre et l'évolution des communautés indigènes d'Auguste à Hadrien," *Klio* 76 (1994) 342–54.

Le Roux (1995)—Le Roux, P., "L'émigration italique en Citérieure et Lusitanie jusqu'à la mort de Néron," *Roma y el nacimiento de la cultura epigrafica en Occidente. Actas del Coloquio . . . 1992*, ed. F. Beltrán Lloris, Zaragoza 1995, 85–95.

Le Roux (1996)—Le Roux, P., "Droit latin et municipalisation en Lusitanie sous l'Empire," *Teoria y practica del ordenamiento municipal en Hispania. Actas del Symposium . . . 1993*, Bilbao 1996, 239–53.

Leveau (1981)—Leveau, P., "La fin du royaume maure et les origines de la province romaine de Maurétanie césarienne," Bull. arch. du comité des trav. hist., Ser. 2, 17 (1981) 314–20.

Leveau (1983)—Leveau, P., "L'urbanisme des princes clients d'Auguste: l'exemple de Cesarea de Maurétanie," *Architecture et société de l'archaïsme grec à la fin de la République romaine. Actes du colloque . . . 1980*, Paris 1983, 349–54.

Leveau (1984)—Leveau, P., *Caesarea de Maurétanie, une ville romaine d'Afrique et ses campagnes*, Paris 1984.

Leveau (1987)—Leveau, P., "Les enceintes augustéennes d'Afrique: à la rencontre de l'archéologue, de l'histoire et du droit," *Les enceintes augustéennes dans l'Occident romain (France, Italie, Espagne, Afrique du Nord). Actes du colloque* . . . 1985, ed. M.-G. Colin, Nîmes 1987, 151–58.

Leveau and Paillet (1983)—Leveau, P., and J.-L. Paillet, "Alimentation en eau et développement urbain à Caesarea de Maurétanie," *Journées d'études sur les aquéducs romains* . . . 1977. *Actes* . . . , ed. J.-P. Bucher, Paris 1983, 231–39.

Levick (1967)—Levick, B., *Roman Colonies in Southern Asia Minor*, Oxford 1967.

Lopez Paz (1994)—Lopez Paz, P., *La ciudad romana ideal*, 1: El territorio, Santiago de Compostela 1994.

Loukopoulou (1996)—Loukopoulou, L. D., "The fortunes of the Roman *conventus* of Chalcidice," *Roman Onomastics in the Greek East. Social and Political Aspects. Proceedings of the International Colloquium* . . . 1993, ed. A. D. Rizakis, Athens 1996, 143–47.

Lugli (1957)—Lugli, G., *La tecnica edilizia romana con particolare riguardo a Roma e Lazio*, 2 vols., Roma 1957.

Lyttelton (1987)—Lyttelton, M., "The design and planning of temples and sanctuaries in the Roman imperial period," *Roman Architecture in the Greek World*, eds. S. Macready and F. H. Thompson, London 1987, 38–49.

MacDonald (1982)—MacDonald, W. L., *The Architecture of the Roman Empire*, 1: An Introductory Study, ed. 2, New Haven 1982.

MacDonald (1986)—MacDonald, W. L., *The Architecture of the Roman Empire* 2, New Haven 1986.

Mackie (1983)—Mackie, N., "Augustan colonies in Mauretania," *Historia* 32 (1983) 332–58.

MacMullen (1959)—MacMullen, R., "Roman imperial building in the provinces," *Harvard Studies in Class. Philol.* 64 (1959) 207–35.

MacMullen (1966)—MacMullen, R., "Provincial languages in the Roman empire," *Am. Jnl of Philol.* 87 (1966) 1–17.

MacMullen (1968)—MacMullen, R., "Rural Romanization," *Phoenix* 22 (1968) 337–41.

MacMullen (1970)—MacMullen, R., "Market-days in the Roman empire," *Phoenix* 24 (1970) 333–41.

MacMullen (1974)—MacMullen, R., *Roman Social Relations* 50 B.C. to A.D. 284, New Haven 1974.

MacMullen (1976)—MacMullen, R., *Roman Government's Response to Crisis* A.D. 235–337, New Haven 1976.

MacMullen (1981)—MacMullen, R., *Paganism in the Roman Empire*, New Haven 1981.

MacMullen (1984)—MacMullen, R., "Notes on Romanization," *Bull. Am. Society of Papyrologists* 21 (1984) 161–74.

MacMullen (1988)—MacMullen, R., Corruption and the Decline of Rome, New Haven 1988.

MacMullen (1990)—MacMullen, R., Changes in the Roman Empire. Essays in the Ordinary, Princeton 1990.

MacMullen (1993)—MacMullen, R., "The unromanized in Rome," Diasporas in Antquity, eds. S. J. D. Cohen and E. S. Frerichs, Atlanta 1993, 47–64.

Magdinier and Thollard (1987)—Magdinier, A.-G., and P. Thollard, "L'enceinte romaine d'Orange," Les enceintes augustéennes dans l'Occident romain (France, Italie, Espagne, Afrique du Nord). Actes du colloque . . . 1985, ed. M.-G. Colin, Nîmes 1987, 77–96.

Magie (1950)—Magie, D., Roman Rule in Asia Minor to the End of the Third Century after Christ, 2 vols., Princeton 1950..

Manderscheid (1981)—Manderscheid, H., Die Skulpturenausstattung der kaiserzeitlichen Thermenanlagen, Berlin 1981.

Mangin (1986)—Mangin, M., "Activités économiques et occupation de l'espace dans une agglomération gauloise et gallo-romaine: l'exemple d'Alésia," Géographie historique des villes d'Europe occidentale. Actes du colloque . . . 1981, ed. P. Claval, 2 vols., Paris 1986, 56–68.

Mar and Ruiz de Arbulo (1993)—Mar, R., and J. Ruiz de Arbulo, Ampurias romana. Historia, arquitectura y arqueología, Sabadell 1993.

Mariner Bigorra (1983)—Mariner Bigorra, S., "Hispanische Latinität und sprachliche Kontakte im römischen Hispanien," ANRW II, 29, Berlin 1983, 819–52.

Marquez (1998)—Marquez, C., "Modelos romanos en la architectura monumental de Colonia Patricia Corduba," Archivo español de arqueología 71 (1998) 113–37.

Martin-Bueno (1987)—Martin-Bueno, M., "Los recintos Augusteos en Hispania," Les enceintes augustéennes dans l'Occident romain (France, Italie, Espagne, Afrique du Nord). Actes du colloque . . . 1985, ed. M.-G. Colin, Nîmes 1987, 107–24.

Mattern (1999)—Mattern, S., Rome and the Enemy. Roman Imperial Strategy in the Principate, Berkeley 1999.

Mattingly (1995)—Mattingly, D. J., Tripolitania, London 1995.

Mattingly (1997)—Mattingly, D. J., "Africa: a landscape of opportunity?" Dialogues in Roman Imperialism. Power, Discourse, and Discrepant Experience in the Roman Empire, ed. idem, Portsmouth 1997, 117–39.

Maurin (1978)—Maurin, L., Saintes antique des origines à la fin du VIe siècle après Jésus-Christ, Saintes 1978.

Maurin (1991)—Maurin, L., "Villes augustéennes de l'Aquitaine occidentale: Bordeaux, Périgueux, Saintes," Les villes augustéennes de Gaule. Actes du colloque . . . 1985, Autun 1991, 45–59.

May (1996)—May, R., *Lugdunum Convenarum: Saint-Bertrand-de Comminges*, Lyon 1996.

Mayer and Velaza (1993)—Mayer, M., and J. Velaza, "Epigrafía ibérica sobre soportes típicamente romanos," *Lengua y cultura en la Hispania prerromana. Actas del V Colloquio . . . 1989*, Salamanca 1993, 667–82.

Mayet (1984)—Mayet, F., *Les céramiques sigillées hispaniques: Contributions à l'histoire de la péninsule Ibérique sous l'Empire romain*, 2 vols. [text and plates], Paris 1984.

M'Charek (1987–89)—M'Charek, A., "Un itinéraire inédit dans la région de Maktar: tronçon de la voie augustéenne Carthage-Ammaedara," *Bull. arch. du comité des trav. hist*, Ser. 2, 22 (1987–89) 153–67.

Mediolanum (1988)—*Mediolanum. Une bourgade gallo-romaine*, ed. L. Roussel, Dijon 1988.

Mellor (1975)—Mellor, R. J., ΘΕΑ ΡΩΜΗ. *The Worship of the Goddess Roma in the Greek World*, Göttingen 1975.

Menzel (1985)—"Römische Bronzestatuetten und verwandte Geräte: ein Beitrag zum Stand der Forschung," ANRW II 12, 3, Berlin 1985, 127–69.

Merkelbach (1974)—Merkelbach, R., "Zu der Festordnung für die Sebasta in Neapel," *Zeitschr. Papyrologie und Epigraphik* 15 (1974) 192–93.

Mertens (1985)—Mertens, J., "Les efforts de l'urbanisation dans le Nord de la Gaule," *Caesarodunum* 20 (1985) 261–80.

Mertens (1994)—Mertens, J., "L'interaction culturelle dans le nord de la Gaule belgique à l'époque romaine," *Caesarodunum* 28 (1994) 2.255–77.

Metzler (1984)—Metzler, J., "Treverische Reitergräber von Goeblingen–Nospelt," *Trier, Augustusstadt der Treverer. Stadt und Land in vor–und frührömischer Zeit*, Mainz 1984, 87–99.

Mierse (1990)—Mierse, W., "Augustan building programs in the western provinces," *Between Republic and Empire. Interpretations of Augustus and His Principate*, eds. K. Raaflaub and M. Toher, Berkeley 1990, 308–31.

Mihaescu (1993)—Mihaescu, H., *La Romanité dans le sud-est de l'Europe*, trans C. Grecescu, Budapest 1993.

Millar (1968)—Millar, F., "Local cultures in the Roman empire: Libyan, Punic and Latin in Roman Africa," *JRS* 58 (1968) 126–34.

Millar (1977)—Millar, F., *The Emperor in the Roman World 31 BC–AD 337*, London 1997.

Millar (1993)—Millar, F., *The Roman Near East 31 BC–AD 337*, Cambridge (England) 1993.

Miret et al. (1991)—Miret, M., et al., "From indigenous structures to the Roman world: models for the occupation of central coastal Catalunya," *Roman Land-*

scapes. Archaeological Survey in the Mediterranean Region, eds. G. Barker and J. Lloyd, London 1991, 47–53.

Mitchell (1993)—Mitchell, S., *Anatolia. Land, Men, and Gods in Asia Minor*, 1: *The Celts in Anatolia and the Impact of Roman Rule*, Oxford 1993.

Moatti (1993)—Moatti, C., *Archives et partage de la terre dans le monde romain (IIe siècle avant—Ier siècle après J.-C.)*, Rome 1993.

Momigliano (1986)—Momigliano, A., "Some preliminary remarks on the 'religious opposition' to the Roman Empire," *Opposition et résistances à l'Empire d'Auguste à Trajan. Entretiens sur l'Antiquité Classique* 33 (1986) 103–33.

Morel (1986)—Morel, J.P., "Céramiques à vernis noir d'Italie trouvées à Délos," *Bull. de Correspondance hellénique* 110 (1986) 461–93.

Moretti (1953)—Moretti, L., *Iscrizioni agonistiche greche*, Roman 1953.

Moretti (1980)—Moretti, L., "Chio e la lupa capitolina," *Riv. di filol.* 108 (1980) 33–54.

Musso (1995)—Musso, L., "Leptis Magna," *Enciclopedia dell'arte antica classica e orientale 4*, Roma 1995, 333–47.

Nash (1976)—Nash, D., "Reconstructing Poseidonios' Celtic ethnography: some considerations," *Britannia* 7 (1976) 111–26.

Nash (1976a)—Nash, D., "The growth of urban society in France," *Oppida: the Beginning of Urbanization in Barbarian Europe*, eds. B. Cunliffe and T. Rowley, Oxford 1976, 95–133.

Nash (1981)—Nash, D., "Coinage and state development in central Gaul," *Coinage and Society in Britain and Gaul: Some Current Problems*, ed. B. Cunliffe, London 1981, 10–17.

Nesselhauf (1960)—Nesselhauf, H., "Zwei Bronzeurkunden aus Munigua," *Madrider Mitt.* 1 (1960) 142–54.

Nicols (1980)—Nicols, J., "*Tabulae patronatus*: a study of the agreement between patron and client-community," *ANRW* II, 13, Berlin 1980, 535–59.

Niemeyer (1968)—Niemeyer, H. G., *Studien zur statuarischen Darstellung der römischen Kaiser*, Berlin 1968.

Niemeyer (1993)—Niemeyer, H. G., "Römische Idealplastik und der Fundort Italica," *Hispania Antiqua. Denkmäler der Römerzeit*, eds. W. Trillmich et al., Mainz 1993, 183–92.

Nigdélis (1994)—Nigdélis, P. M., "M. Insteius L. f., αὐτοκράτωρ et le province de Macédoine au début du second triumvirat: à propos d'une inscription inédite d'Europos," *Bull. de Correspondance hellénique* 118 (1994) 215–28.

Nünnerich-Asmus (1993)—Nünnerich-Asmus, A., "Strassen, Brücken und Bogen als Zeichen römischen Herrschaftsansprüchs," *Hispania Antiqua. Denkmäler der Römerzeit*, eds. W. Trillmich et al., Mainz 1993, 121–57.

Olesti i Vila (1994)—Olesti i Vila, O., "Cadastre, aménagement du territoire et romanisation du Maresme à l'époque républicaine," *Dialogues d'histoire ancienne* 20 (1994) 283–307.

d'Ors (1974)—d'Ors, A., "La condición jurídica del suelo en las provincias de Hispania." *I diritti locali nelle province romane . . . Atti del convegno . . . 1971*, Roma 1974, 253–68.

Oswald (1937)—Oswald, F., *Index of the Figure Types on Terra Sigillata ("Samian Ware")*, Liverpool 1937.

Oudhna (1998)—Oudhna (Uthina). *Le redécouverte d'une ville antique de Tunisie*, eds. H. Ben Hassen and L. Maurin, Bordeaux 1998.

Pairault (1972)—Pairault, F.-H., *Recherches sur quelques séries d'urnes de Volterra à représentation mythologiques*, Rome 1972.

Palarés (1970)—Palarés, F., "La topografia e le origini di Barcellona romana," *Rivista di studi liguri* 36 (1970) 63–102.

Pallí Aguilera (1985)—Pallí Aguilera, F., *La Via Augusta en Cataluña*, Bellaterra 1985.

Palol (1987)—Palol, P. de, "El foro romano de Clunia," *Los foros romanos de la provincias occidentales*, Madrid 1987, 153–63.

Palol (1991)—Palol, P. de, "Clunia, 1974," *Clunia O. Studia Varia Cluniensia*, eds. idem et al., Valladolid 1991, 231–41.

Palol (1991a)—Palol, P. de, "El teatro romano de Clunia," *Clunia O. Studia Varia Cluniensia*, eds. idem et al., Valladolid 1991, 325–39.

Parker (1992)—Parker, A. J., *Ancient Shipwrecks of the Mediterranean and the Roman Provinces*, Oxford 1992.

Passelac (1996)—Passelac, M., "Premières céramiques gallo-romaines," *Dossiers d'archéologie* 215 (1996) 10–17.

Paturzo (1996)—Paturzo, F., *Arretina vasa: la ceramica aretina da mensa in età romana. Arte, storia e tecnologia*, Cortona 1996.

Paunier (1994)—Paunier, D., "Les débuts de l'implantation romaine en Suisse occidentale: un bilan provisoire à la lumière des fouilles récentes," *Caesarodunum* 28 (1994) 2.49–74.

Pavolini (1990)—Pavolini, C., "Les lampes romaines en Gaule aux IIe et Ier siècles avant Jésus-Christ: confrontations chronologiques," *Gaule interne et Gaule méditerranéenne aux IIe et Ier siècles avant J.-C.: confrontations chronologiques. Actes de la table ronde . . . 1986*, eds. A. Duval et al., Paris 1990, 101–112.

Pelletier (1985)—Pelletier, A., "Données nouvelles sur l'urbanisme lyonnais au début de l'empire," *Caesarodunum* 20 (1985) 175–87.

Pelletier (1991)—Pelletier, A., "La société urbaine en Narbonnaise à l'époque d'Auguste," *Les villes augustéennes de Gaule. Actes du colloque . . . , 1985*, Autun 1991, 29–34.

Pensabene (1972)—Pensabene, P., "Considerazione sul trasporto di manufatti marmorei in età imperiale a Roma e in altri centri occidentale," *Dialoghi di archeologia* 6 (1972) 317–62.

Pensabene (1982)—Pensabene, P., "La decorazione architettonica di Cherchel," *150-Jahr-Feier deutsches archäologisches Institut Rom. Aussprachen und Vorträge . . .* 1979, Mainz 1982, 116–69.

Pensabene (1989)—Pensabene, P., "Amministrazione dei marmi e sistema distributivo nel mondo romano," *Marmi antichi*, ed. G. Borghini, Roma 1989, 43–54.

Pensabene (1997)—Pensabene, P., "Maqueta de templo en marmol de Luna," *Las Casas del Alma. Maquetas arquitectónicos de la Antigüedad (5500 A. C./300 D. C.)*, Barcelona 1997, 129–32.

Perdrizet (1900)—Perdrizet, P., "Inscriptions de Philippes. Les Rosalies," *Bull. de Correspondance hellénique* 24 (1900) 299–323.

Pereira Menaut (1995)—Pereira Menaut, G., "Epigrafia 'politica' y primeras culturas epigráficas en el noroeste de la p. Iberica," *Roma y el nacimiento de la cultura epigrafica en Occidente. Actas del Colloquio . . . 1992*, ed. F . Beltrán Lloris, Zaragoza 1995, 293–326.

Perez (1995)—Perez, A., *Les cadastres antiques en Narbonnaise occidentale. Essai sur la politique coloniale romaine en Gaule du Sud (IIe s. av. J.-C.—IIe ap. J.-C.)*, Paris 1995.

Petrochilos (1974)—Petrochilos, N., *Roman Attitudes to the Greeks*, Athens 1974.

Pfanner (1989)—Pfanner, M., "Uber das Herstellen von Porträts. Ein Beitrag zu Rationalisierungsmassnahmen und Produktionsmechanimen von Massenware im späten Hellenismus und in der römischen Kaiserzeit," *Jahrbuch deut. arch. Inst.* 104 (1989) 157–257.

Pfanner (1990)—Pfanner, M., "Modelle römischer Stadtentwicklung am Beispiel Hispaniens und der westlichen Provinzen," *Stadtbild und Ideologie. Die Monumentalisierung hispanischer Städte zwischen Republik und Kaiserzeit*, eds. W. Trillmich and P. Zanker, München 1990, 59–115.

Pflaum (1970)—Pflaum, H.-G., "La romanisation de l'ancient territoire de la Carthage punique à la lumière des découvertes épigraphiques récente," *Antiquités afr.* 4 (1970) 75–117.

Pflaum (1973)—Pflaum, H.-G., "La romanisation de l'Afrique," *Akten des VI. internationalen Kongresses für griechische und lateinische Epigraphilk . . . 1972*, München 1973, 55–68.

Philpott (1993)—Philpott, R. A., "Personal ornaments and burial practices in Roman Britain," *Römerzeitliche Gräber als Quellen zu Religion, Bevölkerungsstruktur und Sozialgeschichte. Internationale Fachkonferenz . . . 1991*, ed. M. Struck, Mainz 1993, 167–79.

C. Picard (1922)—Picard, C., "Les dieux de la colonie de Philippes vers le Ier siècle de notre ère, d'après les ex-voto rupestres," *Rev. de l'histoire des religions* 86 (1922) 117–201.

G.-C. Picard (1963)—Picard, G.-C., "Glanum et les origines de l'art romano-provençal, 1: architecture," *Gallia* 21 (1963) 111–24.

G.-C. Picard (1964)—Picard, G.-C., "Glanum et les origines de l'art romano-provençal, II: sculpture," *Gallia* 22 (1964) 1–21.

G.-C. Picard (1974)—Picard, G.-C., "Une survivance du droit publique punique en Afrique romaine: les citées sufétales," *I diritti locali nelle province romane . . . Atti del convegno internazionale . . . 1971*, Roma 1974, 125–33.

G.-C. Picard (1975)—Picard, G. Charles, "Observations sur la condition des populations rurales dans l'Empire romain, en Gaule et en Afrique," ANRW II, 3, Berlin 1975, 98–111.

G.-C. Picard (1982)—Picard, G.-C., "La sculpture dans l'Afrique romaine," *150-Jahr-Feier deutsches archäologisches Institut Rom. Aussprachen und Vorträge . . . 1979*, Mainz 198, 180–95.

G.-C. Picard (1992)—Picard, G.-C., "L'idéologie de la guerre et ses monuments dans l'Empire romain," *Rev. archéologique* 1992, 1, 111–41.

Plassart (1926)—Plassart, A., "Fouilles de Thespies et de l'hiéron des Muses de l'Hélicon, 6: Inscriptions," *Bull. de Correspondance hellénique* 50 (1926) 383–462.

Poinssot (1959)—Poinssot, C., "Suo et Sucubi," *Karthago* 10 (1959) 93–129.

Polomé (1983)—Polomé, E. C., "The linguistic situation in the western provinces of the Roman empire," ANRW II, 29, Berlin 1983, 509–53.

Potter and Damon (1999)—Potter, D. S., and C. Damon, "The *Senatus consultum de Cn. Pisone patre*," *Am. Jnl Philology* 120 (1999) 13–42.

Price (1984)—Price, S. R. F., *Rituals and Power. The Roman Imperial Cult in Asia Minor*, Cambridge (England) 1984.

Prieur (1986)—Prieur, J., *La mort dans l'antiquité romaine*, Ouest-France 1986.

Princeton Encyclopedia of Classical Sites, eds. R. Stillwell et al., 2 vols., Princeton 1976.

Provost (1994)—Provost, M., "Rapports entre théâtres et sanctuaires gallo-romains. L'apport méthodiques de CAG," *Caesarodunum* 28 (1994) 1.209–21.

Py (1993)—Py, M., *Les Gaulois du Midi. De la fin de l'Age du Bronze à la conquête romaine*, Paris 1993.

Ramage (1997)—Ramage, E. S., "Augustus' propaganda in Gaul," *Klio* 79 (1997) 117–60.

Ramallo Asensio (1989)—Ramallo Asensio, S., *La ciudad romana de Carthago Nova. La documentación arqueologica*, Murcia 1989.

Ramallo (1993)—Ramallo, S. F., "Capiteles Corintios de Cartagena," *Colonia Patricia Corduba. Una Reflexión arqueológica*, ed. P. León, Córduba 1993, 221–34.

Rambaud (1997)—Rambaud, F., "Portus Gaditanus," *Madrider Mitt.* 38 (1997) 75–88.

Ramilli (1973)—Ramilli, G., *Gli agri centuriati di Padova e di Pola nell'interpretazione di Pietro Kandler,* Trieste 1973.

Ramsay (1895–97)—Ramsay, W. M., *The Cities and Bishoprics of Phrygia,* 2 vols., Oxford 1895–97.

Rebourg (1991)—Rebourg, A., "Les origines d'Autun: l'archéologie et les textes," *Les villes augustéennes de Gaule. Actes du colloque . . . 1985,* Autun 1991, 99–106.

Reinert (1993)—Reinert, F., "Nécropoles rurales romaines précoces dans l'ouest du pays trévire (Grand-Duché de Luxembourg et régions limitrophes)," *Monde des morts, monde des vivants en Gaule rurale. Actes du colloque . . . 1992,* ed. A. Ferdière, Tours 1993, 177–84.

Revilla Calvo (1995)—Revilla Calvo, V., "Producción artesanale, viticultura y propietad rural en la Hispania Tarraconense," *Gerion* 13 (1995) 305–38.

Reynolds and Ward-Perkins (1952)—Reynolds, J. M., and J. B. Ward–Perkins, *The Inscriptions of Roman Tripolitania,* London 1952.

Ricardo Mar and Ruiz de Arbulo (1990)—Ricardo Mar, P., and J. Ruiz de Arbulo, "El foro de Ampurias y las transformaciones augusteas de los foros de la Tarraconense," *Stadtbild und Ideologie. Die Monumentalisierung hispanischer Städte zwischen Republik und Kaiserzeit,* eds. W. Trillmich and P. Zanker, München 1990, 145–63.

Riccobono et al. (1968–72)—Riccobono, S., et al., *Fontes iuris Romani anteiustiniani in usum scholarum,* ed. 2, 3 vols, Florence 1968–72.

Richardson (1995)—Richardson, J. S., "*Neque elegantem, ut arbitror, neque urbanum:* reflections on Iberian urbanism," *Social Complexity and the Development of Towns in Iberia from the Copper Age to the Second Century AD,* eds. B. Cunliffe and S. Keay, Oxford 1995, 339–54.

Richardson (1996)—Richardson, J. S., *The Romans in Spain,* Oxford 1996.

Rieks (1970)—Rieks, R., "Sebasta und Aktia," *Hermes* 98 (1970) 96–116.

Rizakis (1990)—Rizakis, A., "Cadastres et espace rural dans le Nord-Ouest du Péloponnèse," *Dialogues d'histoire ancienne* 16, 1 (1990) 259–80.

Rizakis (1995)—Rizakis, A. D., "Le grec face au latin. Le paysage linguistique dans la péninsule balkanique sous l'Empire," *Acta colloquii epigraphici latini . . . 1991,* eds. H. Solin et al., Helsinki 1995, 373–91.

Rizakis (1996)—Rizakis, A. D., "Anthroponymie et société. Les noms romains dans les provinces hellénophones de l'empire," *Roman Onomastics in the Greek East: Social and Political Aspects. Proc. of the International Colloque . . . 1993,* ed. idem, Athens 1996, 11–29.

Rizakis (1997)—Rizakis, A. D., "Roman colonies in the province of Achaia: territories, land and population," *The Early Roman Empire in the East*, ed. S. Alcock, Oxford 1997, 15–36.

Robert (1937)—Robert, L., *Etudes anatoliennes. Recherches sur les inscriptions grecques de l'Asie Mineure*, Paris 1937.

Robert (1940)—Robert, L., *Les gladiateurs dans l'Orient grec*, Paris 1940.

J. and L. Robert (1980)—Robert, J. and L., "Bulletin épigraphique," *Rev. études grecques* 93 (1980) 368–485.

J. and L. Robert (1981)—Robert, J. and L., "Bulletin épigraphique," *Rev. études grecques* 94 (1981) 362–485.

Roddaz (1984)—Roddaz, J.-M., *Marcus Agrippa*, Roma 1984.

Roddaz (1986)—Roddaz, J.-M., "Guerres civiles et romanisation dans la vallée de l'Ebre," REA 88 (1986) 317–38.

Roddaz (1996)—Roddaz, J.-M., "Pouvoir et provinces: remarques sur la politique de colonisation et de municipalisation de Rome dans la péninsule ibérique entre César et Auguste," *Teoria y practica del ordinamiento en Hispanias. Actas del Symposium . . . 1993*, Bilbao 1996, 13–25.

Rodriguez Colmenero (1996)—Rodriguez Colmenero, A., "Pueblos prerromanos del convento juridico lucense: organización sociopolitica y distribución territorial," *Lucus Augusti* 1. El Amanecer de una Ciudad, ed. idem, Coruña 1996, 129–242.

Rodriguez Colmenero (1996a)—Rodriguez Colmenero, A., "Integración administrativa del noroeste peninsular en la estructuras romanas," *Lucus Augusti* 1. El Amanecer de una Ciudad, ed. idem, Coruña 1996, 265–99.

Rodriguez Hidalgo and Keay (1995)—Rodriguez Hidalgo, J. M., and S. Keay, "Recent work at Italica," *Social Complexity and the Development of Towns in Iberia From the Copper Age to the Second Century AD*, eds. B. Cunliffe and S. Keay, Oxford 1995, 395–420.

Roldán Gómer (1992)—Roldán Gómer, L., *Technicas constructivas romanas en Carteia (San Roque, Cadiz)*, Madrid 1992.

Rolland (1958)—Rolland, H., *Fouilles de Glanum 1947–1956*, Paris 1958.

Rolland (1977)—Rolland, H., *L'Arc de Glanum (Saint-Rémy-de-Province)*, Paris 1977.

Roller (1998)—Roller, D. W., *The Building Program of Herod the Great*, Berkeley 1998.

Romanelli (1959)—Romanelli, P., *Storia delle province romane dell'Africa*, Roma 1959.

Romanelli (1974)—Romanelli, P., "Le condizioni giuridiche del suolo in Africa," *I diritti locali nelle province romane*, Roma 1974, 170–215.

Ros (1996)—Ros, K. E., "The Roman theater at Carthage," Am. Jnl Archaeology 100 (1996) 449–89.

Roth-Congès (1987)—Roth-Congès, A., "Fouilles et recherches récentes sur le Forum de Glanum," *Los foros romanos de la provincias occidentales*, Madrid 1987, 191–201.

Roth-Congès—Roth-Congès, A., "Les mausolées du sud-est de la Gaule," *Monde des morts, monde des vivants en Gaule rurale. Actes du colloque . . . 1992*, ed. A. Ferdière, Tours 1993, 389–96.

Rothaus (1992)—Rothaus, R. M., "Omne ignotum pro sacro: quadrisected gameboards and religious graffiti," *Oxford Jnl of Archaeology* 11 (1992) 365–68.

Rouillard (1997)—Rouillard, P., "Les Ibères et leurs partenaires méditerranéens phéniciens, grecs, puniques et romains," *Dossiers d'archéologie* 228 (1997) 14–21.

Rouquette and Sintès—Rouquette, J.-M., and C. Sintès, *Arles antique. Monuments et sites*, Paris 1989.

Rowland (1972)— Rowland, R. J., "Cicero and the Greek world," *Trans. Proc. Am. Philol. Assoc.* 103 (1972) 1–61.

Saddington (1993)—Saddington, D. B., "Preparing to become a Roman: the 'Romanization' of Deiotarus in Cicero," *Charistion C. P. T. Naudé*, ed. U. Vogel-Weidemann, Pretoria 1993, 87–97.

Sahin (1979–82)—Sahin, S., *Katalog der antiken Inschriften des Museums von Iznik (Nikaia)*, 2 vols., Bonn 1979–82.

Samuel (1972)—Samuel, A. E., *Greek and Roman Chronology. Calendars and Years in Classical Antiquity*, München 1972.

Santos Retolazza (1991)—Santos Retolazza, M., "Distribución y evolución de la vivienda urbana tardorrepublicana y altoimperial en Ampurias," *La casa urbana hispanorromana. Ponenciás y comuncaciones*, Zaragoza 1991, 19–34.

Sauron (1983)—Sauron., G., "Les cippes funéraires gallo-romains à décor de rinceaux de Nîmes et de sa région," *Gallia* 41 (1983) 59–110.

Sauron (1988)—Sauron, G., "Le message esthétique des rinceaux de l'Ara Pacis Augusta," *Rev. archéologique* 1988, 3–40.

Scheers (1969)—Scheers, S., *Les monnaies de la Gaule inspirées de celles de la République romaine*, Leuven 1969.

Scheers (1972)—Scheers, S., "Coinage and currency of the Belgic tribes during the Gallic wars," *British Numismatic Jnl* 41 (1972) 1–6.

Scheers (1981)—Scheers, S., "The origins and evolution of coinage in Belgic Gaul," *Coinage and Society in Britain and Gaul: Some Current Problems*, ed. B. Cunliffe, London 1981, 18–23.

Schmitt (1983)—Schmitt, R., "Die Sprachverhältnisse in den östlichen Provinzen des römischen Reiches," ANRW II, 29, Berlin 1983, 554–86.

Schrijvers (1989)—Schrijvers, P. H., "Vitruve et la vie intellectuelle de son temps," *Munus non ingratum. Proc. of the International Symposium on Vitruvius' De Architectura and the Hellenistic and Republican Architecture . . . 1987*, eds. H. Geertman and J. J. de Jong, Leiden 1989, 13–21.

Schubert (1996)—Schubert, C., *Land und Raum in der römischen Republik. Die Kunst des Teilens*, Darmstadt 1996.

Schwartz (1944)—Schwartz, J., "Dies Augustus," *REA* 46 (1944) 266–79.

Schwertheim (1985)—Schwertheim, E., "Neue Inschriften aus Miletupolis," *Epigraphica anatolica* 5 (1985) 77–87.

Sear (1982)—Sear, F., *Roman Architecture*, Ithaca 1982.

Sebastián Hernández Fernández (1998)—Sebastián Hernández Fernández, J., "Los Vibii Pac(c)iaeci de la Bética: una familia de hispanienses mal conocida," *Faventia* 20, 2 (1998) 163–76.

Seston (1967)—Seston, W., "Liber Pater et les curies de Lepti minus," *Cahiers de Tunisie* 15 (1967) 73–77.

Seyrig (1929)—Seyrig, H., "Inscriptions de Gythion," *Rev. archéologique* 29 (1929) 84–106.

Sherk (1969)—Sherk, R., *Roman Documents from the Greek East. Senatus Consulta and Epistulae to the Age of Augustus*, Baltimore 1969.

Sherwin-White (1963)—Sherwin-White, A. N., *Roman Society and Roman Law in the New Testament*, Oxford 1963.

Sherwin-White (1973)—Sherwin-White, A. N., *The Roman Citizenship*, ed. 2, Oxford 1973.

Sherwin-White (1983)—Sherwin-White, A. N., *Roman Foreign Policy in the East 168 B.C. to A.D. 1*, Oxford 1983.

Sillieres (1994)—Sillieres, P., "Le Ianus Augustus," *Caesarodunum* 28 (1994) 1.305–11.

Smajda (1978)—Smajda, E., "L'inscription du culte impérial dans la cité: l'exemple de Lepcis Magna au début de l'Empire," *Dialogues d'histoire ancienne* 4 (1978) 171–86.

Smeaton (1793)—Smeaton, J., *A Narrative of the Building and a Description of the Construction of the Edystone Lighthouse with Stone*, ed. 2, London 1793.

Snyder (1938)—Snyder, W. F., "Ἡμέραι Σεβασταί," *Aegyptus* 18 (1938) 197–233.

Snyder (1940)—Snyder, W. F., "Public anniversaries in the Roman Empire. The epigraphical evidence for their observance during the first three centuries," *Yale Classical Studies* 7 (1940) 225–317.

Snyder (1964)—Snyder, W. F., "Progress report on the Ἡμέραι Σεβασταί," *Aegyptus* 44 (1964) 145–69.

Solier (1973)—Solier, Y., "Notes sur les galeries souterraines de Narbonne," *Les cryptoportiques dans l'architecture romaine. Colloque internationale . . . 1972*, Rome 1973, 315–24.

Soricelli (1995)—Soricelli, G., *La Gallia Transalpina tra la conquista e l'età cesariana*, Como 1995.

Spaeth (1994)—Spaeth, B., "The goddess Ceres in the Ara Pacis Augustae and the Carthage relief," *Am. Jnl Archaeology* 98 (1994) 65–100.

Spawforth (1996)—Spawforth, A. J. S., "Roman Corinth: the formation of a colonial elite," *Roman Onomastics in the Greek East. Social and Political Aspects. Proc. of the International Colloquium . . . 1993*, ed. A . D. Rizakis, Athens 1996, 167–82.

Stamires (1957)—Stamires, G. A., "Greek inscriptions," *Hesperia* 26 (1957) 236–70.

Ste. Croix (1981)—Ste. Croix, G. E. M. de, *The Class Struggle in the Ancient Greek World from the Archaic Age to the Arab Conquests*, London 1981.

Stefenelli (1995)—Stefenelli, A., "Remarques sur le structure socioculturelle du latin vulgaire protoroman," *Latin vulgaire—latin tardif IV. Actes du 4e colloque international . . . 1994*, ed. L. Callebat, Hildesheim 1995, 35–45.

Stylow (1990)—Stylow, A. U., "Apuntes sobre el urbanismo de la Córduba romana," *Stadtbild und Ideologie. Die Monumentalisierung hispanischer Städte zwischen Republik und Kaiserzeit*, eds. W. Trillmich and P. Zanker, München 1990, 259–82.

Stylow (1993)—Stylow, A. U., "De Córduba a Colonia Patricia. La fundación de la Córduba romana," *Colonia Patricia Corduba. Una Reflexión arqueológica*, ed. P. León, Córduba 1993, 77–85.

Stylow (1995)—Stylow, A. U., "Los inicios de la epigrafía latina en la Bética," *Roma y el nascimiento de la cultura epigrafica en Occidente. Actas del Colloquio . . . 1992*, ed. F . Beltrán Lloris, Zaragoza 1995, 219–38.

Suic (1976)—Suic, M., *Anticki Grad na Istocnom Jadranu*, Zagreb 1976.

Sznycer (1975)—Sznycer, M., "L'assemblée du peuple' dans les cités puniques d'après les témoignages épigraphiques," *Semitica* 25 (1975) 47–68.

Tamassia (1984)—Tamassia, A. M., "Riflessi della confisca dei terreni," *Misurare la terra: centuriazione e coloni nel mondo romano*, ed. R. Bussi, Modena 1984, 89–94.

Tchernia (1986)—Tchernia, A., *Le vin d'Italie romaine: essai d'histoire économique d'après les amphores*, Rome 1986.

Thébert (1978)—Thébert, Y., "Romanisation et déromanisation. Histoire décolonisée ou histoire inversée?" *Annales* 33 (1978) 64–82.

Thevenot (1955)—Thevenot, E., *Sur les traces des Mars celtiques entre Loire et Mont Blanc* (Diss. arch. Gandenses 3), Bruges 1955.

Thill (1966)—Thill, G., "Ausgrabungen bei Goeblingen-Nospelt," *Hémecht* 18 (1966) 482–91.

Thompson (1987)—Thompson, H. A., "The impact of Roman architects and architecture on Athens: 170 B. C.–A. D. 170," *Roman Architecture in the Greek World*, eds. S. Macready and F. H. Thompson, London 1987, 1–17.

Tierney (1959–60)—Tierney, J. J., "The Celtic ethnography of Posidonius," *Proc. Royal Irish Acad.* 60 c2 (1959–69) 189–275.

Tilhard (1992)—Tilhard, J.-L., "Les céramiques sigillées italiques à Saintes (Mediolanum Santonum) (Charente-Maritime, France)," *Rei cretariae Romanae fautorum acta* 31–32 (1992) 231–54.

Tomaschek (1868)—Tomaschek, W., "Uber Brumalia und Rosalia," *Sitzungsber. der phil.-hist. Cl. der Kaiserlichen Akad. der Wiss.* 60 (1868) 351–404.

Tovar (1973)—Tovar, A., *Sprachen und Inschriften. Studien zum Mykenischen, Lateinischen und Hispanokeltischen*, Amsterdam 1973.

Tranoy (1988)—Tranoy, A., "Du héros au chef. L'image du guerrier dans les sociétés indigènes du nord-ouest de la péninsule ibérique (IIe siècle avant J.–C.— Ier siècle après J.–C.)," *Le monde des images en Gaule et dans les provinces voisines. Actes du colloque . . . 1987*, Paris 1988, 219–27.

Trillmich (1976)—Trillmich, W., *Das Torlonia-Mädchen. Zur Herkunft und Entstehung der kaiserzeitlichen Frauenporträts*, Göttingen 1976.

Trillmich (1986)—Trillmich, W., "Ein historisches Relief in Mérida mit Darstellung des M. Agrippa beim Opfer. Ein Rekonstruktionsversuch," *Madrider Mitt.* 27 (1986) 279–304.

Trillmich (1990)—Trillmich, W., "Colonia Augusta Emerita, die Hauptstadt von Lusitanien," *Stadtbild und Ideologie. Die Monumentalisierung hispanischer Städte zwischen Republik und Kaiserzeit*, eds. W. Trillmich and P. Zanker, München 1990, 299–316.

Trillmich (1993)—Trillmich, W., "Hispanien und Rom aus der Sicht Roms und Hispaniens," *Hispania Antiqua. Die Denkmäler der Römerzeit*, eds. idem et al., Mainz 1993, 41–47.

Troso (1991)—Troso, C., *Il ceramista arretino Publius Cornelius: La produzione decorata a rilievo*, Firenze 1991.

Trousset (1995)—Trousset, P., "Les centuriations romaines," *Dossiers d'archéologie* 200 (1995) 70–81, 135.

Tuffreau-Libre (1994)—Tuffreau-Libre, M., "La céramique dans les sanctuaires gallo-romains," *Les sanctuaires de tradition indigène en Gaule romaine. Actes du colloque . . . 1992*, eds. C. Goudineau et al., Paris 1994, 128–37.

Tuffreau-Libre (1996)—Tuffreau-Libre, M., "La romanisation de la céramique commune," *Dossiers d'archéologie* 215 (1996) 58–61.

Vallette and Guichard (1991)—Vallette, P., and V. Guichard, "Le forum gallo-romain de Feurs (Loire)," *Gallia* 48 (1991) 109–64.

Van Nostrand (1937)—J. J. van Nostrand, "Roman Spain," *An Economic Survey of Ancient Rome*, ed. T. Frank, 3, Baltimore 1937, 119–224.

Varène (1987)—Varène, P., "L'enceinte augustéenne de Nîmes," *Les enceintes augustéennes dans l'Occident romain (France, Italie, Espagne, Afrique du Nord). Actes du colloque . . . 1985*, ed. M.-G. Colin, Nîmes 1987, 17–23.

Vasari (1965)—Vasari, G., The Lives of the Artists. A Selection, trans. G. Bull, Harmondsworth 1965.

Ventura et al. (1993)—Ventura, A., et al., "Análisis arqueológico de la Córduba romana: Resultado e hipótesis de la investigación," Colonia Patricia Corduba. Una Reflexión arqueologica, ed. P. León, Córdoba 1993, 87–118.

Vermeule (1963)—Vermeule, C., "Augustan and Julio-Claudian court silver," Antike Kunst 6 (1963) 33–40.

Vernhet (1979)—Vernhet, A., La Graufesenque, atelier de céramiques gallo-romain, Millau 1979.

Verzar (1974)—Verzar, M., "Frühaugusteischer Grabbau in Sestin (Toscana)," MEFRA 86 (1974) 385–444.

Veyne (1961)—Veyne, P., "Le Marsyas 'colonial' et l'indépendance des cités," Rev. de philol. 87 (1961) 87–98.

Veyne (1976)—Veyne, P., Le pain et le cirque. Sociologie historique d'un pluralisme politique, Paris 1976.

Veyne (1979)—Veyne, P., "L'hellénization et la problématique des acculturations," Diogène 106 (1979) 3–29.

Veyne (1988)—Veyne, P., Les mystères du gynécée, Paris 1988.

Veyne (1990)—Veyne, P., Bread and Circuses. Historical Sociology and Political Pluralism, trans. O. Murray, London 1990.

Vicente Redon et al. (1991)—Vicente Redon, J. D., et al., "La Caridad (Caminreal, Teruel)," La casa urbana hispanorromana. Ponencias y comunicaciones, Zaragoza 1991, 81–129.

Visscher (1963)—Visscher, F. de, Le droit des tombeaux romains, Milano 1963.

Vittinghoff (1951)—Vittinghoff, F., Römische Kolonisation und Bürgerrechtspolitik unter Caesar und Augustus, Mainz 1951.

Volterra (1952)—Volterra, E., "L'adozione testamentaria ed un'iscrizione latina e neopunica della Tripolitana," Ren. Accad. Lincei, Ser 8, 7 (1952) 175–88.

Waelkens (1987)—Waelkens, M., "The adoption of Roman building techniques in the architecture of Asia Minor," Roman Architecture in the Greek World, eds. S. Macready and F. H. Thompson, London 1987, 94–105.

Waelkens (1990)—Waelkens, M., "Technique de carrière, préfaçonnage et ateliers dans les civilisations classiques (modes grec et romain)," Pierre éternelle du Nil au Rhin. Carrières et préfabrication, ed. idem, Bruxelles 1990, 53–72.

Walbank (1997)—Walbank, M. E. H., "The foundation and planning of early Roman Corinth," Jnl Roman Archeology 10 (1997) 95–130.

Walker and Burnett (1981)—Walker, S., and A. Burnett, The Image of Augustus, London 1981.

Ward-Perkins (1970)—Ward-Perkins, J. B., "From Republic to Empire: reflections on the early provincial architecture of the Roman West," *Jnl Roman Studies* 60 (1970) 1–19.

Ward-Perkins (1981)—Ward-Perkins, J. B., *Roman Imperial Architecture*, Harmondsworth 1981.

Ward-Perkins (1982)—Ward-Perkins, J. B., "Town planning in North Africa during the first two centuries of the Empire, with special reference to Lepcis and Sabratha: character and sources," *150-Jahr–Feier deutsches archäologisches Institut Rom. Aussprachen und Vorträge . . . 1979*, Mainz 1982, 129–44.

Ward-Perkins (1992)—Ward-Perkins, J. B., *Marble in Antiquity. Collected Papers of J. B. Ward-Perkins*, eds. H. Dodge and B. Ward-Perkins, London 1992.

Wells (1977)—Wells, C. M., "Manufacture, distribution and date: some methodological considerations on the dating of Augustan terra sigillata," *Rei cretariae Romanae fautorum acta* 17–18 (1977) 132–40.

West (1931)—West, A. B., *Corinth. Results of Excavations . . . VIII, ii: Latin Inscriptions*, Cambridge 1931.

Whittaker (1997)—Whittaker, C. R., "Imperialism and culture: the Roman initiative," *Dialogues in Roman Imperialism. Power, Discourse, and Discrepant Experience in the Roman Empire*, ed. D. J. Mattingly, Portsmouth 1997, 143–63.

Wightman (1976)—Wightman, E., "Il y avait en Gaule deux sortes de Gaulois," *Assimilation et résistance à la culture gréco-romaine dans le monde ancien. Travaux du VIe Congrès international d'Etudes Classiques . . . 1974*, ed. D. M. Pippidi, Paris 1976, 407–19.

Wightman (1985)—Wightman, E. M., *Gallia Belgica*, London 1985.

Wild (1985)—Wild, J. P., "The clothing of Britannia, Gallia Belgica and Germania Inferior," *ANRW II, 13, 3*, Berlin 1985, 362–422.

Wilkes (1969)—Wilkes, J. J., *Dalmatia*, Cambridge (England) 1969.

Will (1984)—Will, E., "Damas antique," *Syria* 71 (1994) 1–43.

Wilson (1966)—Wilson, A. J. N., *Emigration from Italy in the Republican Age of Rome*, Manchester 1966.

Woodward (1923–24)—Woodward, A. M., "Excavations at Sparta, 1924–25, 2: The theater," *Ann. Brit. School Athens* 26 (1923–24) 119–58.

Woodward (1925–26)—Woodward, A. M., "Excavations at Sparta, 1926," *Ann. Brit. School Athens* 27 (1925–26) 173–209.

Wörrle (1988)—Wörrle, M., *Stadt und Fest im kaiserzeitlichen Kleinasien; Studien zu einer agonistischen Stiftung aus Oinoanda*, München 1988.

Woolf (1994)—Woolf, G., "Becoming Roman, staying Greek: culture, identity and the civilizing process in the Roman East," *Proc. Cam. Philological Society* 40 (1994) 116–43.

Yavetz (1983)—Yavetz, Z., *Julius Caesar and his Public Image*, London 1983.

Yegül (1992)—Yegül, F. K., *Baths and Bathing in Classical Antiquity*, New York 1992.

Zanker (1983)—Zanker, P., *Provinzielle Kaiserporträts. Zur Rezeption der Selbstdarstellung des Princeps*, München 1983.

Zanker (1988)—Zanker, P., *The Power of Images in the Age of Augustus*, trans. A. Shapiro, Ann Arbor 1988.

Zanker (1990)—Zanker, P., "Einleitung," *Stadtbild und Ideologie. Die Monumentalisierung hispanischer Städte zwischen Republik und Kaiserzeit*, eds. W. Trillmich and P. Zanker, München 1990, 9–24.

Zanker (1991)—Zanker, P., "Immagini e valori collettivi," *Storia di Roma*, ed. A. Schiavone, 2: *L'impero mediterraneo*, 2: *I principi e il mondo*, Torino 1991, 193–220.

Zulueta (1932)—Zulueta, F. de, "Violation of sepulture in Palestine at the beginning of the Christian era," *Jnl Rom. Studies* 22 (1932) 184–97.

INDEX